THE CASTLES OF THE ASSASSINS

The Castles
of the Assassins

BY PETER WILLEY

with a Foreword by
FIELD-MARSHAL SIR CLAUDE AUCHINLECK
G.C.B. G.C.I.E. C.B. C.S.I. D.S.O. O.B.E.

and with a new Preface by the Author

A Craven Street Book
Linden Publishing
Fresno, CA

124689753

THE CASTLES OF THE ASSASSINS
by
Peter Willey

Cover Art by James Goold

First published in Great Britain by George G. Harrap & Co. Ltd. 1963
Copyright ©1963, 2001 by Peter Willey

ISBN 0-941936-64-3

Library of Congress Cataloging-in-Publication Data
Willey, Peter.
    The Castles of the Assassins / by Peter Willey.
       p.cm.
    Originally published: London : G. G. Harrap, 1963.
    ISBN 0-941936-64-3 (pbk.:alk paper)
    1. Elburz Mountains (Iran). 2. Iran—Descriptions and travel. 3. Assassins (Ismailites) I. Alamut Valley Expedition (1960) II. Title.

    DS324.E4 W5 2001
    955'.2—dc21
    2001029240

A Craven Street Book

Linden Publishing Inc.
2006 South Mary, Fresno CA 93721 USA
800-345-4447   www.lindenpub.com

This book is dedicated
to the members of the expedition
and the people of the valleys

Foreword by

FIELD-MARSHAL SIR CLAUDE AUCHINLECK, G.C.B.

HAVING HAD the privilege of watching the enterprise described in this book from the start, I count it an honour as well as a pleasure to have been asked to write this Foreword.

The author is known to me not only as a man of enterprise and endeavour, but also as a leader and trainer of youth.

The story is a fascinating one, not merely because of its great historical interest, but also for the vivid light it throws on the life and times of great peoples and personalities long forgotten. It shows us, too, how even to-day there are people who can still live simply and naturally, much as their forefathers did a thousand years ago.

This is a tale of initiative, imagination, perseverance, and determination, which succeeded in the face of frustration, difficulty, and, at times, danger.

The results must, I think, add greatly to our knowledge of this most ancient and still remote part of the world. It is interesting, too, to think that the Ismailis of to-day, descendants of those who built the fabulous strongholds described in this book, have become a most enlightened and prosperous community, not only in Asia, but also in Africa and elsewhere.

It is indeed invigorating to learn that the spirit of enterprise and adventure still lives and that there are those who, without dependence on wealth or influence, are eager and able to prove that the qualities that made this country great are not dead.

Preface

IN THIS book I have tried to tell the story of the Alamut
Valley Expedition, which set out in June 1960 to explore
the castles of the Assassins in Persia. My aim has been to
say something about the Assassins and their part in
history; to tell the story of our expedition and about those
who took part in it; to depict the way of life of the present
inhabitants of the valleys; to describe our archaeological
findings; and to present a comprehensive, first-hand
description of the valleys of the Assassins as they are
to-day.

To strike a happy balance in these aims was no easy task,
as I am a schoolmaster and not a professional writer. But
I hope, nevertheless, that those who read this account will
be able to share, in their imaginations, the comradeship
and pride in achievement that our small group knew on our
journey into this historic and legendary part of the world.

During the writing of this book I have been constantly
supplied with material and friendly criticism by the other
members of the expedition, especially Richard Mordaunt,
Roddie Dugmore, and Robert Moss. Most of the photographs were taken by Ragnar van Leyden, but some were
supplied by Richard Mordaunt and Michael Oliver. The
maps and plans are by Roddie Dugmore. The drawings
that appear in Appendix C were made by Mrs D. M.
Wilson. I am deeply indebted to Paula Monk for her
sympathetic intuition, without which she could neither
have interpreted my notes nor typed the manuscript.

I must also thank Dr J. A. Boyle, of Manchester
University, as well as the Manchester University Press
for permission to quote extensively from *The History of*

the World Conqueror, his translation of Juvayni's history.[1]

To our patron, Field-Marshal Sir Claude Auchinleck, who has written the Foreword, I should like to express my deep respect and sincere gratitude. I am also indebted to Dr S. M. Stern, Fellow of All Souls College, Oxford, our historical adviser, for his constant advice and help, as well as to Mr Ralph Pinder-Wilson, of the Department of Oriental Antiquities at the British Museum. Finally, I should like to express my warm thanks for the encouragement and support of so many friends, without whose help this book would never have been written, especially Elizabeth Ellem, who has seen this book through the press.

Throughout the time we were in Iran the expedition received great help from the Iranian authorities, and it is our pleasant duty to express to them our warmest thanks. In particular we should like to mention H. E. Husain Ala, the Minister of Court; H. E. Dr Mahmud Mehran, Minister for Education; the High Council of Antiquities of Iran and the Council of the Museum of Iran-Bastan; H. E. the Minister for Health; the head of the Internal Security Organization; H. E. the Minister for War; and Major-General Muhammad Behruz, head of the Geographical Department of the Imperial Armed Forces. We also received much help from Mr Abul Fazl Albuyeh; Mr Alamuti; Dr Hasan Alavi, Professor of Ophthalmology at the University of Teheran; Mr Ali Hannibal and Dr Minasian, as well as the National Iranian Oil Company.

We should like to offer our sincere thanks to all the members of the staff of the British Embassy in Teheran, especially to Sir Geoffrey and Lady Harrison and Mr and Mrs Arthur Kellas for their great kindness and help.

We have received special help from the following: H. E. the Iranian Ambassador and members of the Imperial Iranian Embassy in London; the Army Council; B.B.C.

---

[1] Dr Boyle uses the spelling 'Juvaini,' but 'Juvayni' is equally used.

Television and the Independent Television companies; the directors of Barclays Bank, Ltd, Reading; Messrs Bevington, Vaizey, and Foster; Sir George Binney; the Department of Oriental Antiquities, British Museum; Brigadier J. G. Carr, R. E.; Mr Miles de Vries; Foyle's Lecture Agency; Mr F. J. Girling; Mrs Cynthia Holley; Professor W. Ivanow; the Ismaili Society of Great Britain; the London Hospital for Tropical Diseases; Dr L. Lockhart; Professor V. Minorsky; the Commandant and Quartermaster of Mons Officer Cadet School; General Sir Cameron Nicholson; the Persian Air Services and Middle East Airlines; the Pilgrim Trust; the Royal Central Asian Society; Mrs J. H. Rudkin; Mr W. F. Russell; Miss Freya Stark; Mr D. Stronach; the School of Military Survey; the Governors and Master of Wellington College; Miss Kay Whalley; Mr A. E. Yuill; the Editors of *The Times, Daily Telegraph, Daily Mail,* and our other friends in the Press.

We are very grateful to all of these and also to our many other friends.

Below is a list of firms whose generosity and kindness enabled us to set out for the valleys of the Assassins.

Acrow, Ltd; Benson and Hedges, Ltd; Alfred Bird and Sons, Ltd; British Bata Shoe Co., Ltd; British Ropes, Ltd; British Oxygen Co., Ltd; Bronco, Ltd; Bryant and May, Ltd; Cadbury Fry; Carlsberg Distributors, Ltd; Chubb and Son's Lock and Safe Co., Ltd; Colibri Lighters, Ltd; Cooper, McDougall and Robertson, Ltd; Coty, Ltd; E. B. Dive and Co., Ltd; Dunlop Rubber Co., Ltd; Ever Ready Co., Ltd; Ferodo, Ltd; Gillette Co., Ltd; Glaxo Laboratories, Ltd; Halex, Ltd; George G. Harrap and Co., Ltd; Thomas Hedley and Co., Ltd; Horlicks, Ltd; Horniman and Co., Ltd; Imperial Chemical Industries, Ltd; Imperial Tobacco Co., Ltd; Jeyes-Ibco Sales, Ltd; Kodak, Ltd; R. Lehmann and Co., Ltd; Macfarlane Lang and Co., Ltd; Marmite, Ltd; Metal

Box Co., Ltd; Nestlé Co., Ltd; Oxo, Ltd; Phillips Scott and Turner, Ltd; Polarizers, Ltd; Rediffusion, Ltd; Rose Kia-Ora Sales Co.; Rover Co., Ltd; Rumble, Crowther, and Nicholas Ltd; The Ryvita Co., Ltd; J. Sainsbury, Ltd; Smiths Clocks and Watches, Ltd; W. Symington and Co., Ltd; Tate and Lyle, Ltd; Valor Co., Ltd; Van den Berghs, Ltd; J. Walter Thompson Co., Ltd; A. Wander, Ltd; and Watney Combe Reid and Co., Ltd.

P.R.E.W.

WELLINGTON COLLEGE
Spring 1963

Preface to the 2001 Edition

When I wrote my preface to the first edition of *The Castles of the Assassins* in 1963, I could not possibly have foreseen that almost half a century later I would be sitting in my study in a Wiltshire village in England writing an introduction to a new impression of my book to be published in the United States. It is, of course, a pleasant task and I hope the reader will enjoy this account of two expeditions I led to Iran all those years ago. And I must, of course, express my warm thanks to Richard Sorsky of Linden Publishing for making this possible.

I am naturally glad that the book will now be freely available to readers again, as it has been out of print for a long time and has been much sought after by historians and the general public. It has in fact become the standard work on the Alamut castles and the Ismailis, or Assassins as they are popularly called, and will remain so for a long time.

I have now spent more than 40 years researching the history of the Assassin state (1090-1258), locating and describing their formidable castles, examining their infrastructure and their agriculture, and evaluating the numerous legends and myths which have circulated about them since the days of Marco Polo. I have also tried to understand what made this formidable sect so feared and respected that their very name is still an alarm bell in our modern world. I have also tried to understand their deep sense of loyalty to their leader, their imam, which is still very much in evidence today in their utter devotion to the present Aga Khan.

How did this all begin? In 1959 I was invited by the British Ambassador in Tehran to spend the summer vacation with him. The lure of a visit to Persia was very strong and I had already read Freya Stark's excellent account of her courageous visit to the Valley of the Assassins in 1930. I met Freya Stark and she encouraged me to continue her work. I also had the advantage of meeting a famous orientalist at Oxford, who urged me to examine carefully the fortress of Alamut and to see if I could find the long "lost" castle of Maymun Diz, where the Assassins were finally defeated and put to death by the Mongols under Hulagu Khan. I gladly accepted the challenge, but I did not realize how dangerous it would turn out to be. Although, as I describe, my first expedition, called the Oxford Expedition to the Elburz Mountains, was almost brought to an abrupt halt right at the beginning, we did in fact examine Alamut Castle and discovered the site of Maymun Diz. With the help of Oxford University and the British Museum our follow-up expeditions were equally successful.

In this book I try to relate in a readable form the history of the Assassins, who will probably be little more than a name to most readers, and to do justice to their great achievements as architects, craftsmen, and farmers. In many respects their castles are technicallly greater achievements than even those built at roughly the same time by the Crusaders. I also try to describe the excitement, the difficulties, and the dangers of the expeditions and to portray the lives of the simple Ismaili mountain folk among whom we lived.

After the publication of the original *The Castles of the Assassins,* I continued to lead many more expeditions to locate Ismaili castles in other parts of Iran, Afghanistan, Central Asia, Pakistan, and Syria. The Iranian revolution of 1979 interrupted this work until 1996. Our most recent expedition was to the mountain valleys of northern Pakistan, especially Hunza, in 1999. As a result of all this work we have now been able to make a fairly accurate and complete plan of the Ismaili state as it developed in the years 1090-1258. Although there are still some minor forts to be located, we have succeeded in describing all the major castles. This research will form the theme of a second book, but it will in no way supersede the descriptions of the castles in this book. Alamut was the core of the Ismaili state. I also like to think that the background description of the valley and its inhabitants, as well as the trials and tribulations of the expeditions I led, has lost none of its freshness over the years.

My most recent visit to the valley was in 1996 with my research partner, Adrianne Woodfine. No Westerner had been given permission to examine the castles there since the revolution of 1979. In 1996 and 1997 Adrianne and I were able, despite considerable difficulty with the authorities, to do some research on other Ismaili castles in the east of the country and we were naturally anxious to revisit Alamut on our way to the province of Khorasan on the Iran-Afghanistan border. We were driven there by our taxi driver, Ali Moradi, who was an Ismaili himself and an invaluable help. We chose to go by an ordinary taxi, as this would make us less conspicuous to the authorities.

When we arrived at the village of Gazur Khan, just below Alamust castle, everything seemed the same as 40 years before. Even the fleas bit as furiously as ever! I was unable to manage the difficult ascent to the fortress. So Adrianne, our driver, Ali, and a local guide climbed their way to the top of the great rock outcrop on which the fortress stood. And to my utter dismay they sadly reported that hardly any vestige of the ruined castle remained. I can only assume that local people, or complete strangers perhaps, had heard of my previous research and thought that we were looking for hidden treasure inside the castle. Archaeology meant little to them and they would not understand that we were interested only in the historical evidence the castle provided. So during the years after the revolution, parties of treasure-seekers must have gone to the fortress and in their attempts to find anything of value they had destroyed all that remained of the walls and rooms.

Later in our stay we went to the castle of Maymun Diz, which I describe at length in this book. The same thing had happened there and the caves, which formed the core of the castle, have now been sealed off on grounds of safety. So the information in this book is invaluable and important from the archeological point of view, as it presents the only record of the Alamut castles before they were vandalized. The Ministry of Cultural Heritage has now stationed officials and gendarmes in the valley to prevent further damage to the castles, but this step was taken far too late. Alamut is now very much a tourist attraction, both for foreigners and Iranians. There is now an excellent road from Tehran to the Alamut Valley and so it has become much more accessible. It was interesting to hear local people telling the history of the Assassins based on my own discoveries and interpretations.

In my original preface I had thanked all the organizations and individual sponsors, both Iranian and British, who had helped to make my first expeditions such a success. I now renew my thanks to them. Many of these Iranian sponsors were killed during the revolution or fled into exile. Whatever role they played in the politics of the time, I am immensely grateful to them for the support they gave me and the real contribution they made to historical research. Their friendship and practical help was both generous and genuine. During our recent visits to Iran both Adrianne and I were struck by the many Iranians who now regret the violence and bloodshed of the early days of the revolution and who show a greater understanding and appreciation of their former rulers, including the last Shah.

I also warmly renew my respect and affection for the people of the valleys and the Ismaili community, who, under the guidance of their imam, the Aga Khan, are among the most progressive Muslims, eager to see an end to the distrust and suspicion that has persisted between Christians and Muslims since the Crusades. In all the 40 years I have known them they, together with many other Iranians, have gone out of their way to help us and our research.

Finally I must extend my good wishes to my new American readers, who, I hope, will find interest and pleasure in reading this book.

Peter Willey
Upavon, Wiltshire
Autumn 2000

Contents

Illustrations

MAPS AND GROUND-PLANS

1

The Assassins

THE VALLEY of the Assassins, or, to give it its more prosaic name, the Alamut valley, lies in the Elburz mountains, in the north of Iran, about half-way between Teheran, the capital, and the Caspian sea. The valley is some 30 miles long and 3 miles wide at its broadest, and the present population is about 20,000. It was here that the infamous Ismaili sect known as the Assassins,[1] founded by Hasan-i-Sabbah at the end of the eleventh century, flourished and spread until, in 1256, the valley was overrun and most of the inhabitants massacred by Mongol invaders under the "World Conqueror," Hulagu Khan.

[1] The Assassins are normally referred to as Nizari Ismailis in order to distinguish them from the Ismailis of the Fatimid caliphate. The term Nizari is used to apply to the supporters of Prince Nizar, a claimant to the Egyptian caliphate, who was defeated and imprisoned in Cairo in 1095 and subsequently murdered. After his murder Hasan became the acknowledged leader of the Nizaris, using this position to further his own purposes. Ismailism as such has a far older history (see Appendix A). The Ismailis formed part of the Shi'ite branch of Mohammedanism, and Shi'ism is the official religion of modern Iran.

C.A.–B

Al-Hasan b. Al-Sabbah, commonly known as Hasan-i-
Sabbah, First Grand Master of the Assassins, and dignified
by such honorific titles as Our Lord and Old Man of the
Mountains, came from obscure origins. He was born of
lower middle class parents at Rayy, an old city a few
kilometres to the south of modern Teheran. Unfortunately
we do not know the exact date of his birth, nor are there
any precise details about his education or early youth.
Legends there are in plenty and one of the most famous
and well established may be found in the preface to Edward
FitzGerald's translation of *The Rubáiyát* of Omar Khayyám.
The great Persian astrologer-poet was a contemporary of
Hasan-i-Sabbah's, and the two were law students together
at Naishapur. They were joined by a third young man of
similar intellectual gifts and aesthetic tastes named Nizam-
al-Mulk, who later, in his "Testament," told their story.

The teacher of the three friends was the famous Imam
Mowaffak, and they firmly believed that they, in common
with Imam Mowaffak's other pupils, would eventually
attain considerable eminence. One day when Hasan was
talking with Nizam and Omar he suggested that they all
should make a solemn vow to the effect that whosoever
should achieve fame and fortune first would share it equally
with the other two. The compact was made, and, in the
course of time, it was Nizam-al-Mulk who first achieved
fame and fortune when he was elevated to the office of
Vizier by Sultan Alp Arslan. Some years passed before
Omar Khayyám came back to Naishapur and sought out
the Vizier. He reminded Nizam of their vow, but did not
ask for title, honour, or office. He would be content, he
said, if he could but live in the shadow of the Vizier's
fortune, devoting his life to science and the arts. This boon
was readily granted.

When Hasan in his turn came to Naishapur, he adopted
quite a different tone. He demanded a place in the Government, and this the Vizier granted. His endless ambition,
however, drove him to seek greater and greater power,

until he instigated an intrigue against the Vizier and the Sultan, which aimed at deposing them. The plot was discovered, and Hasan was fortunate to escape with his life. Showing considerable clemency, the Vizier was satisfied with exiling him from the country. Whether this story is true or not, it certainly is typical of the person Hasan later showed himself to be, and the sequel is even more illuminating, for two years later Nizam-al-Mulk was murdered on Hasan's orders as a wanton and spiteful act of revenge.

Shortly after his infamous plot against the Vizier it seems that Hasan was converted to Ismailism through, the *Sar-gudhast-i-Sayyidna*[1] tells us, the influence of a holy man who cared for him when he was dangerously ill. Thereafter, Hasan devoted his considerable talents to the cause of Ismailism and soon attracted the attention of his superiors. In 1071 (when he was about thirty) he was ordered to Isfahan by the chief *da'i* (or "summoner to the truth," a senior member of the Ismaili hierarchy) to further his studies, and a few years later he was sent to Cairo, the capital of the splendid and luxurious Ismaili Fatimid caliphate which had been established in the preceding century with the avowed intention of reuniting the whole of the Mohammedan world under the House of the Prophet and conquering the lands of the infidels. By this time the once magnificent empire, distinguished not only for its power, wealth, and luxury but also for its tolerance (even of Christians) and love of the arts, was weakened by wars and disputes about the succession. Its principal external enemies were the Turkish Seljuk tribes who had risen to military power in the Middle East in the eleventh

---

[1] Or *History of our Lord*. This included autobiographical notes written by Hasan-i-Sabbah, and was destroyed by the Mongols when they sacked the castle of Alamut in 1256 and burnt its priceless library. Juvayni was able to study the documents before they were destroyed, and, in his *History of the World Conqueror*, he quotes extensively from the *Sar-gudhast-i-Sayyidna*.

century and were supporters of the orthodox Sunni beliefs. The Fatimid state was the very incarnation of Ismailism, but now it seemed it was doomed. If Ismailism was to survive in the face of the attacks of its enemies a leader of exceptional calibre was needed. Hasan was not slow to realize that here was his opportunity to seize power.

In 1080 Hasan returned to Persia. He soon attracted followers by his powers of oratory, his powerful personality, and his extreme asceticism. At this time he supported the claims of Nizar, the eldest son of the ruling Fatimid caliph, to the succession, but Hasan himself received support from Persian Ismailis partly because of his personal magnetism; partly because many Ismailis felt the need for a strong leader; and partly because his teaching that the rulers of the day should be disposed of appealed to people of all classes with grievances against them.

In order to seize and hold power, Hasan chose means that were not uncommon in his day—political intrigue and murder. What was uncommon was his complete ruthlessness and his ability to attract followers who would follow him blindly.

In 1090 he established himself, by trickery, in the castle of Alamut. Here he gathered around him a corps of disciples, or *fida'is*, willing and eager to serve his cause by any means. So successful were the *fida'is* in carrying out their lord's commands that by the beginning of the twelfth century the name Assassin, which was applied to any follower of Hasan, had become a synonym for political murder and intrigue throughout the Middle East. The word 'Assassin' came from 'Hashishin,' or 'Eater of Hashish.' According to legend, this drug was extensively used by Hasan during the training of the *fida'is*. He was supposed to have built a secret garden within the precincts of the castle of Alamut. There the *fida'is*, after they had been instructed in the art of murder, were drugged with hashish and, under the influence of this powerful narcotic, spent three days enjoying a foretaste of the delights of paradise, consisting mostly of purely sensual pleasures. They never knew how they had entered the garden or when they had emerged; it all seemed like a dream, but a dream of such power and reality that they were fully convinced that they had actually been in paradise. Henceforth no terrors or tortures would deflect them from spreading Hasan's influence throughout the Mohammedan world. These were the blind fanatics who, armed with dagger and poison, struck at caliphs, emirs, and viziers.

It is not surprising that Hasan chose the valley of Alamut as his headquarters. Set in the forbidding Elburz mountains, it was sufficiently remote to be the ideal site for the headquarters of a rebellion and yet not too far for messengers or *fida'is* to slip into the important cities of Rayy or Kazwin. It was easily defended, self-contained, a viable economic area and strategically placed between the capital and the Caspian. The castle itself had first been constructed in the years 860–861 and was already a formidable fortress, and Hasan set about making it impregnable. Storerooms were hewn out of the solid rock, a stream was diverted to give the garrison an adequate water-supply in times of siege, and the fortifications were strengthened. Hasan remained here for the rest of his life, directing and controlling the Nizari policy of expansion by subtle penetration and terrorism. Juvayni relates that in the course of thirty-five years Hasan left his house in Alamut twice only, and then just for a walk on the roof! By this time practically all ties with the Fatimid empire had been severed—the Assassins were everywhere referred to as the Nizaris—and their chief enemies were the Seljuk Turks and Sunni orthodoxy. Spurred on by Hasan's seizure of Alamut and the surrounding districts of Rudbar, revolts flared up all over the Seljuk domains. Hasan's strategy was to seize existing castles either by trickery or force of arms, and from these firm bases undermine the morale of his enemies by means of political terrorism. The sheer brazen success of this policy is well illustrated by

the taking of the fortress of Shahdiz, which actually overlooked the Seljuk capital of Isfahan and held out for some
fifteen years. The three main areas of Nizari activity were
Daylaman (which included Rudbar and Alamut), Quhistan,
and the south-western district of Fars. Most of the
fortresses were in inaccessible, mountainous areas where
the garrisons could hold out against Seljuk expeditions
sent to subdue them. In 1101 Hasan's armies took the
important fortress of Lammassar to the west of Alamut,
thus securing effective control of the shortest routes
through the Elburz mountains to the Caspian.

Hasan died in 1124, after a long and prosperous rule,
and was succeeded in the office of Grand Master by his
chief *da'i*, Buzurg-Ummed, who reigned for the next
fourteen years. During this period the Assassins were able
to extend their power to Syria and thus founded the
Syrian side of the movement. They were often defeated in
battle, and sometimes their castles were taken and
plundered, but as long as the castles in the home valley of
Alamut stood firm their power could not really be shaken.
The early years of the twelfth century were the greatest
period of the Assassins' evil renown, and it was during this
time that the most important assassinations took place.

In the years immediately preceding the destruction of
the Assassins' strongholds the use of assassination as a
political weapon diminished, and for some time there was
a period of almost liberal government. It was at this time
that the Syrian branch made themselves independent and
fought against the Crusaders. The Grand Masters themselves often suffered the same violent death by poison or
assassination as they meted out to their enemies. For
example, the last Grand Master of the Assassins, Rukn-ad-
Din, had his father killed, and this act of parricide was by
no means an isolated incident. Gradually, however, the
line became enfeebled, until the last ruler was unable to
put up more than a token resistance to the Mongol hordes
under Hulagu Khan when they invaded the Alamut valley

in 1256. He surrendered with the bulk of his army at
Maymun-Diz, the 'invincible' stronghold built by his
father, and one after the other the rest of the castles,
including Alamut, followed suit. After a short interval
Rukn-ad-Din and about 12,000 of his followers were put to
death in a particularly barbarous way, and Juvayni, the
Mongol historian, was able to relate with smug self-
satisfaction: "Of him and his stock no trace was left, and
he and his kindred became but a tale on men's lips and a
tradition in the world."

Altogether there had been over sixty castles in the
valley, the three most important being Alamut, meaning
"Eagle's Nest," which had been captured and rebuilt by
Hasan-i-Sabbah; Maymun-Diz, or "Happy Castle"; and
Lammassar. After the Mongols had overthrown the
Assassins, they proceeded to destroy every fortification,
large or small, with utmost zeal. Small groups of Assassins
who had survived the massacre attempted to recapture the
valley in 1275 and 1389, but they did not succeed.

To the Western world (which had heard of the Assassins
through the tales of returning Crusaders, and, later, through
the traveller Marco Polo, who was born probably in the year
before the fall of Maymun-Diz), the tyranny of Alamut had
ended in the mid-thirteenth century; the Assassins had
become legendary figures, and their castles were forgotten.

During medieval times feudal lords took possession of
parts of the valley of Alamut, and some of the castles were
rebuilt.

In the seventeenth century the castle of Alamut was
used as a prison and thus described by Chevalier Chardin
in his *Les Voyages du Chevalier Chardin en Perse*:

> Alamouth est un fort château proche de Casbin, bâti sur un
> haute roche, aux bords d'un précipice, qui sert de tout temps
> de prison aux illustres disgraciez, et où, dans les siècles
> précédents, les rois relégoient les personnes de leur sang, et
> d'autres, dont on vouloit se défaire sans éclat.

The first serious attempt to tell the story of the Assassins was in 1697, in a series of articles in d'Herbelot's *Bibliothèque Orientale,* and these were the main source of information for many years to come.

Then in 1833 an article appeared in the *Journal of the Royal Geographical Society* by a British officer, Colonel Monteith. Monteith had some knowledge of the history of the Assassins, and knew that the castle of Alamut was in the mountains near Kazwin. From the town of Menjil he followed the course of the Shah Rud, and eventually came to the entrance to the Alamut valley, though he did not reach the village of Gazur Khan above which the castle of Alamut is situated. He also seems to have confused the fort of Shir Kuh, at the entrance to the valley, with the main castle.

To Lieutenant-Colonel Sheil belongs the honour of being the first Westerner to have identified the castle itself, and he gave an account of his visit in the *Journal of the Royal Geographical Society* in 1838. Another British officer, Stewart, also visited the castle, only slightly later.

Strangely enough, there was a lull of another century before the second great period in the exploration of Alamut began. In 1927 the eminent archaeologist, Professor Herzfeld, visited the area, but unfortunately he did not publish anything about his journey. Then, in 1928, Dr Lockhart of Cambridge went there too, and published a valuable article entitled "Hasan-i-Sabbah and the Assassins" in the *Bulletin of the School of Oriental and African Studies,* 1928–30. In this article he gave a detailed and clear description of the physical features of the site, and this has been the basis of all subsequent modern work.

Professor W. Ivanow, the historian of the Ismaili Society and author of *Alamut and Lamasar* (published in 1960), first visited the area in December 1928, and contributed an article entitled "Alamut" to the *Geographical Journal* of January 1931.

The name most frequently associated in this country

with the Assassins is that of Miss Freya Stark, who published in her charming book *The Valleys of the Assassins and other Persian Travels* (Murray, 1934) an account of her journey made in May 1930. This work, which holds its place among the classics of travel, also adds one other most important piece of information to our knowledge. Her main achievement was the discovery of the site of Lammassar, and so the second great Assassin fortress was identified.

But the site of the fortress of Maymun-Diz, which played such an important part in the last days of the Assassins, had not yet been established. To add to the difficulties, the name had been forgotten by the local inhabitants, whereas Alamut and Lammassar continued to be used throughout the centuries. If the site of Maymun-Diz could be identified, this would be a very important link in our knowledge of the area—and this is where our story really begins.

The first time that an expedition to Persia set out from Wellington College was in 1959, when I led a reconnaissance party which actually succeeded in finding the site of Maymun-Diz. But by the time we accomplished our mission we were so exhausted and ill that we were able to enter only a small part of the steep rock fortress. As the 1959 expedition led to our attempt in 1960 to make a thorough survey of Maymun-Diz and of all the other castles in the valley, I shall briefly relate the story of this expedition.

In 1959 I was invited by the British Ambassador in Teheran, Sir Geoffrey Harrison, to spend the summer holidays in Iran with his son, Bruce, and Richard Mordaunt, both of whom had been boys in my house at Wellington. Our original intention was to drive out in my own car, a project that, while undoubtedly exciting, filled me with no small degree of alarm for the well-being of my car. Soon after this invitation I was appointed to a Schoolmaster

Studentship at Balliol for the spring term of 1959. Among the many friends I met there two were to have a special influence on the forthcoming expedition. The first, Michael Gwynne, was a young don at Balliol, a professional botanist, and an ardent explorer. He had already taken part in an Oxford expedition to Socotra, an island in the Indian Ocean, and was on the committee of the Oxford Exploration Club. When I told him of my intention to spend two months in Persia, he suggested that I might go farther afield than Teheran and explore the desert of Dasht-el-Kebir. On the map this is a vast salt desert to the south-west of Teheran in which there are few roads or tracks. He was full of enthusiasm for the adventurous training of the young, and assured me that I would not lack support from Industry, both in the way of funds and of supplies. He threw himself into the planning with tremendous ardour, and it was from him I learnt a great deal about the vital preliminary stages which contribute to the success of an expedition. My second mentor, Dr S. M. Stern, Fellow of All Souls College, Oxford, was a man of quite different type, and it was largely due to him that I forsook the great salt desert for the valleys of the Assassins. I had recently read Freya Stark's book and it seemed to me that much more valuable work could be done here than in the south. Stern, who has a considerable reputation in the field of Oriental studies, soon convinced me that I was right. Although primarily a scholar, he has a boyish appreciation of anything unusual or adventurous, and, sitting beside the fire in his oak-panelled room at All Souls, he told me something of the legends that surrounded Hasan-i-Sabbah and of the mystery of the fortress of Maymun-Diz. "Why not go and look for it yourself?" was his challenge. "You cannot fail to have an exciting time, and you may come back with something intensely worth while." He agreed to become our historical adviser, and soon I had two or three notebooks filled with comments and suggestions which, together with Freya Stark's books

and Juvayni's *History of the World Conqueror*, translated by
Dr Boyle of Manchester University, became our Bible.

When I first met Stern I had little idea of the course I
was embarking on and that what at first seemed fascinating
tales of a legendary figure would, in fact, lead me, in
company with the other members of both expeditions, to
the pursuit of something that was at the same time tangible
and precise and yet full of doubts and uncertainties. When
we drew up our list of objectives they read as follows:

1. To carry out a thorough investigation of the rock of
   Alamut.
2. To find, if possible, the site of Maymun-Diz.
3. To investigate the castles of Lammassar and Shir Kuh.
4. To recover and bring back any archaeological finds
   —pottery or coins, for example—dating from Assassin
   times that we might find at these sites.

The next task was to choose suitable members to
accompany me. Gwynne suggested a young geographer,
Colin Volk, who was in his last year at Oxford. Bruce
Harrison told me that his brother John wanted to come,
and we soon enlisted another undergraduate from
Brasenose, Michael Downham, who was reading medicine.
Then we had to find an interpreter, and Stern suggested an
undergraduate at Keble, Brian Spooner, who had originally
read classics and had then switched to Persian. With
Digby Brindle-Wood-Williams of Worcester as our
administrative officer the party was now complete.
Altogether we would be nine including Richard Mordaunt,
who was still at Grenoble University.

The eight Oxford representatives met in my rooms at
Balliol to draw up our plan of campaign. Our first task was
to provide transport for ourselves. Gwynne reported that
a firm in Oxford was willing to lend us a bus, and we all
trooped down to see it. The bus turned out to be a vintage
Commer that had first seen service during the Second
World War and was now residing in a garage near

Oxford. We looked at it and our hearts sank. How on earth could this decrepit old thing possibly convey us the 10,000 miles to Teheran and back? But we decided to take the risk, and, with our administration complete, the expedition left Wellington at the beginning of August 1959.

Our journey down to Dover was uneventful. The bus was decorated with brightly painted headboards showing the words "The Oxford Assassins." On the side was painted in large white letters, "Oxford—Teheran—and return." We enjoyed very much the way in which people looked at us as we bowled down the main road to Dover, and, having arrived safely at Calais, we began our long overland journey to Istanbul. The bus seemed to be behaving extremely well until just south of Paris, at Châlons-sur-Marne, it came to a grinding halt outside one of those funny little petrol-stations that are dotted around the French countryside. I was driving at the time and, feeling that something serious was wrong, I put the bus into neutral and came to a stop. The garage manager saw us and promptly came out to inquire what was the matter. I told him that I did not know and asked him to listen to the engine and to give his expert opinion.

As soon as I pressed the starter there was a most peculiar noise under the bonnet. It sounded just as though a Polaris missile was about to take off. Sadly the garage manager shook his head. "Il est mort," he said. "Why was it dead?" we asked, and would it not be possible to revive it? No, he replied, six *têtes de bielles* were broken. We looked at one another questioningly. What on earth were *têtes de bielles*? None of us had ever met this expression and our pocket dictionaries proved of no use at all. Then, slowly, the magnitude of the disaster dawned upon our numbed brains. A *tête de bielle* was a big-end, we discovered from the manager's crude diagrams. Six of them. "How long would they take to repair?" we asked in despair. He did not know, but promised to phone to Châlons and get us towed to the largest garage there the next day. We set up our tents by the side of the road and passed the night in utter dejection.

The next morning the breakdown lorry arrived and towed us to the garage. There the engine was stripped and we were shown the six big-ends, which undoubtedly would never work again. Châlons-sur-Marne did not possess big-ends of the pattern we wanted, nor, as we discovered from frantic telephoning, did any town in the whole of the north of France. They would just have to be made, and this would take at least two weeks. Our gloom was indescribable. Before we had set out the chaplain at Wellington had presented us with a bottle of champagne that was to be opened on the top of Maymun-Diz. Maymun-Diz now seemed far away, and in order to relieve our gloom and depression we decided to broach the champagne there and then. It was perhaps due to the excellence of this drink that our spirits revived. After all, the main point of the expedition was not to get there by bus but to get there, and if the bus failed us there were other means of transport. Paris was not so far away, and we decided that we would leave the bus at Châlons to be repaired and proceed by train to Istanbul. This meant the complete reorganization of our equipment; but within twelve hours we found ourselves on the Orient Express bound for Venice, Sofia, Istanbul.

From Istanbul we travelled across Turkey in the Trans-Anatolian Express as far as Erzerum, and there changed into one of the so-called 'dust buses' which eventually delivered us, battered and filthy, in Teheran. Here we stayed in the British Embassy compound, recuperating from our long journey and getting the last of the stores that we needed. Three days later we were able to leave for Alamut in two Land Rovers lent to us by the Embassy. We struck north-west from Teheran along the main road to Kazwin, following the foothills of the Elburz mountains for 70 miles, then turned north along a mule-track for another 15 miles. From this point it was impossible for the

Land Rovers to proceed any farther into the foothills, and they returned to Teheran.

We camped for the night in a draughty wadi, and the next day arranged for our first mule-team to take us over the Chala Pass into the Alamut valley. The path rose sharply and it took us a good six hours of solid slogging to reach the top of the pass at 8000 feet. The day was extremely hot, there was little water, and even our muleteers were beginning to flag.

Suddenly our mule-train came to the top of a crest, and there, laid out before us, we saw the entire length of the valley of the Assassins. The predominant colours were brown and red, but a few patches of luxuriant green showed the sites of the villages. Up in the sky, as if messengers of Hasan-i-Sabbah, there wheeled two eagles, and far away on the horizon we could see the outline of Solomon's Throne, a mountain peak of 12,160 feet, resembling the throne-bed of an Oriental potentate. Dusk was falling, and we postponed our descent until the next day. The journey down took us another six hours until we came to the entrance to the Alamut gorge. This is hidden even from the top of the Chala Pass and stands at the confluence of two rivers—the Taliqan (or Upper Shah Rud) and the Alamut Rud. To reach the gorge two rivers have to be forded. In summer, the water, a beautiful grey-green but icy cold, comes only up to one's waist, but in the winter the valley is entirely cut off from any communication with the outside world. The gorge itself is just less than a mile long. On each side tower up red sandstone rocks to a height of some 500 feet. The complete silence and lack of vegetation, combined with the burning heat, conjure up in the mind the impressions of how this valley must have looked 700 years ago. On the left and right are two little ruined forts, which must have served as look-outs for the Assassin sentries, and which Freya Stark noted. But we decided to leave them for the moment and to push on to the fortress of Alamut itself.

The castle of Alamut is situated above the village of Gazur Khan, and it was here that we set up our first base-camp. Every evening we questioned the villagers closely about any other castles in the vicinity, but no one seemed able to throw any fresh light on the possible site of Maymun-Diz until, on our last evening, we were told that near Mu'allim Kilaya, the 'capital' of the valley, there was a big rock on the top of which some ruins were still thought to exist. This did not seem at first sight a very likely place for Rukn-ad-Din's castle to be placed, but nevertheless we felt it would be well worth a visit. We arrived at the 'capital' in the evening, and there, towering above us, was a great mass of conglomerate rock, looking for all the world like some Gothic cathedral with pinnacles and buttresses.

The headman greeted us, and we asked him if the rock was the castle. Yes, it was, he said, but he knew nothing about it at all. He did not even know the name. We asked if anybody else had been there, and he said no. Had he ever been inside, was our next question. He replied that a few villagers had climbed into some of the caves about fifteen years before, but that the ascent was extremely difficult, and he did not think that we would be able to make it. However, he promised to let us have the assistance of two guides.

On the next day we set out with ropes to see if we could get inside. Our chief guide was called Shukrallah, and we soon christened him the Ape-man. This nickname he earned by climbing and scampering over the steepest slopes with such ape-like agility that no height seemed too difficult for him. Like most of the rest of the villagers, he never wore shoes, and advised us to do the same, but five minutes on razor-sharp pebbles and stones, interspersed with very sharp thistles, made walking barefoot so uncomfortable that we insisted on putting our shoes on again. When we got to the foot of the rock we could clearly see the openings of caves and what, from ground-level,

appeared to be a well-preserved arch and traces of plaster.
The Ape-man said that inside one of the holes he had seen
some bones, and people had also picked up daggers and
swords from the foot of the mountain. We decided to try
the easiest opening first. The Ape-man shinned up a
narrow chimney, tied a rope firmly round a boulder, flung
it down, and told us to climb up. Downham was the first
to have a go. He was about half-way up when there was a
shower of dislodged pebbles and stones and down he
tumbled. Fortunately he did himself no harm, apart from a
few superficial grazes and cuts. But this episode convinced
the Ape-man and his fellow-guides that we needed to be
handled rather more carefully than they had at first
thought. Their final solution was to tie the rope round our
waists and to haul us up like bundles of hay, and in this
way three of us managed to get inside one of the caves.

To our astonishment we did in fact see plaster inside
and were able to explore a considerable number of rock
chambers and corridors that were obviously man-made.
Try as we would, however, we could get no farther than
our original opening. The following day we made two
fresh attempts, but without success. Ill-health was already
beginning to take its toll, and most of the party were now
beginning to feel weak through dysentery and incipient
jaundice. From a close study of Juvayni it seemed to us that
Mu'allim Kilaya was almost certainly the site of Maymun-
Diz. In any case we could tell that this was a vast castle,
far bigger than Alamut. If it was not Maymun-Diz, what
was it?

On our return to England we submitted our results to
the British Museum and to Dr Stern, and were delighted
when they confirmed our findings and informed us that we
could announce that we had discovered the site of Maymun-
Diz. What had begun as a light-hearted attempt to extract
(as *The Times* put it) the "maximum enjoyment from an
adventurous summer vacation in Persia with an archaeological flavour" had now turned through our unexpected

success and discoveries into something far more serious. More than this, our success was such that both Dr Stern and Ralph Pinder-Wilson of the British Museum (the latter was advising me on the pottery) thought it would be well worth our while to go again and attempt to get inside Maymun-Diz and make complete sketches and ground-plans.

2

The Beginnings

W E H A D been back in England a bare two months when the final decision was taken that another expedition should go out in 1960 to the valleys of the Assassins. It was at once clear to us that the expedition would have to include rather more experts than we had had before. I was asked to be the leader, and Richard Mordaunt would be my deputy. In addition we planned to have an archaeologist, a mountaineer, a photographer, a surveyor and carto-grapher, a quartermaster, and a medical officer. The last we felt to be quite vital. Three of the 1959 members had spent quite a long period in the London Hospital for Tropical Diseases after their return from Persia, and we did not want this to happen again.

Our next step was to get out a leaflet describing who we were and what we intended to do. In this we stated that the purpose of the 1960 expedition was to verify and make a more detailed investigation of the discoveries of 1959, and to ex-tend our explorations to include all aspects of the valleys of the Assassins, many of which had not been explored by Westerners. We went into greater detail about the scientific programme, and this we divided into five main headings.

1. *Historical.* A detailed investigation, including ground-plans, etc., of the principal fortresses of the Assassins, with particular reference to Maymun-Diz in the Alamut valley, and penetration into other un-explored valleys, especially the valley of Ashkavar which should give evidence of earlier fortresses and civilizations.
2. *Archaeological.* The recovery of pottery and other objects from the sites to be investigated.
3. *Geographical.* The study of the economy, agricultural methods, and way of life of the inhabitants of the region.
4. *Medical.* A medical survey of the area.
5. *Photographic.* The making of ciné films and tape-recordings of the life of the valleys, and recording on film the location and topography of the Assassin castles.

We sent this programme to the Royal Geographical Society and asked for their support and help. Field-Marshal Sir Claude Auchinleck had again agreed to be our patron, and our other sponsor was Sir George Binney, the well-known industrialist in the steel world and a great explorer himself. We filled up the R.G.S. form and waited for an interview. On the appointed day I was unfortunately unable to be present myself, and so Richard went in my place. The Committee of the R.G.S. were undoubtedly extremely interested in the expedition, but we were not sufficiently geographical for them to be able to support us financially. To make up for this, Ralph Pinder-Wilson agreed to provide us with some invaluable credentials and references, and with this backing we felt we could go ahead and ask for support from industry and elsewhere.

The selection of the members of any expedition is, of course, one of the most important tasks of the leader. The teaching staff at Wellington was fortunate to include several men who had proved their courage and ability in

dangerous and difficult feats in war and in peace. I asked
two of them to join us. Gerald Hawkins, still fit, tough,
and wiry at 47, was to be our medical officer. But before the
expedition left England he was unfortunately compelled
to withdraw. Robert Moss, a housemaster, who had taken
part in the Oxford University Expedition to North East
Land in 1936, was thrilled with the idea of exchanging the
Polar snows for the sunbaked plains and mountains of
northern Persia. I asked him to be our mountaineer, and
he was soon busily writing round for the necessary equipment. As quartermaster we chose Michael Oliver, who
was working with Rediffusion in Bristol and who had also
been a pupil at Wellington. He was the youngest member
of the party, barely 20, but tough and efficient at his job.
These men seemed to me to make a very satisfactory
nucleus for the expedition.

Shortly afterwards I was introduced to a young and
intelligent Persian doctor, Minou Sabetian, who was
working at a hospital near London. He had left Persia
eight years before and come to England to continue his
medical studies. His aim was to gain his Master's degree in
surgery at a British university, and then return to a
teaching post at the University of Teheran. Although
this meant we should have two doctors, we felt this would
be an advantage. If the expedition had to split into two
parties, which seemed very likely, each party would have
a competent doctor at its disposal, but it was agreed that
officially Gerald Hawkins should be our medical officer and
Minou Sabetian our interpreter. When Gerald had to
withdraw from the expedition, Minou was asked to
combine the posts of doctor and interpreter.

In order to find our surveyor, who would be responsible
for all cartographical matters, we approached the Army.
The Directorate of Military Survey enthusiastically gave
its blessing to the idea of a young Engineer being seconded
to the expedition. A notice was published in Army Orders
asking for all volunteers to write to London. The chief

qualifications we wanted were that the candidate must be a first-class surveyor and cartographer and also have some knowledge of explosives. At this stage we felt that if we were to penetrate farther into Maymun-Diz we could do this only by clearing the galleries with small explosive charges. These would have to be very carefully controlled, as otherwise we might destroy valuable pottery inside as well as bring down more rubble than we should be able to move. Altogether about twenty candidates applied for this post. A short list was drawn up and in the end we appointed Roddie Dugmore, a captain in the Ordnance Survey Office at Edinburgh.

The choice of a photographer was more difficult. In order to help raise some money, I put an advertisement in the Personal column of *The Times* which said: "Unexplored territory. Expedition penetrating to the valleys of the Assassins urgently requires funds. Are there any en-lightened benefactors in this utilitarian age?" The B.B.C. noticed this and in "From To-day's Papers" mentioned it the morning that it appeared. This produced quite an avalanche of letters, mostly from people who wanted to join the expedition in some capacity or other, and every one seemed to be a top-class photographer. However, on closer investigation, no one quite suited our book. We were really wondering what we should do when Richard heard of a young American, Ragnar van Leyden, who had spent four years making documentary films in Hollywood and who was now in Venice on a short holiday. We wrote to him, and he replied that there was nothing he would like to do better than come to the valleys of the Assassins. It was agreed that Richard and he would meet in Italy, and it was there that Ragnar was signed on.

We still did not have an archaeologist, and despite all our efforts—and those of Ralph Pinder-Wilson—we eventually had to leave without one. This was not so much of a handicap as it might seem at first sight. The study of the Assassins is a highly specialized one, and I suppose

there are only three or four people in the world who are
competent to undertake it. Although I was very much a
newcomer in this field I had by now acquired sufficient
experience to be able to evaluate with reasonable accuracy
the significance of anything we might find. Rather than
add to the expenses of the expedition by taking an
archaeologist who was a specialist in a field other than
medieval Persia we felt that I might just as well take the
plunge and be personally responsible for the archaeological
work. In the end I think this decision was justified.

Among letters I had received as a result of *The Times*
advertisement was one from the representative of the
National Iranian Oil Company in London. The word oil at
once conjured up thoughts of money-bags bursting with
dollars that would be placed unreservedly at our disposal!
Mr Nabavi, the London representative, asked me to go
and see him. He had, he said, already read in the Teheran
papers that another expedition was going to Persia, and his
company would be very willing to help in whatever way
they could. Unfortunately, they could not make any direct
financial grant, but they could promise to give us all the
petrol we should need in Persia, to maintain our Land
Rover and any other vehicles we might acquire, and to
provide us with a substantial amount of stores and equipment. In addition, they would probably be able to lend us
the services of a second interpreter and an engineer if we
wanted them.

We then turned our attention to the problem of equipment. We decided to cut our food-supplies down to a
minimum as transportation across Europe and through the
Elburz mountains would be a headache in any case, and we
felt that our equipment should have first priority. Gerald
Hawkins, however, insisted that we should take an
adequate supply of tinned and preserved foods. He was
quite sure that in 1959 we had contracted jaundice and
dysentery from eating polluted meat that we had obtained
from the villagers, and he was emphatic in his insistence

that this must not happen again. Ralph Pinder-Wilson suggested that we approach Mr Sainsbury (now Lord Sainsbury), and this we did. He told us that he was an amateur archaeologist himself, and that he would be delighted for his firm to supply us with £100 worth of tinned food at wholesale prices. This news brought in from every member a list of his own personal requirements and tastes, ranging from canned chicken to caviare and *pâté de foie gras*. We sternly refused to allow any such exotic tastes, and, in the end, spent £50 on bully beef, and the rest on food that Gerald recommended for its high nutritional value. We did, however, spend £5 on fruit salad, so we could give ourselves a special treat on Sundays. Other firms contributed in a very generous way also, and showed a keen interest in the expedition. In the course of our negotiations we were staggered to find that in 1960 over 300 expeditions were setting out from England to different parts of the world. Many came from universities, and were not serious expeditions at all. They write in and ask for goods, which they are then given, but nothing more is ever heard of them. Such jaunts can really spoil the market for those whose expeditions are of a serious nature.

Originally we had contemplated taking two Land Rovers, but this would have doubled our requirements of petrol, oil, and spare parts. So we bought, at a very reasonable price, a second-hand Land Rover, originally registered in 1958. It was a long-based model, and we had a special roof-rack fitted by Acrow, so that we could sleep either inside with the gear or on the rack.

In May, the *Daily Telegraph* printed an article on the forthcoming expedition, saying that no one had yet penetrated inside the castle of Maymun-Diz, and that this year some Britons would attempt what had been impossible for over 700 years. Put this way, it made us feel rather heroic, but any tendency to being swollen-headed was soon knocked out of me by my own colleagues in the Masters' Common Room! They probably thought I was being rather

rash; but underneath their mockery there was sincere
encouragement and friendly co-operation. As the days
passed, things became more and more hectic. Wellington
was our headquarters, and we had a meeting nearly every
week at which a progress report would be given and we
considered the next steps. It was decided that Richard,
Mike, and Minou would take the equipment and stores in
the Land Rover (picking up Ragnar van Leyden in Venice
if he agreed to join us), and the rest of the party would
fly out and join them in Teheran. The next thing to do was
to have two large signs painted by the works staff at
Wellington College: one said "Alamut Valley Expedition
1960" and the other "London, Teheran, and Return." The
Land Rover was serviced, given new tyres and a spare set,
and was fully guaranteed (rather a rash thing for the
garage to do) for a period of six months.

On June 29 Richard and Mike arrived and the process of
loading up began. It was then that we discovered that we
had in fact got far more stores than we could possibly
carry in the Land Rover. A hasty council-of-war ensued
and it was decided that the lighter goods would be taken
out by air with the main party. Insurance agents came
down to make a final check and were helpful in drawing up
a complete inventory of all that we possessed. We packed
and re-packed the Land Rover and trailer five times before
we were finally satisfied. The Land Rover looked perfectly
sturdy under its heavy load, but the trailer[1] certainly did
not, and so we decided to put in the latter anything that
was not absolutely vital. There was a long argument as to
whether beer came under this heading or not, and eventually it was split between the two vehicles. Loading was
finally finished about 2 A.M. on July 1. Richard had already
drawn up a shorter itinerary. He would drive straight to
Venice, where he would meet Ragnar, and then push on
through Yugoslavia and Bulgaria to Istanbul. There he

[1] This trailer was not made by the Rover Company.

would take the usual route through Turkey to Teheran. This, if all went well, would allow him ten days in Teheran for making certain that all our papers and passes were in order. Two days earlier we had received an offer from an archaeologist in Teheran to join us out there, and Richard was to brief him fully once he arrived, but unfortunately this offer came to nothing.

The following morning at 6 the Land Rover slipped quietly away. Robert Moss and I got up early to see Richard and Mike off. Sabetian was to meet them in London and they were due at Dover by 11. We took the first photograph of the expedition: the start. Followed by cries of "See you in Teheran," the Land Rover purred down the main drive of Wellington, and the 1960 expedition had begun. I returned to my room for a cup of coffee and the telephone rang. It was Minou Sabetian. In a voice full of genuine regret he said that family circumstances compelled him to stay for a week longer in England, and so he could not go out with Richard after all. Instead Minou intended to follow the party by plane, and he would meet Richard in Erzerum. We just had time to ring up the Port Authorities at Dover and ask them to warn Richard, and received a phone message in reply saying that all had gone well, except for a few minor hitches, such as the loss of one Bulgarian visa. Later it was picked up in a London street.

All expeditions have their teething troubles!

3

The Advance Party

I T   H A D   been decided some six weeks before that Richard
would take with him on his outward journey two of his own
friends. These were Myles de Vries, an Old Wellingtonian
of Richard's vintage, and Simon Orr-Ewing, who lived near
Richard in Hertfordshire. Myles de Vries wanted to go to
Iran to see something of the country and hoped to spend
two or three months in Teheran teaching English before
he returned to England to start his career in Lloyd's.
Orr-Ewing wanted a lift only as far as Geneva, but they
were both prepared to pay their share of the petrol. Also it
seemed wise to have as many qualified drivers and capable
spare hands as possible.

Richard and Mike picked up these two supernumeraries
in London, and also had to make a last-minute call to
collect some specially designed boxes, which were intended
for storing pottery. When the advance party was complete,
there were four altogether—Richard in charge, Mike
Oliver, Myles de Vries, and Simon Orr-Ewing. Collecting
the stores in London took longer than they had anticipated,
and their first task was to cover the 72 miles from London

THE CASTLE OF SAMIRAN

bove: An aerial view. *Below:* From the base, which, in 1962, was flooded by the
*w Menjil dam.

THE EASTERN MAUSOLEUM AT SAMIRAN

The remains of this mausoleum are on a rise near the castle (in the background.
Part of an inscription on a frieze (enlarged below) can be seen.

SAMIRAN

This minaret, about a mile from the castle, contains a double spiral staircase. A person ascending will never meet another person descending.

The staircase
of the
minaret.

SAMIRAN

The main
mausoleum.

Three-storey apartments built into the fortifications of the castle.

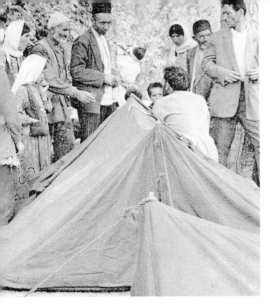

Left: Surgery hour at base-camp below Maymun-Diz.

Right: Minou Sabetian at Samiran.

Below: The Alamut Valley Expedition: (left to right) Roddie Dugmore, Mike ?ver, Minou Sabetian, Jah Kurlu, the ?dman, Shukrallah (front), the author, ?hard Mordaunt, Ragnar van Leyden.

Some of the contents of a small grave near Shuileh.

LOTOSAN

Above: The excavation of the bath-house.

Below: Clay conduit pipes from the bath-house.

The bath-house at Lotosan. Note the three fire holes and the tiled bench.

A blacksmith
at Alamut.

to Dover in something under two hours. From the start the trailer proved a doubtful asset. It lurched badly and made the Rover very hard to steer. However, they just made it and had time to telephone to us before embarking without Sabetian.

The route that the advance party intended to follow went through France, Italy, Yugoslavia, Bulgaria, and Turkey, with an early detour to Geneva to drop Simon Orr-Ewing. Although much is written about the bad state of the European road network, the main trunk roads are in fact very good. There is now a plan to link Europe and Asia together by a highway known as the Trans-Asian Motorway, and future travellers will not need to fear running into any undue hazards. In any case it is not until one reaches the Iranian frontier that one encounters the most appalling corrugated dust-tracks that wind through the sandy mountains. Obtaining petrol is not a great problem until the Afghan border, although it is always wise for motorists to carry a good supply of petrol in jerry cans. Often one comes across petrol-pumps that have been empty for some time, and the quality, of course, varies very much from country to country.

The advance party now had a little over a month to get to Teheran and make certain that all our permits were in order. To begin with, they moved in rather a slow and leisurely fashion towards Geneva. Later, they were to regret that they had not gone somewhat faster, as all the delays due to mechanical troubles or administrative reasons occurred in the middle or towards the end of the long journey and not at the beginning. The journey to Geneva was uneventful. Orr-Ewing was safely dropped and the party started to move south towards France.

The first hitch occurred at the frontier between France and Switzerland at Annemasse. There the Land Rover was stopped at the customs, and, although all documents were completely in order, the authorities found it difficult to believe that all the kit was intended merely for our personal

use. They politely requested that everything be unloaded
from the Rover and trailer, and in a short time approximately £5000 worth of technical apparatus, film, food,
and beer was piled up outside the Rover. The customs
officials clustered inquisitively around, looked into the
different sacks and kitbags, and then climbed up on the
luggage-rack to examine the camping equipment that was
stacked up on top. This was very frustrating because loading the vehicle had taken a long time, and now everything
would have to be restacked. However, the officials
insisted, and they were rewarded when a sentry unearthed
two 12-bore shotguns, two revolvers, and a Very pistol
from beneath a pile of camp-beds. The 12-bores were
intended for supplementing our supplies of canned meat,
the revolvers were for our own personal protection (in
1959 a brigand had shot at me with the obvious intention
of robbing me of the binoculars and camera that I was
carrying—fortunately he missed!), and the Very pistol was
in case we were lost when crossing the mountains by night.
All these weapons were perfectly legal, but apparently we
had neglected to obtain an ammunition licence, and it was
this that caused a major hold-up. The chief customs officer
said that it would be impossible for the party to continue
unless a licence signed by the authorities in Geneva was
produced. It was a Friday, and a licence could not be
obtained until the following Monday. This would mean
too long a delay, so Richard decided that it would be better to
withdraw and try another frontier-post. This he did, and after
making a detour of some 20 miles the advance party again
approached the familiar red-and-white barrier. A friendly
salute from the guards, "Vos passeports, messieurs. Ah!
bon, vous êtes Anglais, ça va." A polite wave of the hand,
the barrier was raised, and the Land Rover was through.

   The party moved quickly through France to Grenoble
and Modane, and so through the tunnel under the Alps
from Sestrières to Turin. The mountain passes are
difficult to negotiate with a Land Rover and trailer, and

this route seemed easier. The tunnel was originally built for a local branch railway-line. Cars are put on board a miniature train-ferry and the journey takes about half an hour. Most of the cars that use this route are rather luxurious American-type vehicles, with sparkling chromium. Above the entrance to the railway there is a kind of U-shaped notice hanging down from a chain. There is nothing to say what it indicates, but it is, in fact, the height of the tunnel through the mountains. Our party discovered this after it was too late, and then realized to their horror that the trailer was a good six inches above the permitted height. In addition, the roof-rack was square while the tunnel was curved. However, there was nothing they could do, and there followed an anxious half-hour as they sat in the passenger coaches in the forward part of the train expecting to hear at any moment an ear-splitting crash. Fortunately, all was well, as the railway authorities had wisely allowed a very large safety-margin.

Bardonecchia was reached. The air was crisp, and Richard and Mike were happily conscious that they were moving farther east all the time. The Land Rover purred beautifully along. Petrol consumption was good, about 20 miles to the gallon. But Italy is an expensive country to cross on this type of expedition. Very understandably the officials rarely meet with a vehicle such as ours, and ironically they classified it as a luxury coach. Needless to say, Richard and his party could not understand how the words "luxury" or "coach" came in at all. There was also a certain amount of trouble about the capacity of the engine for tax purposes. In the end it was agreed that the Land Rover should be downgraded from the category of luxury coach to that of super racing-car!

At Milan, the first mechanical trouble developed. A slipping clutch held up the party, but the Land Rover agents in the city were able to put it right. Nevertheless the chief mechanic rather gloomily forecast that the whole vehicle was so overloaded that it would never reach

Teheran, and he was prepared to back his opinion with a substantial wager. Richard, to his regret afterwards, declined, but he received in addition the useful information that there had been heavy floods in Turkey, and that he might meet very adverse motoring conditions. The state of the trailer was now becoming definitely worrying. The original U-springs had sagged to a hump-backed position, and it seemed likely that it would have to be ditched before very long.

The party arrived in Venice on July 18, some ten days before their scheduled arrival in Teheran. Here they were due to interview Ragnar van Leyden, and a meeting was arranged in San Marco Square. Although giving full heed to my warning that it would be unwise to engage further manpower unless it was absolutely essential, Richard at once took to this tall, thin American. His professional qualifications were excellent, and he had a chain of contacts that would obviously stand us in good stead from Venice to Teheran. He and his wife were visiting his parents in Italy, and he had, in fact, planned to go to Greece within the next two days. On hearing of our romantic destination and the obvious photographic possibilities of the expedition he at once enthusiastically volunteered to sign on as a full member. Everything was arranged with the minimum of delay. The formal contract was signed, and Ragnar was ready to leave at 6.30 the following morning. The heavily laden Rover and its green, lumbering trailer slipped back across the causeway that links Venice to the mainland and turned north to Trieste. Ragnar lost no time in showing how useful he could be in a dozen capacities apart from the one for which he had been engaged. He spoke Italian, Greek, German, and Turkish fluently. By nature an extremely orderly person, he soon insisted on reorganizing the somewhat chaotic conditions prevailing inside the Land Rover after the encounter with the authorities at Annemasse. The clutch continued to give trouble, but somehow Ragnar managed to repair it.

The Yugoslav frontier was soon reached, and it is with considerable justice that this country boasts of its fine autobahn from Belgrade to Nis. The only trouble is that the road is unfenced. Ragnar was driving during the early hours of one morning when Michael and Richard, who were peacefully sleeping in the back, were rudely awakened by a screech of tyres and a thud. They had hit a cow that had wandered on to the road. Fortunately it did not seem to mind, and got to its feet, wobbled unsteadily, then rather sulkily moved away. The Land Rover moved on, but the offside wing had crumpled into a convulsive, fried-egg pattern. Richard did not know to whom he should report this incident, and in any case the only damage that had accrued was to our own property; but after ten minutes he realized that the vehicle was moving considerably faster than previously and, looking back, he saw the reason why. The trailer was no longer there. They turned and went back the way they had come and saw the trailer sitting rather sadly by itself in the road. At the impact of the collision with the cow the tow-bar had snapped. This was the beginning of the end. Various garages tried to weld it together. With each fresh operation it became heavier and heavier, and it parted company for good near the Bulgarian township of Hermanlitz, in the mountains near the eastern border of the People's Republic. The Rover was gently free-wheeling downhill when Ragnar saw sparks leaping from the road. The tow-bar had parted once again and the trailer was doing its best to catch up the Land Rover. It almost succeeded, and there was danger of a collision, but with great presence of mind Ragnar pulled in to the side and let the trailer hurtle past. Fortunately, it soon came to a halt by a bend in the road and was prevented from crashing over a precipice by a mound of stones. The party emptied it of all its contents, which they loaded on to the Land Rover, and then lumbered into Hermanlitz. They called at police headquarters to inform the authorities of the accident and to suggest that the trailer could be broken up or be put to some use by the municipal authorities. Here, however, they ran into a great snag. By the laws of Bulgaria anything that is taken into the country must be taken out, and with the greatest goodwill the authorities could not make any exception without reference to the Ministry of Internal Affairs in Sofia. It was, however, agreed that in these special circumstances Richard should be allowed to put his case before the local Chief of Police, and an appointment was made for 11.30 the following morning.

Punctually at 11.30 the party arrived at the local Prefecture, and were politely received by the Prefect. He regretted that the Chief of Police had been detained on urgent business, and he suggested that to while away the time he and Richard should play draughts. Richard is quite good at this game and so was the Prefect. For two solid hours a contest went on; soon it became clear that each man was representing the prestige and ambitions of his own side of the Iron Curtain. Richard was sufficiently tactful to allow the Prefect to win the majority of games. At 3 o'clock the Chief of Police with many apologies turned up. He spoke a kind of German and Ragnar acted as interpreter. He firmly insisted that the law could not be broken, but, realizing that this would mean that the expedition would be held up indefinitely in Bulgaria, he hit on a brilliant compromise. The town of Hermanlitz, he said, had a museum. Why not present the trailer on long loan to the museum? It could be picked up when the expedition returned, and in this case everybody's honour would be satisfied. This was a stroke of genius and was enthusiastically accepted by Richard and the advance party. A formal agreement complete with seals was drawn up and signed. The local militia went out and collected the trailer, which was duly placed in the municipal museum. A bottle of wine was opened and speeches were made. So efficacious were the celebrations that the Chief of Police agreed to telephone to the frontier and request the authorities there to give the Land Rover every facility for crossing into Turkey. He was as good as his word. When the party arrived they were given treatment that even Mr Khruschev might have envied. The sequel to this story was that on Richard's return to Bulgaria he was told that some one had stolen the trailer!

It was now July 21, and fortunately the journey through Turkey proved uneventful and much quicker without the lumbering trailer. The Turks were helpful and friendly and did everything in their power to speed on the party, who soon saw before them the deep blue waters of the Bosporus as they approached the ancient city of Istanbul. It was about 4 o'clock in the morning when they arrived, and the twinkling lights of the Sea of Marmara gave way to the silhouette of mosques and towers limned against the skyline in the morning light. The streets of Istanbul were empty, even the station and the Galata bridge—normally seething with shoe-cleaners, paper- and food-sellers, and animals—were peaceful under the patient gaze of Aya Sofya, which was built as a Christian church, then used as a mosque, and is now a museum. The steep, twisting streets of the old eastern side of the city led upward to the Embassy quarter and here the party decided to park their vehicle. Ragnar had no visa and therefore had to visit the Iranian Embassy.

Meanwhile Richard made a lightning visit to Radio Turkey. Oh, yes, they had heard of him and the expedition, they said, and would like a programme in three days' time. But this, alas, was impossible.

Few people remember that Turkey is more than 1000 miles across. The cosmopolitan capital of Ankara is linked to Istanbul, the nerve-centre of the country's economic life, by a great arterial road carved through the mountains, but east of Ankara the country becomes brown, desolate, and arid, and the roads act only as highways to the Black Sea coast in the north where life begins again. Richard

C.A.–D

decided that it would take less time if they drove along the mountain roads through central Turkey; and so it was agreed that when they reached Ankara, Ragnar should board a train to Erzerum with ten or twelve kitbags, thus lightening the Rover for its difficult journey over the mountains. By train from Ankara to Erzerum takes two days, and, with his Press card, Ragnar was entitled to a reduced fare of only fifteen shillings.

The Rover threaded its way through the mountains and on over the plain. In these parts the menace of robbers and thieves is very real and a strict guard is necessary at all times. One evening after a very long drive, the Rover was parked by the side of the road as usual so that the party could have a few hours' sleep. As usual, Richard slept on the front seat of the vehicle and the others in the back. The following morning they woke to find that one window of the Rover was open; all the papers from the pocket in the door had been quietly removed during the night, except for one vital yellow folder which Richard had put under his head while he slept. This folder contained all the money and passports. They could now see that they had stopped on the fringe of a small village, so they walked into it and had tea in the only tea-house in the place, which was crowded with the early-rising villagers. Although everybody must have known what had happened, they all appeared cheerful and innocent and merely said that a passing robber must have attempted to loot the Rover.

It was near this village that they passed the early Christian rock-temples at Avanos and decided that it would be well worth while leaving the main road to explore them. Though they are now a State monument, few travellers visit this remarkable site. Altogether over three hundred churches lie hidden amongst curious volcanic pinnacles, and in them can still be seen the remnants of paintings of Christ and the Virgin Mary and many other religious scenes. The walls are lined with mosaics, and tombs have been excavated beneath the naves. The party was escorted round by a little wizened Turk; at first he complained that Richard had arrived after visiting hours, but he later confessed that he had seen no one for ten days. He collected a candle and they followed his shuffling feet.

After visiting the rock-temples they motored on and spent the night in a village some 25 miles from Avanos, in the house of a man named Mohammed. Learning of the interest shown by the party in the rock-temples, he collected together the wise men of the village, and these whispered that not far from their own village they had even more remarkable caves, which showed evidence of a rich and powerful civilization. According to schedule there were only three days in which to complete the journey to Teheran, but rather than risk missing the discovery of what might prove to be interesting antiquities of considerable value Richard decided to rise early the following morning and visit these new caves. As if to give further proof of their good intentions the villagers brought *objets d'art* of varying periods and descriptions into the room and said that all these had been discovered around the caves.

The party got up at 4.30 the following morning and tumbled into the Land Rover, which now contained sixteen villagers as well, and headed towards the mountains. As they went, their guide pointed out two huge rocks jutting out from the mountains and explained that here, too, were man-made caves far greater than those at Avanos, but that he was taking the party to a special one. After two more hours they arrived at their destination and looked around for the opening of the caves. But now they had to climb up into the rocks, and after a time they reached a gaping hole. Here Mohammed announced that inside were the dwellings of many men. Leaving half their escort above, the party crawled down into this underground world. On and on they crept. A few rough markings were cut into the rock, and that was all they could see at the moment. The guide smoked and laughed; deeper and deeper they went, now standing, now crawling on hands and knees, and finally inching their way along the ground. The light became dimmer and dimmer, but still Mohammed insisted that the great houses were a little farther on. Water dripped down the walls, and the rocks were slippery with moisture. By this time there were still no signs of the end of the passage and several hours had passed. The air was revolting and torches barely picked out the man in front.

Richard and his party had had enough, and so, without wishing to hurt Mr Mohammed's feelings, they explained that the find was quite remarkable, but that it was now time to return. They turned and headed back and, after climbing for two or three hours, they realized that this was not the way they had come. No one had marked the route on the way in, and it now seemed that they were hopelessly lost. At this juncture the torches went out, but fortunately Mike had a box of matches. Panic took hold of the Turks when they realized their predicament, and a babble of shrill voices echoed around the caves, followed by deep silence. They decided to move on, only to find after an hour's further search that they had made a complete circle and had come back to the same room. It was then that Richard hit on the only plan that could show them where the real exit lay. Each man was to take one of the exits out of the room, marking his route with a pile of stones wherever there was a branch in the passage. They would explore for fifteen minutes and then return. At the end of fifteen minutes everybody was back with very long faces except for one Turk. Fortunately, he arrived some five minutes later, announcing that he had felt a draught of air, and this the whole party followed. Eventually they reached daylight again at about 5 o'clock, some nine hours after they had gone underground.

Many valuable hours had been lost in this fruitless search and, in order to make up time, the advance party took it in turns to drive for the rest of the day and night to Erzerum. The roads in Turkey are maintained by the Army, so if one is travelling between two garrison towns the roads will probably be excellent; otherwise in mountainous areas only a broken dust-track confronts the traveller. Some lorries passed from time to time, and these were all hopelessly overladen, their great loads towering sometimes up to 25 feet. On steep inclines the driver must make his way up in a series of jerks. Torrential rain had flooded all the roads approaching Erzerum and most of the bridges had been washed away. However, the Land Rover seemed to take things in its stride. The party passed quite a few vehicles in trouble, but if they had stopped to help every one they would have turned themselves into a day-and-night breakdown-service and made no headway at all. As they were approaching Erzerum along a tortuous and slippery stretch of road, they slowed down almost to a halt behind a group of cars. Here the road had been washed away by a stream that had broken its banks higher up in the valley. As it flooded along the road, it had forced a large Mercedes, which had been cautiously rounding a curve, to the extreme outside edge. The car contained a party of Iranians returning from Germany, and was heavily laden with polythene-covered suitcases. All the occupants—three veiled women and two men—were trying to manoeuvre the car back on the road, but in so doing each time they came a few inches closer to the edge of the cliff. The Rover once again proved its worth, and soon with the aid of ropes the car was back on the road and moving once more.

The party arrived in Erzerum at midday on July 25. The Rover was stopped at a checkpoint outside the town and a military escort was provided. The same thing happened when it left the town. Old city walls encircled this rapidly growing, but unattractive, frontier town which swarmed with troops and dusty armoured cars. Erzerum lacked the lustre and bustling activity that seem typical of most Middle Eastern towns. In some ways it had almost a Russian flavour. Carriages, sometimes pulled by as many as six horses, rattled through the streets. These

carriages are often used for weddings, when they are piled
high with gaily coloured carpets and rugs—the customary
wedding presents.

As well as these carriages, heavily curtained small cabs
ply up and down the main street. At first sight they appear
to be ordinary hackney carriages, but in fact they are used
mostly by prostitutes. Richard wished to get a lift to the
Trebizond Hotel where he was to meet Minou Sabetian:
he hailed an oncoming cab, which strained to a halt. After
making his destination clear with considerable difficulty,
not helped by the interruptions of a crowd that had quickly
gathered and was trying to be helpful, he climbed inside.
Fascinated by this unusual mode of transport, he sat back,
and for several seconds remained unaware of the highly
scented lady who was reclining in one corner of the
carriage. Suddenly he realized the situation in which he
had unwittingly landed himself, and his small Turkish
vocabulary soon proved quite inadequate for the occasion.
From the noises outside he realized that he was not, in fact,
being taken to the Trebizond Hotel, but was being gently
shanghaied to the bazaar area where, presumably, this lady
had her headquarters. He leapt for the door, and the driver,
anxious not to lose his fare, saw what was happening and
came to a halt. The lady, however, was not prepared to
relinquish her quarry quite so easily and started a scene. A
crowd gathered very quickly, but fortunately for Richard
a policeman soon arrived who was able to speak a little
French. The situation was cleared up, although everybody
seemed to think that Richard was to blame, and no word of
reproach was uttered against the driver of the cab or its
occupant. Naturally, Richard's only desire was to get
away as soon as possible, and with a deep sigh of relief he
slipped through the bazaar and eventually found his way
to the hotel.

Minou Sabetian was waiting dismally when Richard and
Michael arrived, and they were soon joined by Ragnar. It
transpired that Minou had been waiting in Erzerum for

three days, his mother and two brothers, who had accompanied him from England, having gone on to Teheran. In the interval Minou had had plenty of opportunity of talking with Iranian students and travellers who were on their way back to Iran from abroad. They had repeated to him numerous stories—highly coloured and exaggerated —of arrests by the Iranian authorities of returning Iranians whom they considered to be Communists. This term, they said, was applied to anyone who had spoken against the Government during his stay in the West or who had been concerned with student politics among the considerable Iranian student population in Western universities. Minou, who had been European Secretary to the Iranian Student Federation, considered himself particularly vulnerable. It is true that he had in fact been active politically, and had probably been unwise in some of his actions, but we had always felt that he had exaggerated the extent of his own activities. The Iranian authorities are not monsters: they are perfectly reasonable men, but naturally they do take a dim view of anybody, particularly in an influential position, who indulges in anti-Government propaganda, even if he has no real wish or intention of overthrowing the regime. Richard and Michael tried to reason with Minou, and pointed out that it would be a real blow to the expedition if their principal interpreter and medical adviser withdrew at this moment, but there was no dissuading him. He had made up his mind that as soon as he crossed the frontier he would be arrested. And so, dejectedly, he returned to Italy, promising that he would write me a letter. Richard sent me a cable and then pushed on. At this time Richard did not know that Gerald Hawkins would not be able to come with us after all, and so the situation was even worse than he thought.

They covered the distance from Erzerum to the Iranian frontier in thirteen hours, which is very good time considering the state of the roads. As they crossed the last stretches of the Anatolian Plain, they again passed by

Mount Ararat and a solitary signpost which said: "Russia
—30 kilometres." Needless to say, few people take
advantage of this invitation, and practically every car
bumps its way along the dusty road until it reaches the
Iranian frontier. They arrived there at 8 A.M., and thus
avoided having to stay the night in the comfortable but
expensive tourist hotel run by the Iranian authorities. The
customs proved amiable and helpful, as they had been
previously informed that the advance party would be
arriving about this time. From the frontier they drove to
the small town of Maku, which is built at the foot of a
mountain. Half-way up the mountain there is a most
remarkable fortification, which seems to hang suspended
on the sheer rock-face beneath a great overhang.

A hundred miles from Maku the road forked, and there
was no signpost to say which was the right route. The
advance party stopped and waited to see if a passer-by
would appear; it seemed pointless to try one of the forks
at random as this might waste several hours or even days.
For two hours nothing happened, and so they thought
they would fill in the time by stripping and cleaning parts
of the engine. Then an old man and a boy came struggling
over the brow of the hill in front of them. Richard and
Michael tried to make the old man understand they
wanted to go to Tabriz, the city of heroes. Which road
should they take? The old man pointed first in the
direction of one fork and then solemnly pointed to the
other. This made no sense at all and it was only after a
while that they realized that the old man was both deaf
and dumb. He went on his way.

Not long after, a small cloud of dust appeared on the
skyline behind them and a large lorry panted down the
road. It was crowded with women, dogs, and children, and
in reply to questioning the driver seemed to be indicating
that they were making their way to Tabriz. Ragnar said
that he would like to go on this lorry as he would probably
get some good shots. So he climbed up and managed to

find himself a place to lean with his camera. It was agreed that the party would meet again in Tabriz. Richard and Mike started up the Land Rover and a few minutes later set off in the wake of the lorry. After ten minutes they found that the two roads met! This is quite a common occurrence in these parts, and why there should be two parallel tracks for a distance of two or three miles nobody quite knows. Devastation following severe floods continued to hamper the Land Rover's progress, and often big detours had to be made to cross a stream where a bridge had been washed away. The Land Rover often threatened to stick hard in the muddy stream beds; but somehow this was avoided—although only just. When the advance party arrived in Teheran, they read in the papers that the floods had been particularly severe around Tabriz. Whole stretches of the railway-line had been washed away and many heavily laden lorries had been abandoned in the water.

They reached Tabriz safely, and then Kazwin, which had been the Persian capital under the great Shah Abbas in the sixteenth century until he transferred the seat of government to Isfahan. The distance from Kazwin to Teheran is about a hundred miles. The road is a fine, metalled one running almost completely straight along the southern foothills of the Elburz mountains. It is lined with small villages, flea-ridden tea-houses, and wooden huts advertising "Pepsi-Cola" on huge, gaudy signboards. The traffic is heavy, and consists of lorries, private cars, and overloaded buses. On each side of the road the dusty plain stretches out, and on it one can see camel-trains plodding patiently along, carrying great burdens of goods. I suppose that there are more accidents on this stretch of road than anywhere else in Iran. When a lorry has a breakdown, or an accident has occurred, the custom is to put a small pile of stones a few yards in front of and behind the broken-down vehicle. When the vehicle is repaired, the driver moves off again, but hardly ever does he replace the stones at the side of the road. Consequently, these stones are a constant menace to fast-moving traffic. A driver will suddenly see them, brake hard and swerve to avoid them, and crash into another vehicle coming in the opposite direction. The advance party decided that they would move slowly along the road. Having come some 5000 miles in safety, they did not wish to jeopardize their lives in the last stretch. They passed one very nasty accident in which a bus had overturned and four or five people had been killed. This accident had just occurred, and yet no one seemed to be doing very much about it. The rest of the travellers from the bus were standing around in a rather helpless way, and no one had attempted to tend the injured. Richard said that as soon as he reached the next village two or three miles down the road, he would at once try and telephone for the police and an ambulance. This he did, but could not wait to discover how long it was before these emergency services came into operation.

They arrived in Teheran late on the evening of the 27th—tired, filthy, and badly in need of a rest. There was nowhere for them to camp, and so they spent the night on the outskirts of the city, parked in a side road. The next morning they headed straight for the British Embassy to see what letters and cables had arrived. Having collected the messages that we had sent telling them the latest situation in London and the urgent need for getting another doctor, they were about to set off in the Land Rover to find a place to eat when they saw a tall, dark figure coming out of the Embassy and walking up to the Land Rover. The tall man introduced himself to Richard as Roddie Dugmore. As Roddie had been appointed to the expedition after Richard had left with the advance party, and Richard had not yet had time to read all my letters, this name meant nothing to him at all. At first Richard thought he must be the archaeologist who was to have joined us in Teheran, but was unable to come at the last minute, and it was only after a bit of polite fencing on his part that he discovered who Roddie really was. Over some food they were able to give each other the latest information about the progress of the expedition. Roddie painted a gloomy picture of how things were going in Teheran. The Foreign Ministry and the Museum seemed to know nothing of our plans, and the letters of recommendation that the Iranian Embassy in London had promised to send had not arrived. This meant that they now had to find a doctor instead of Gerald, an interpreter instead of Minou, and to obtain all the necessary permits! All this had to be done in the two or three days before I arrived in Teheran with Robert—definitely a tall order.

Their first visit was to Mr Arthur Kellas, the Oriental Counsellor at the British Embassy, with whom I had previously been in touch. This scholarly and charming diplomat, who has the ability and character that one associates with officials of the British Foreign Service, could not have been more helpful. He saw that the whole success of the expedition was in jeopardy almost before it started, and he set out with great skill and efficiency to help us. He promised that he would have a word with the Ministry of Health and try to persuade them to lend us a doctor. Then Richard must meet Mr Hannibal, a well-known figure in the intellectual and cultural world of Teheran, who would smooth the way for him with the Museum authorities. After that he would provide an introduction to the Ministry of Education, who alone had the power to issue excavation permits. Finally, he would see that the Ministry of Foreign Affairs was also informed.

In spite of the fact that the authorities did not seem to be aware of the presence of the expedition in Teheran, there was no doubt that everybody else was. In fact, *Kayhan*, a daily newspaper, which publishes the two English and the French-language newspapers in Teheran, had already printed two articles about us, and had given us a great deal of publicity. A reporter had quickly discovered that

Richard, Mike, Ragnar, and Roddie had arrived, and came round to the Embassy requesting an interview; this was given, and then invitations started to pour in from people who wanted to know more about the expedition. In particular, they were invited to meet Dr Hafiz Farman, of Teheran University, and Dr Sotudeh, an authority on Persian fortresses. These two gentlemen explained that permits to dig would have to be obtained from the High Council of Antiquities and promised to back our case. An interview with the Director of Iran-Bastan followed. He was polite, but said that it would be necessary for me to bring letters of recommendation from England, explaining exactly what our objectives were. Accordingly, Richard sent a cable, asking me to bring as much evidence of official support as I could.

The other great source of help at this juncture, apart from Mr Kellas, was the National Iranian Oil Company. The head of their Publicity Department was obviously pleased at the idea of N.I.O.C. helping our expedition, and he had received letters from Mr Nabavi, the company's representative in London, requesting that we be given all possible assistance. His first and most practical offer was to lend the advance party an interpreter, as without an interpreter their attempts to sort out the complications in Teheran would be limited, to say the least. The company also agreed to service the Land Rover and to lend us various articles of kit that we should need, such as pressure lamps and certain survey instruments.

I suppose the real turning-point in the fortunes of the expedition came with a cocktail party that Mr and Mrs Kellas gave in the garden of their house in the Embassy compound. It was officially given as a farewell party for a member of the Embassy staff, but it almost seemed as if the Oriental Counsellor had invited every influential person in the capital so that the advance party could meet them. First the advance party met a director of N.I.O.C., who renewed the guarantee given earlier that his company would do everything in its power to help the expedition. Then they met Dr Alavi, who had been ophthalmologist to Reza Shah Pahlavi, and is now a professor in the Faculty of Medicine at the University of Teheran. Dr Alavi promised to lend us one of his personal assistants, Dr Jah Kurlu, who was working at his eye clinic. Besides being a doctor, Jah Kurlu could also speak some English and this would help a little in solving the problem of interpreters. With a broad grin Dr Alavi said that the clinic would benefit from the expedition, as Jah would come back with a greater knowledge of the medical problems of the area as well as improving his English. Then a senator came up and introduced himself. He was interested in our archaeological programme and said that he would put in a good word for us with the different ministries. There and then he sought out the Director of the Archaeological Institute in Teheran, who was also at the party, and who promised to help.

As well as the Iranians there were, of course, a large number of the Embassy staff present, and everybody made helpful suggestions in one form or another. It seemed that all the loose ends were now beginning to be tied up, and a most useful introduction—as it later turned out— came at the end of the party. There were few ladies there, but Richard was introduced to one of them, who was a most striking personality and the daughter of a senator. She told him that she had met me in England and that she had already promised to help in any way she could. Richard told her exactly how things now stood, and she replied that there was one man above everybody else who could help resolve all our difficulties with one stroke of the pen. This was His Excellency, the Minister of Court. She knew the Minister well and had, in fact, an invitation to his house the following day. She would tell him all about us and she felt confident that she would be able to enlist his aid.

The last person of special significance for the expedition that they were to meet was a Mr Albuyeh. He was

obviously a highly influential man and he told Richard
that his estates were mostly situated in the area of Daylaman to the north of Alamut. He then talked long and
passionately about the great kings of Daylaman who had
ruled over this area long before Hasan-i-Sabbah came to
Alamut and from whom he was directly descended. The
party was by this time breaking up, and Mr Albuyeh said
that he would be delighted if two members of the expedition
would call on him the following day for tea. He had something of special significance that he wished to tell them, he
said, but time was now too short. The party had been a
great success, and the advance party felt that now they
were really launched. The Kellases were obviously pleased
that the preparations were moving into clearer waters and
they very generously offered the use of their garage as a
storeroom for the expedition. Richard accepted their offer
with alacrity, and the following morning unloaded the
Land Rover.

The next day Richard had an appointment with Dr Alavi
at his clinic at 11 o'clock. Kurlu was there and already fully
briefed. He was thrilled with the idea of accompanying the
expedition and it was agreed that he should come to the
Embassy later in the day to inspect the drugs that we had
brought and to meet the other members of the expedition.
Richard told Dr Alavi of his meeting with the senator's
daughter at the party and her promise to inform the
Minister of Court of the difficulties of the expedition in
getting the necessary permits. Dr Alavi thought that this
move would certainly help and, as he too knew His
Excellency, Husain Ala, the Minister, he picked up the
telephone and was soon speaking directly to the Minister's
office. He then said that the Minister would give Richard
an appointment to see him, probably the following day.

During the afternoon Roddie and Richard hunted high
and low for Mr Albuyeh's house in the western suburbs
of the city. The houses of most rich men in Teheran are
tucked away down small side streets, and it is often difficult

to find them. On this occasion, they were reduced to ringing him up on the telephone saying where they were and that they were lost, whereupon Mr Albuyeh sent out two servants to meet them. They were led to a villa surrounded by a high wall; inside was a large garden planted with rose bushes, fruit-trees, and every kind of sweet-smelling flower. In the centre of the garden four chairs stood around a table heaped high with fruit; Mr Albuyeh rose to welcome his visitors and introduced them to his brother. Refreshed by tea and cool fruit-juice, they conversed in French. Mr Albuyeh's brother then started to talk about the excavations that had been made in Daylaman. It turned out that for most of the year he lived there himself, looking after the family estates, returning only occasionally to Teheran to give a report to his brother. Four years ago the villagers in a small side valley had been digging a trench to improve the irrigation-system. As they dug down, they had struck a large stone covered with inscriptions, which they could not read. They had moved the stone with some difficulty, and underneath they had found pottery, bronze plates, and swords. This discovery had started an epidemic of digging around the villages of the area. The local landlords had collected teams together, and at night opened what are now known to be tombs. Bronzes, statuettes made of various metals, and exquisite pottery—mostly in the shape of animals—had come to light. Dealers from Teheran had begun to make excursions into the mountains along the Caspian and had bought the most valuable articles in secret. If we could obtain an official permit to dig, Mr Albuyeh assured us that with his co-operation and knowledge we could achieve much; there was great wealth in the ground just waiting to be dug up.

Roddie asked if he could put any date to the objects that had been recovered; he replied that he could not. At that particular moment one of his servants happened to cross the garden carrying a bulging sack, and, as if sensing their

disbelief, Mr Albuyeh summoned him and asked him to
empty the sack on the ground. It was filled with swords,
daggers, spears, and axes made of bronze. From another sack
he produced grey pottery bowls shaped like birds, water-
containers, and even some examples of crystal. This
seemed to be sufficient proof that these objects were in fact
being recovered, and it was agreed that after our return
from the valleys of the Assassins it would be worth going
into Daylaman and exploring for ourselves. At the word
"Assassins" Mr Albuyeh suddenly remembered why his
guests had come. He asked Richard which way we
intended to approach the valley, and when Richard replied
that we should be entering it through the Chala Pass he
inquired whether we could alter our route to include the
town of Samiran. There, he said, was a castle that had
never been visited. This was no ordinary castle like
Alamut, but had been the centre of a great city, as great as
Persepolis. These were extravagant words. Persepolis is,
after all, the finest memorial of the glorious Persian past,
known throughout the world as the capital of Darius and
Xerxes. However, Mr Albuyeh insisted that four years
before, at the same time as the initial digging had started
at Daylaman, he had read in an ancient manuscript the
description of an ancient capital that had been situated to
the west of Daylaman. He had at once begun to search for
it, and had found it near the village of Menjil. Again and
again he tried to interest the Council of Antiquities in
Teheran, but, overloaded by other tasks and constantly
hearing stories of lost cities from all corners of the country,
they had never been able to spare the time to visit the site.
It seemed that it would be well worth including a visit to
this castle and site among the tasks of the expedition. The
party decided to wire to me to inquire of Stern if he had
ever heard of the name Darband—as this was the name
that Mr Albuyeh used for Samiran—but the name was unfamiliar to him. By now it was getting late, and the guests
took their leave, promising Mr Albuyeh that they would

pass on to me all that he had said, and that we would certainly meet at Darband.

On their return to the Embassy the following morning they found an urgent letter from Dr Alavi informing Richard that he had an appointment with the Minister of Court at 11 o'clock at His Excellency's private residence inside the grounds of the Shah's Palace at Shimran. This gave him only an hour and a half to get there. He hastily changed into a suit and took a taxi to Shimran, a pleasant and wealthy suburb of Teheran to the north of the city. At 10.30 he arrived at the Palace gates clutching in his hand the letter from Dr Alavi. He was stopped by the guards, to whom he handed the letter. A guard looked at it and then, motioning to Richard to remain outside, disappeared inside the great gates of the Palace. A few minutes later the guard came back, returned the letter to Richard unopened, and asked him to leave. Richard was filled with anger at the man's stupidity and demanded to see an officer. After a while this request was granted and he was allowed inside. There he saw a big courtyard surrounded by flower-beds and fountains. On the other side of the courtyard was the guardhouse, and radiating from it were avenues lined with young saplings. The guard went into the guardhouse and spoke to some one on the telephone. His expression at once changed as he realized that Richard indeed had an appointment with Husain Ala. He barked an order at another sentry who rapidly disappeared round the corner. In a few minutes an expensive American car appeared in the courtyard, the door was opened, and Richard was bowed into it. He says that in a twinkling he felt that he was transformed from a Cinderella in rags to a Very Important Person.

The Minister of Court's villa is situated amongst terraced flower-beds within easy reach of the Palace. When Richard arrived at the villa, he was escorted from one room to the next until eventually he arrived in a small anteroom, beautifully furnished and decorated with old tapestries.

C.A.–E

The door was opened, and he walked into the Minister of Court's room. The Minister was seated at his desk and at once rose and made Richard welcome.

Husain Ala is a remarkable man, shrewd yet kindly, and obviously devoted to his master, the Shah, and to the interests of his country. He speaks excellent French and English and has, of course, travelled widely. Richard first asked him if he would care to read a short synopsis that we had prepared for just such an occasion, outlining the main tasks of the expedition. He read it carefully and then said in a friendly and sympathetic voice that he was glad we had come to carry out this important piece of research, and that His Imperial Majesty's Government would do all it could to smooth our path. He then started to discuss with Richard the history of the Assassins and showed remarkable knowledge of this period and of the authorities such as Stern, Minorsky, and Ivanow, who have contributed so much to it. Tea scented with rose petals was brought in and served in exquisite old silver vessels. As they talked on, a gleam of boyish delight lit up the Minister of Court's face when he recalled his own adventurous youth.

Outside, the fountains flashed in the sunlight, birds wandered lazily on the lawns, and occasionally a big American car rolled past the large, open windows. It was difficult to believe that here was the hub of Persia, one of the centres of power of this great country stretching from Turkey to Afghanistan and from the Caspian sea to the Persian Gulf. The setting seemed too peaceful and undemanding. An occasional pyjama'd servant would patter past the door and return with a watering-can. A few discreet officials glided past, and only the bark of a sentry broke the almost monastic calm. His Excellency repeated his promise of full support to the expedition and wrote letters of introduction to various ministries. Then the telephone rang with an urgent summons from the Shah asking to see his Minister of Court, and the meeting was at an end. One of the royal cars was placed at Richard's disposal and, as he drove back to the capital, his thoughts remained centred for a long time on the figure of this remarkable man, who appears to have defied old age and revolutions alike and, with his royal master, seems to be one of the great men of modern Iran.

The next day or two were taken up with visiting ministries, using Husain Ala's letters of introduction. The advance party was received everywhere in a courteous and friendly fashion, but it was difficult to force the pace in the rather leisurely atmosphere of Teheran. Even with high-powered credentials, not everything could be sorted out immediately, and periods of optimism were followed by even longer periods of frustration. Before the final arrangements for issuing the necessary passes could be settled the authorities naturally wished to interview me as leader of the whole expedition, and so nothing more could be done for the moment. Meanwhile Richard and the advance party set about reorganizing all our kit. Two main stacks were made, one of reserve supplies, which would be left behind in Teheran, and another of supplies that would be taken up with us on the Land Rover and later transferred to mules. Many of the goods had to be repacked into smaller containers, and at one stage the lawn in the Embassy compound looked rather like a bargain counter. But, with goodwill on the part of everybody concerned, the chaos was soon resolved into a big pile of boxes and packages all carefully labelled. This operation was finished by the early morning of August 8.

I was expected that evening, and Richard had called a conference of all the advance party to draw up provisional plans of campaign. They were all seated on the lawns by the Kellases' garage when Roddie looked up and saw two neatly dressed men approaching down the Embassy path—Robert and I had arrived.

4

Teheran

WHILE RICHARD and Michael were making their way across Europe to Teheran, the pace of things at home began to speed up considerably. First, there was still some equipment to be obtained. Chief among this was a supply of oxygen. We felt that this would be very necessary if we were able to get inside Maymun-Diz and wanted to explore some of the caves lying quite a distance beneath the surface. In 1959 we had been driven back by foul air, and when the candles we were carrying went out we had felt that it would be prudent to withdraw. This time we were determined to explore everything as thoroughly as we could, and had decided that the weight on the mules of half a dozen oxygen-cylinders would be justified by increased results. Secondly, the medical kit had not arrived. Sabetian had ordered several drums of instruments and dressings, as well as a large quantity of drugs. Getting film, too, presented certain difficulties, and I had received the telegram from Richard at Venice saying that Ragnar van Leyden had joined the expedition and wanted certain special types of film as well as lenses. Kodak could not have been more helpful, and even arranged for a special lens to be sent over from America in order to meet van Leyden's requirements.

The end of a summer term at a school is always an extremely busy time for a schoolmaster, and, apart from end-of-term examinations and reports, I was having to cope with a mail that was most days full of letters demanding immediate replies. Various newspapers asked if we wanted advance publicity, but this we declined as we felt it much better to save everything up until we came back and could see if our results really justified any large-scale publicity. About July 20 I had to go off to Corps camps, and when I left, everything seemed to be reasonably under control. I spent three days in Wales and two at Tidworth, and it was there that I received the news of Sabetian's withdrawal. The news somehow reached our insurance brokers almost immediately, and their representative rang up in a very worried state of mind saying that the absence of a qualified medical officer might well lead to increased premiums, bearing in mind the large claims they had had to meet as a result of illness on the previous expedition.

Roddie was due to fly out on July 25, and so Robert and I went up to London to brief him about the latest complication. We told him that his first job when he arrived in Teheran must be to contact the Minister of Health and ask him to provide the expedition with a doctor. Failing this, the British Embassy might be able to suggest some one. Roddie's second task was to make sure that all our documents and permits were in order. The Iranian Embassy in London had assured us that they had requested the Ministry of Foreign Affairs to issue us with everything that would be necessary and they were quite sure we should need only a very short time in Teheran before we set off for the mountains. Robert and I did some last-minute shopping in London, and then went to the airport to see Roddie off. He was flying on a charter flight, and the plane was full of families going back to Teheran after the end of the school term. He promised to send us a telegram as soon as he arrived, telling us the latest position, and, full of confidence, we bade him farewell, saying that we would meet again in ten days' time in Teheran.

On the next day I had started to sort out my own kit when the promised telegram arrived from Roddie. The Iranian authorities had heard nothing of our expedition at all, and it seemed unlikely that they would issue any permits. This was a complete bolt from the blue. I cabled back "You must get permits," and that was as much as I could do. I knew that Roddie would be moving heaven and earth to break through the deadlock that had obviously arisen, and I felt I had better take with me a complete set of fresh documents to substantiate our case. These last three days after I returned from camp were a nightmare. I visited Stern and begged him to write as flattering an account as he could of the aims of the expedition; he could not have been kinder. Ralph Pinder-Wilson also turned up trumps. In the end I had collected quite an impressive pile of documents referring to our expedition in very flattering terms. This most generous support from the authorities in our own country made me feel a lot happier, particularly as it was given at such short notice and couched so persuasively. Our various setbacks had tended to undermine morale a bit, and it was a tonic to know that other people appreciated the importance of what we were trying to do. Some of the national newspapers from time to time criticize the British Museum, saying that this institution is too stuffy, old-fashioned, and tangled with red tape. In our experience nothing could be farther from the truth. At every stage we received from the staff the greatest support possible, and in this particular instance they could not have acted with greater speed or determination.

We were also delighted to receive a telegram from Richard saying that he had arrived in Teheran and had met Roddie. He also asked us to bring a "fine detector" with us. This puzzled us for a little until we suddenly realized he must mean a mine-detector, and even this we were able to procure at very short notice from a store dealing with Government surplus goods. Richard thought that with the help of a mine-detector we should be able to locate metal objects beneath the ground much more easily and conveniently. In order to restore our good spirits we decided that we ought to have a final party on the Wednesday evening, and it was heart-warming to see how many of our friends came to wish us good luck and success.

Thursday, August 4, dawned. I had been up all the previous night finishing my correspondence, and Robert and I spent the morning packing up the last of the things that had to go. Among them was a crate of soap and powder given to us by Coty. This seemed to us to be complete luxury, and the thought of washing with this beautiful, scented soap in the middle of the awful smells of the valleys was wonderful. Gerald Hawkins nobly offered to drive us to London Airport, and we left Wellington at about midday. This was a thrilling moment, but, looking forward into the next six weeks, I wondered exactly how successful the expedition would be. I could not help feeling a little bit doubtful, despite Stern's assurances and support, whether the site of Maymun-Diz was in fact where we claimed it to be. There seemed to be so little evidence to go on. We had found very few traces of brickwork, and the pottery that we had recovered might after all not be of the twelfth century. Would we find nothing at all in the valley of Ashkavar? Would it be possible to climb into Nevisar Shah and the other Assassin fortresses we had come to explore? Would our health be better than it was last year? We had taken all the precautions we could and hoped that we had learnt by past lessons, but I was worried about Richard. I knew that although he was tough, this kind of living was a greater strain physically on him than the rest of us. How would the members of the party get on together? Apart from Robert, Richard, and myself, we knew so little of each other. Would personal relationships be able to bear the strain and stress of the long journey and the rigorous conditions?

All these thoughts were going through my mind as I sat beside Gerald in the car. Again, there was the question of actual physical danger. I knew that part of what lay in store would be dangerous and I knew that the responsibility for any decision must ultimately rest with me alone, and that I might perhaps have to decide matters that would entail the risk of human life. I do not think that any leader of an expedition can really feel elated at the moment of departure; he is bound to be reviewing in his mind all these and allied problems. And then I wondered if some of the decisions we had taken had been made in too much of a rush. Had everything been decided wisely? Only the future could tell. It is at such a moment that one can only put one's confidence in God, and trust in the integrity of one's companions, relying on their wisdom and advice. On this matter I had no worry at all. The expedition included men of ripe experience, like Robert, and younger men, Richard and Mike, who had all the dash and vigour of youth. I felt that we should be able to arrive at balanced decisions, but, at the same time, I believed that we would all be prepared to take calculated risks if we felt that they would be justified.

We arrived at London Airport at about 2 o'clock to find that a parcel of film Ragnar had specially requested had not been delivered to our plane. The extraordinary co-operation of the airport authorities enabled us to recover it in a matter of minutes, and we boarded our plane for Brussels knowing that it was safely on board as well as the mine-detector, oxygen, medical supplies, food, and extra cigarettes. Our journey was completely uneventful. We changed planes at Brussels, where we boarded a DC4 belonging to Persian Air Services, and, after stopping at Paris and Geneva, sped through the night to Teheran. At about 7 o'clock the next morning we had our first view of the Elburz mountains. From the plane they look intimidating enough—red-brown rock jutting up starkly against the interminable high plateau that stretches south right down to Abadan. Teheran from the air appears as a very straggly town. The modern buildings and green squares in the centre as well as the long, straight avenues built by the present Shah's father are easily picked out, but the outlines of the city become blurred and indistinct as concrete dwellings give way to mud-and-plaster huts. Brown is the predominating colour—a rather dirty, unsavoury brown.

We stepped out of the plane and at once felt the tremendous heat, although it was quite early in the morning. We had hoped that the rest of the party would be at the aerodrome to meet us, but they expected us on the evening plane. We waited for an hour, and then decided to take a taxi into the centre of the town. Mehrabad Airport is like any other large international airport, and was obviously designed as a showpiece—cool, air-conditioned lounges, sleek bars, and the well-designed customs building give a first impression of Western cos-mopolitan luxury. It is only when you get outside and travel on the long, straight road to the centre of the city that you realize that by contrast with other buildings the airport is, in fact, a showpiece. Beside the road there are countless melon shops: outside are high piles of melons of every kind. Inside there are always two portraits: one of the Shah eating a melon, which he manages to do with becoming royal dignity, and the other of the Prophet looking at a bed of remarkably seedy and withered specimens.

The only vehicles on the road are taxis painted in all sorts of colours and huge, American-style Army lorries, which drive along at a furious rate, hooting incessantly. The taxis do the same, and as there are no pedestrian crossings or traffic lights the confusion is exactly what you would expect. At any intersection you may well see a taxi overturned or damaged, with its driver gesticulating furiously at a lorry that has suffered hardly any damage at all. On this particular short journey we counted no less than six accidents.

Half an hour later we arrived at the Embassy compound,

and there I received a warm greeting from the Pakistani
guards who remembered me from last year. I was not even
asked to sign the usual visitors' book, which I felt to be a
great distinction. The Embassy itself is situated in one of
the most fashionable quarters of Teheran. It was built
during the reign of Edward VII by a company of Royal
Engineers from India. The obvious intention is to impress
and also to rival its Russian counterpart across the way. It *is*
impressive, in a mixture of British and Oriental styles, and
the cool compound inside is a wonderful haven from the burning light and dust of the rest of the city. It was there that
we found the rest of the expedition assembled, and their
astonishment at seeing us mingled with their evident delight.

They were having a council-of-war and they at once put
Robert and me in the picture. We agreed that in order
to save time Richard and Mike should drive out in the
Land Rover to carry out a preliminary investigation of
Samiran, setting up their headquarters at Menjil, a near-by
town, while the rest of the party remained behind in
Teheran to complete our formalities. Mike would come
back in the Land Rover in two days' time and report
progress. By this time it was hoped that the rest of us
would be ready to leave and join Richard. From Samiran
we planned to go to the Caspian, send the Land Rover back
to Teheran, and start our long trek through the Elburz
mountains. We would first explore the valley of Ashkavar,
and then cross the 11,000-foot peaks and descend into the
valleys of the Assassins. Here we would set up our first
base-camp at Maymun-Diz, and then move on to the other
castles of Alamut and Nevisar Shah.

The advance party had been camping some 10 miles to
the north of Teheran in a park that had been originally
constructed by the Government as a headquarters for a
World Scout Jamboree, and it was big enough even for the
Olympic Games. Unfortunately it was never used for its
original purpose, and the park, with half-completed
swimming-pools, an athletics track, and numerous

hutments, was used as the headquarters for the Youth Movement of Iran. We decided that we should continue to make this our headquarters, but that during the day we should work from the Embassy.

There are three main religions in Teheran, and as each one has its own holy day—the Moslems on Friday, the Jews on Saturday, and the Christians on Sunday—business becomes virtually impossible over this long week-end. Anything important must be accomplished between Monday and Thursday, as practically every one except the most conscientious takes three days' holiday, saying that it's no use working on the two other days because all their colleagues will be out of town. Our own work in Teheran was very much hindered by this, for, as luck would have it, Robert and I arrived on a Friday.

Teheran was in the middle of a heat wave, but I felt it incumbent upon myself as leader of the expedition to wear a suit and collar and tie. We decided that the official calls would be made by Roddie and myself, and that the rest of the party would complete the sorting of the stores while we were thus engaged. Robert was now showing signs of suffering from the intense heat and he was left to acclimatize himself in the comparative shade of the British Embassy compound making up lists of all the stores that we should take with us.

Our first call was at the Museum. I asked to see the Director and was politely received. When I told him who I was and the purpose of the expedition he replied that he had never heard of us at all despite Richard's visit a few days before! So I produced our credentials from Pinder-Wilson and the British Embassy and the sight of so much paper covered with red seals finally convinced him of our identity and real purpose. He said that the High Council of Antiquities was meeting the next day (a Sunday), and that if we could contact the Minister of Education in the meantime we could present our case. This was no time for half measures and, following Richard's example, we got into a

taxi, dashed to the ministry, and asked for an audience with
the Minister. In England, of course, one would be politely
shown the door or asked to fill in a form or come back in
three weeks' time; but here, somehow or other, our bull-
dozing tactics seemed to work. In half an hour I was sitting
in the Minister's very comfortable office sipping tea and
explaining to him in French that we had come to Iran to
make archaeological investigations that could only benefit
Iran as well as ourselves. He did not hesitate at all, and
promised me that I could appear before the Council the
following morning and that he would be prepared to back
our case, provided that the Minister of War agreed.
Another hectic taxi journey to the Ministry of War, and,
by employing the same technique, we came away half an
hour later with an impressive document, affirming that the
Ministry of War had no objections to our being issued with
all the necessary papers. The following day I attended the
meeting of the High Council of Antiquities. This was a very
gentlemanly affair. They studied our credentials, asked
one or two questions and then said that the Government
would be most happy to give us all the facilities we needed.
Our passes were made out then and there.

I suppose the most startling thing was the suddenness
with which our requests were granted after so many setbacks. Many people complain of the incompetence of the
Iranian civil service, and even hint at the necessity for
bribery before anything is done. I think it worth putting
on record that our experience was completely different.
There were, of course, maddening delays and incon-
sistent attitudes, but we were everywhere treated with a
respect and courtesy that left a lasting impression. And,
in addition, we found that once a promise had been given
it was always honoured. The Iranian authorities could not
have been more helpful, and we acknowledge with
gratitude the help and assistance they gave us. Our greatest
difficulty was getting the stock of film we had brought with
us on the plane from England out of the customs. It took

two days of combined effort on the part of Robert and Minou Sabetian, but in the end even this hurdle was overcome. Minou had, by this time, rejoined us. On sober reflection he had realized that the situation in Iran was not as bad as he had feared, and had cabled us from Venice saying that if we could send him a hundred pounds he would catch the next plane to Teheran. So we now had our medical adviser and interpreter.

Our official business over, my next call was to the chiropodist. I had not had time during the summer term to have my feet properly attended to, and I knew that I ought to have some treatment before starting on our long trek over the Elburz mountains. As a result of war wounds I tend to get large corns on my right foot, and these had already been pretty troublesome in Teheran. I asked Roddie to accompany me. The outside of the premises looked conventional enough. Corn plasters, special shoes, supports—all were there, graphically described in French and Farsi. The inside, however, seemed to me to resemble a medieval torture chamber. The room was low and badly lit, and at one end stood an immense chair. I almost turned round and ran away, but Roddie told me that it could not be as bad as all that, and, feeling very nervous, I seated myself on the chair in much the same state of mind as some poor criminal of the Middle Ages when he was put upon the rack.

Presently the chiropodist appeared. He was an old man with hardly any teeth, and I thought he picked up his knives with an air of great relish. I explained to him that I was an important person, and that if he hurt me I would at once tell the Shah. He replied that all the best things in life hurt a little, and then proceeded to carve away at my feet. At any moment I expected to see the blood gush. Roddie, meanwhile, was taking photographs. This was quite a mistake, as the chiropodist evidently thought that he must show all his skill, or the lack of it, to its best advantage. The worst moment came when he produced an enormous pair of pincers, which looked rather like tongs, and said that he must now pull out the root of the corn at the bottom of my foot. This would hurt, he said with unction. I gripped the chair, there was a moment of excruciating agony, I felt dizzy, and he then told me that all was over. He proceeded to drown my foot in iodine, which I thought was quite a wise move on his part, and then asked me for his fee. In England a service like this costs twelve-and-six, in Teheran £2. A crowd of sight-seers had gathered at the door and as we left they gave a little cheer. They had never seen a European undergoing this treatment before and begged us for money. For five minutes I felt as though I were walking on hot irons, and I was quite sure my leg would have to be amputated, but then the pain suddenly went away, and for the remainder of the expedition my feet gave me no bother at all.

All our official passes now secured, there were two other matters to be cleared up. First, the question of the Press and publicity. We were still sticking to our line that we would say very little until we had some concrete results, but the Persian Press would not be put off. All this had to be handled rather delicately. On the one hand we wanted to avoid offending them, and yet if we gave them too much information before we set off, we were afraid it might be exaggerated. The Press Office at the Embassy was very helpful, and it was agreed that we should send a dispatch by muleteer from the Alamut valley to be released to the local Press and published in the Embassy information bulletin, and a copy sent to London. I also received a message from Iran Television saying that they would like me to appear on one of their programmes. Roddie and I set out to see them. Iran Television had been transmitting programmes for two years only, and its reception is limited to Teheran and a few surrounding villages. The Director had been trained in London by the B.B.C. He spoke fluent English and showed us round the centre with considerable pride. He said that they were extremely short of material for live telecasts and half the transmitting time was normally taken up by films. We told him our plans and said that we should be delighted to give a half-hour programme on our return in a month's time, and asked him if this would fit in with his own plans. To our astonishment he told us that there was no advance schedule of programmes, but that a programme was given out at the beginning of each day, and even then was liable to last-minute alteration. However, this fitted our book quite well until, just before we left, he said that he must have the complete script forty-eight hours before our appearance on TV. As we had no idea when we should be returning to Teheran, and in all probability I should have only twenty-four hours in town, we could give no guarantee of this. To our surprise the Director said he was sure the matter could be arranged to the satisfaction of every one.

The Americans also run their own TV station and we had only just got back to the Embassy when they rang up, rather indignant that we had gone to the Persian service first; and so, in order to placate them, we promised them an interview too. Rather surprisingly during all our conversations with Government officials we heard very little about the Americans, but this may just have been accidental, as the United States has, of course, a great deal of influence in Iran. Russia was a name that was on everybody's lips, but after the Russians we heard most about ourselves and the French.

The remaining problem was that of our doctors. When Minou had refused to enter Iran, the Ministry of Health had promised to lend us two doctors. After Minou's arrival it looked as though the party would consist mostly of medical advisers and interpreters! Our two local doctors, Kurlu and Hatemi, arrived at the Embassy on the morning of our departure. We liked Kurlu at once. Hatemi was a much older man of about fifty, rather plump and, as one might expect in a man of his age, did not seem in prime condition, though his medical qualifications were good. He was a nice man and knew something of the Western way of life as he had completed his medical studies in Paris and had visited South America. He appeared to be suspicious of the unknown or unfamiliar. He regaled us for half an hour with his tales of poisonous snakes, scorpions, and tarantula spiders, all of which he thought would be swarming in droves in the Elburz mountains. We had, incidentally, ordered antivenene from Bombay, but this had failed to arrive in Teheran, although Gerald Hawkins had paid for it in sterling in London. We did not think that there would be many snakes, but we had asked the Natural History Museum in London for their opinion. We also wrote to the Haffkine Institute in Bombay and asked what they could recommend. The snakes we were likely to encounter were all vipers, and although a bite from one could be most painful it was unlikely to be fatal. There is no comprehensive antivenene, as each snake has its own toxic peculiarities. However, every one seemed to agree that if we did run into trouble a polyvalent which is used as an antidote for the bite of South American vipers would do. Hatemi did not agree, and for the next six hours he went through all the chemists' shops in the bazaar collecting every kind of antivenene he could find.

Kurlu, in a rather more practical way, examined our drugs and was impressed by the list that Gerald Hawkins had drawn up, commenting that it was most unusual for a Western doctor to have such a knowledge of Iranian diseases. This was a feather in Gerald's cap, and demonstrated the efficiency of the London School of Hygiene and Tropical Medicine, which had advised us and supplied some of the drugs. These included penicillin, cortisone, blood plasma, gamma-globulin, and, of course, a variety of sulfa drugs for malaria and dysentery. In addition we had quite a large number of surgical instruments for dealing with possible appendicitis and fractures, anaesthetics, and some very strong disinfectants. There were also three bottles of a solution with which we could kill, without mutilating, insects that we wanted to bring back for further examination.

Needless to say, we took the utmost care to see that these three bottles were kept separate. The drugs filled three large suitcases, which were appropriately marked with a red crescent, the Eastern equivalent of the Red Cross, and a large skull-and-crossbones to warn anybody who thought of tampering with them. We were always very careful to keep the keys of these cases ourselves, as their contents could have killed off almost the entire population of the Alamut valley.

We had decided that we would set off at 6 o'clock in the evening of Tuesday, August 9, and risk a hair-raising drive through the night, when at least it would be cool, rather than be choked with dust during the blinding heat of midday. Mike had meanwhile returned in the Land Rover from Menjil and reported that Richard was safely installed, although he was getting a little bored and was anxiously awaiting our arrival. In the morning and afternoon we loaded up the stores.

At the stroke of 6 Hatemi arrived, immaculately dressed in his best suit. There were wild expostulations from us when he told us that he had not brought any other clothes with him at all, but we could not persuade him to go back and change. We showed him our own suits carefully put away in polythene bags and told him that all we intended to wear were shirts and shorts, but he insisted that as the representative of the Iranian Ministry of Health, and consequently of the Government, he must be properly dressed in a dignified way if he was to discharge his duties with full decorum. We shrugged our shoulders, dusted off the seat in the front of the Land Rover, and hoped for the best. There was quite a little knot of people and some photographers at the main Embassy gate. A microphone was put in front of my mouth and I spoke a few totally incomprehensible words into it. Little boys asked for our autographs. Two women said that they were praying for us as they were sure they would never see us again. The bar swung up and we were out.

Five minutes later we stopped with a puncture.

C.A.–F

5

Samiran

OUR IMMEDIATE destination was the fortress of Samiran. To reach it we took the main road to Kazwin, then crossed the western end of the Elburz mountains. This is a very old road and was part of the original trade route from the south of Persia to the Caspian sea and Russia. The mountains do not rise to more than 8000 feet, and in recent times the road has been built up and reinforced for military purposes, but the surface is excruciating, and there are numerous hairpin bends. For considerable stretches there is a one-way-traffic system only, with every now and then a passing place cut out of the hill. There is quite a lot of traffic on this road, mostly American-built army vehicles and some private cars belonging to the border officials. Most Persians when they travel to the Caspian take the modern road at the eastern end of the mountains.

We left Kazwin at about 10 at night and it took us four hours to get to Menjil. Although the night was cool we were almost blinded and choked by clouds of red dust sent up by other vehicles or whipped off the hills by a fresh breeze. Half-way along there is a tea-house, very dirty and primitive, but frequented by most travellers. Here we stopped at midnight to refresh ourselves and change drivers. Shortly afterwards we hit the Sefid Rud, or White River, which flows into the Caspian.

The town of Menjil stands at the confluence of the Qizil Uzun Rud and the Sefid Rud. The Persians have just completed a great dam at Menjil to irrigate the parched lowlands to the west. In 1960 the dam was still under construction and the French engineering company carrying out the work had erected a colony of well-built bungalows near the site of the dam. Richard had seen the head of the enterprise, and he had agreed to lend us a bungalow for as long as we wished. When we arrived at Menjil, Mike could not find it, and it was only after we had woken up two or three French families that we were at last directed to our new headquarters. Richard was fast asleep in bed, but we soon unloaded all our gear, and after a quick meal fell exhausted on our camp-beds.

The next day we set out early in the Land Rover to make our first proper reconnaissance of Samiran. The site itself is some 12 miles to the west of Menjil and lies on the Qizil Uzun, a tributary of the Sefid Rud.

The French company was making a fresh road higher up the valley of the Qizil Uzun, as the existing one would be flooded by the rising water-level. After travelling for about 10 miles we left the Land Rover and walked for the rest of the way until, rounding a promontory, we suddenly saw the magnificent silhouette of the castle.

The reader will recall that we had first heard of Samiran from Mr Albuyeh, and Richard had persuaded him to come and take us round the site. He had made his own way there, and when we at last found him in a small hut about half a mile from the castle he had been waiting for two days. He was somewhat naturally in a very bad humour. Through Minou we asked him how he knew that the castle and city had originally possessed temples, mosques, and buildings that, so he claimed, made it the

equal of Persepolis. It was difficult to get anything concrete
out of him, but he assured us that he had read all about it in
ancient manuscripts. As we were to discover later, the
term "ancient manuscript" can cover anything from a
genuine MS. of Zahir-ad-Din of the fifteenth century to a
faded Victorian calendar of the nineteenth. Although we
felt that a lot of what he said was highly coloured, we
gratefully accepted his services as a guide.

The first person to visit the site (although he did not
realize what it was) was the famous English explorer
Sir Henry Rawlinson, who travelled down the Sefid Rud
in 1838. He noted the impressive ruins, and in a paper to
the Royal Geographical Society gave the following very
brief account of it:

> About 3 miles below Gílawán, a ridge of low hills runs
> across the valley from one range of mountains to the other.
> The Sefíd rúd forces its way, by a narrow gorge, through the
> ridge, and at this point, on an isolated and most precipitous
> hill upon the right bank, immediately overhanging the river,
> are the remains of a large and very strong fort, which, from a
> distance, have a most imposing appearance. The place is
> called Derbend, and forms the boundary between Táromi-
> Khelkhál and Táromi-Páyín; the fort is known by the name
> of Kal'ehi-Kohneh; and, strangely enough, is ascribed by the
> peasantry, to Khaliph Omar; it seems of some antiquity, and
> would be well worth examining.[1]

The curious thing about this account is not only its
paucity but also that Rawlinson locates the main castle ruins
on the right or southern bank of the river, whereas in fact
they are all situated on the left or northern bank. However,
there can be little doubt that this castle described by

[1] H. C. Rawlinson, "Notes on a Journey from Tabriz, through
Persian Kurdistán, to the Ruins of Takhti-Soleïman, and from there by
Zenján and Tárom, to Gilán, in October and November, 1838"
Journal of the Royal Geographical Society, vol. x (1840).

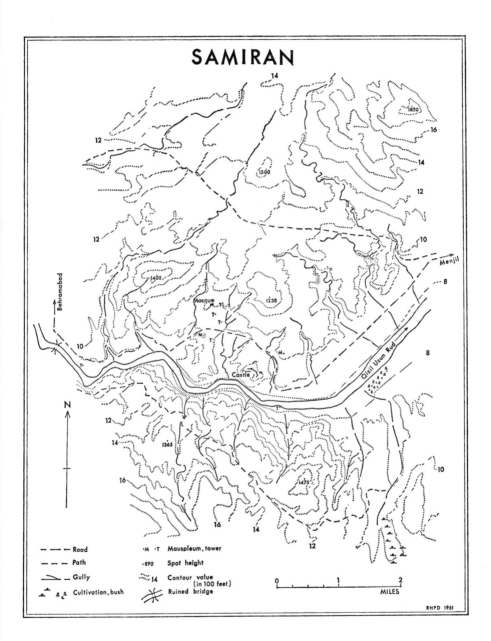

SAMIRAN

1850

1590

Behramabad

Menjil

Qizil Uzun Rud

Mosque

Castle

1400

1238

1365

1475

N

Road

Path

Gully

Cultivation, bush

·M ·T **Mauspleum, tower**

·890 **Spot height**

14 **Contour value**
     (in 100 feet)

Ruined bridge

0   1   2

MILES

RHPD 1961

Rawlinson is Samiran, and we can only conclude that for
some odd reason he got mixed up in his directions.

A German doctor delighting in the name of Julius
Caesar Häntzsche passed through the same district in 1859.
H. Brugsch, in his *Reise der k. preussischen Gesandschaft nach
Persien, 1860 und 1861,* described the site and quoted from
a letter written by Dr Häntzsche (my translation):

> The rock castle of *Kal'a-i-dukhtar,* or Maidenhead Castle,
> which has already been described in Volume I, pp. 183 ff., and
> again in Volume II, p. 371, is situated above the foaming
> waters of the *Kyzyl-üzen* Rud and seems to have been the
> strategically important final link in a chain of fortresses
> which run along this valley, and which guarded the entrance
> into the Province of Gilan from the south. The author of the
> publication, as is well known, was a doctor in Persian
> employ, and for years lived in the unhealthy city of *Resht* not
> far from the Caspian Sea. He has examined with great
> attention similar remains in the valley and has given the
> following description of them which refers to a visit he made
> on 19th October 1859.
>
> Three *fersach* (*i.e.,* about 15 miles) west-south-west of
> Menjil and at much the same altitude there can be found in
> the mountain district of *Tarum* in North Persia, in the valley
> of the Kyzyl-üzen, in a gorge between barren mountains
> covered with pebbles and scree, the remains of an old castle
> and, apparently, of a somewhat newer town, called in the
> local dialect *Gorkalah* or sometimes *Schehr-e-Berberi.* Here
> are scattered on several hills the remains of an old city and
> on one in particular those of a fortified castle, which is
> certainly pre-Islamic, and many octagonal tall towers still
> partly preserved. In the dips between the hills there are
> several remains of Moslem baths etc. The majority of the
> ruins lie on the left bank of the *Kyzyl-üzen.* The general
> direction of the castle is almost due south, that of the towers
> SWS, which indicates the Moslem period.
>
> Near by on a slope in the mountains there is a great heap
> of stones called *Gabr-e-Gor* on to which muleteers throw fresh
> stones as they pass by: immediately adjacent to the ruins on a

hill is the *Imamzardeh* (or shrine) *Kasim*, and, near the remains of the baths, asbestos can be seen on the sides of the hills.[1]

Dr Häntzsche seems not to have heard of Rawlinson: and his account is also very brief, doing less than justice to the significance of the place. No other travellers had, as far as we knew, visited the castle in the century between Dr Häntzsche's visit and ours, although Professor V. Minorsky described it in two articles in the *Encyclopaedia of Islam.*

Until our visit no photographs had been taken or plans drawn of the castle and its environs. We did not know this until our return, but we instinctively felt that here was a site of great importance and we must linger for two or three days in order to do it justice. Even then we realized that we had not investigated it as fully as we should have liked, but as time was running short it was agreed that we should press on to Ashkavar and Alamut and that a rear party should then return to Samiran to finish the work. The account that follows is a composite one, combining the results of both visits.

The mountainous area to the west of the Sefid Rud had been inhabited for centuries by the Daylamites, who had given their name to the area. The famous geographer, mathematician, and astrologer Ptolemy mentions them in the second century A.D. They were known as particularly hardy and ferocious warriors, and their name was often surrounded by an aura of fear and awe. Pushing beyond the limits of their barren and inhospitable homeland, they took over parts of the more fertile districts of Rudbar and Alamut and made Shahrak, in the valley of Alamut, their capital. Lammassar was the cemetery of their kings, and Marshall Hodgson, in his excellent book *The Order of Assassins,* notes that Buzurg-Ummed (the Assassin peasant-general designated by Hasan-i-Sabbah as his successor)

[1] Appendix No. 2, *Ruins of Tarum,* Vol. II, pp. 471–472 (Leipzig, 1862–63).

took especial pleasure in laying out a garden on the site
after he had captured the castle. The dynasty of the
Buyids represents the peak of Daylamite power. In the
first half of the tenth century they were in control of Rayy
and Isfahan, and even extended their influence to Bagdad
(according to Minorsky in *Studies in Caucasian History*).
It was probably the Daylamites who first realized the
strategic significance of the narrow gorge at Darband.

At Darband (the name means "gorge") the river runs
through a narrow gorge a mile long and no more than
100 yards wide. On the southern bank the mountains rise
to a height of some 1200 feet above the stream, and on the
northern bank there is a mile-wide plateau. On the other
side the land drops precipitously to a similar gorge formed
by another tributary of the Sefid Rud. Over this plateau
came the caravans from Azerbaijan, making their way
northward towards the Caspian or southward to the old
Persian capital of Rayy. The Daylamites in all probability
built the first castle there. The castle then became an
important staging-post for these caravans, and gradually a
city grew which, while not comparing in size or magnificence with Persepolis (Mr Albuyeh exaggerated far too
much when he said this), was nevertheless an important
town in the north of the country. The Daylamites suc-
cumbed to the invading armies of the Assassins, but this
particular outpost managed to maintain its independence
under its own princes. That they must have been rich can
be seen by the magnificence of the buildings and, in
particular, the mausoleums.

When the Assassins decided to extend their power westward they soon came across this fortress. Their intelligence
system seems, curiously enough, in this instance to have
been extraordinarily bad. Normally Hasan-i-Sabbah and
his successors were supplied with extremely full information about the morale, numbers, and movements of
potential enemies. We were told that he believed that
Samiran was an ordinary castle and he dispatched a

relatively small army against it. When his general arrived before the castle he sent a message back to his head-quarters in Alamut urgently asking for reinforcements, and said: "I have been sent to take a castle, and now find I must invest a city."

There are no records of the siege of the city or of its destruction, and we could only attempt to piece together its subsequent history from our investigations. The original buildings were almost totally destroyed, but we noticed to the west of the city some towers and foundations of buildings whose construction was so different from that of the main castle and so like the Assassin fortresses in Alamut that it seemed reasonable to suppose that the Assassins had established themselves here for a considerable number of years. Whether they, in their turn, were driven out by the Mongols after the main fortress of Alamut had fallen, or whether they vacated the city of their own free will, must remain a matter for conjecture. Again there are no records, and the only evidence we have is our own plans and photographs.

The site, which covers an area of approximately half a square mile is dominated at the eastern end by the castle. According to Rawlinson, when he visited the site it had three outer walls. We could trace the remains of two and possibly a third, although it was difficult to be sure about the third one. Rawlinson was certainly an accurate observer, and his record of a triple wall is confirmed in contemporary texts. Although the stone from which the castle is con-structed is particularly hard and not liable to erosion by weather, the third wall may have disappeared in this way during the last hundred years—or else been quarried by the local inhabitants for their own use.

The castle is situated on the top of a tilted bluff of sand-stone rock covered with a layer of loose stones and gravel, and overlooks the gorge of the Qizil Uzun, which at this point runs roughly east-west. This, too, is the general lay of the castle. The greatest height of the bluff at the eastern end is not more than 150 feet above the valley below. On the northern and eastern sides, from which the most impressive view of the castle can be obtained, it was a fairly uncomfortable scramble for us up the scree slope with its outcrop of rock in the middle, and the ascent would have been far more difficult and hazardous for an attacking force.

At the foot of the bluff there is a narrow, flat piece of ground, along which a track now runs, before the hills rise again, and this depression would also have served as a dry moat. The triple wall must have run along the northern and eastern sides of the castle, and possibly curled round to the western side too. All that remains now is a sub-stantial wall built about 90 feet down the slope from the castle on the north-eastern corner. This wall is con-structed of undressed stone and is about 20 feet high and 8 feet thick. The remains do not extend for more than 50 feet. At the southern side there is a steep descent of almost sheer rock dropping some 300 feet to the river. About a third of the way down, and built on an outcrop of rock, there is a well-preserved tower from which it would have been possible with the aid of a rope to scramble down a chimney in the cliff-face to the river. This tower could have been used as an emergency exit in time of siege, or as a means of getting additional water from the river by buckets. On the western side, the ground sinks in a series of terraces, each of which was fortified. The lowest terrace is about a hundred feet above the encircling track or dry moat.

Seen from a distance the most impressive thing about the castle is the silhouette of its formidable ochre-coloured walls and crenellated towers and battlements, which stand out sharply against the dark-blue sky. There is a proportion and harmony in its shape which are both pleasing and surprising. I personally derived considerable aesthetic satisfaction from gazing at the noble symmetry of its outline. Windsor Castle seen from a distance against the sky has always seemed to me to be an almost perfect

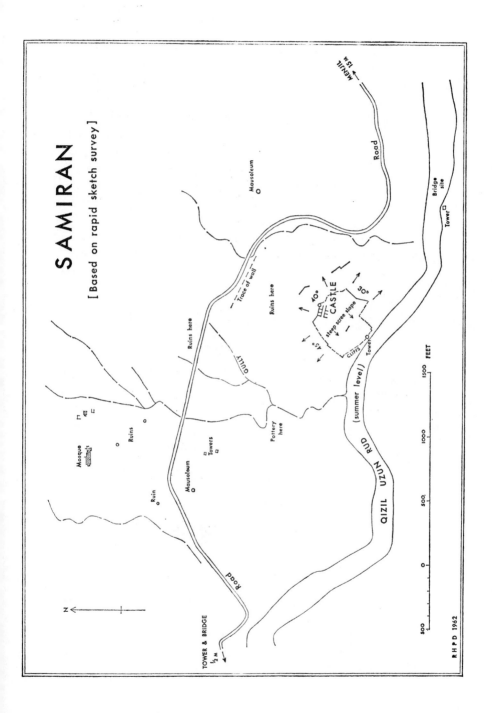

SAMIRAN

[Based on rapid sketch survey]

Mausoleum

Road

MENJIL
15 M

Bridge
site

Tower

Trace of wall

Ruins here

Ruins here

GULLY

Pottery
here

40°

CASTLE

30°

steep scree slope

45°

CLIFFS

Tower

QIZIL UZUN RUD (summer level)

Mosque

Ruins

Ruin

Mausoleum

Towers

Road

TOWER & BRIDGE
½ M

N

FEET

500   0   500   1000   1500

R H P D 1962

example of what a castle should look like. Samiran, in its way, does not fall far short of this standard, although, of course, it is on a smaller scale, comparing roughly in size with Warwick Castle. Nor did this impression of great strength combined with a certain grace and elegance diminish on closer inspection. Its very size indicates that it was meant to be a residence of considerable magnificence in times of war. Thus its builders had tried to soften the harsh outlines of its military architecture with the supple grace of Oriental curves and even arabesques.

We first examined the main fortifications at the eastern end of the castle. They have been extensively destroyed, and virtually only the shell of the outer walls remains. These walls are 30 to 40 feet high and 5 to 10 feet thick. From the rather narrow, wedge-shaped, eastern neck of the bluff, they run back in a zigzag line along the northern and southern slopes. In effect, the walls form a series of rectangular or square towers interspersed with rounded bastions. This meant that any attacking force would have to break up and disperse, as it would have been impossible to launch a concentrated assault on any one point—there just wasn't room. Each of the towers could support at least two others, and a devasting cross-fire could be brought to bear by the defenders. This system of defensive architecture also helped to lessen the damage that could be caused by the standard siege weapons of the time, mangonels or catapults which hurled stones, rocks, or arrows with considerable velocity. Large smooth surface areas that could be destroyed by projectiles were reduced to a minimum.

Most of the main living-quarters seemed to be built into the walls at the eastern end of the castle. Generally these were three storeys high, and wooden joists can still be seen at the different floor-levels. The wood is extremely hard and looks like olive-wood, in spite of the fact that there are no olive-trees in this part of the country. We noticed that the stone and mud-brick at the bottom of the walls was reinforced with beams of the same wood. Some of the windows puzzled us as they were far bigger than we expected and remarkably similar to the late European Gothic style in appearance, with considerable decoration in the form of ornamental tracery in the stonework. There were very probably more rooms beneath ground-level, as we saw the remains of staircases; but we had neither the time nor the equipment to excavate. At the western end of the castle the bluff drops by a series of terraces, each of which contains the remains of a large number of rooms. Here the destruction is even more complete, and it was very difficult to trace the original ground-plan. It was in this part of the castle that we found the greatest number of shards of pottery, mostly small, brown, glazed fragments. In addition, we came across some examples of Caspian grey ware which must have survived from the most primitive period of the potter's art.

We had hoped to find the remains of water-cisterns hewn out of the rock and similar to those built in the castles in the Alamut area, or qanat-channels which collect the rain-water and eventually drain into cisterns built on the slopes of hills—but in this we were unsuccessful. During the winter, water could easily have been obtained from the Qizil Uzun, and there were probably wells, but we could not discover what the source of the water-supply in the summer was. While we were at Samiran the river was very low, only about a foot in depth, and the water was dis-coloured by a yellowish clay which forms alluvial deposits. We waded across the river in order to examine a square tower on the southern bank, about 350 yards from the eastern tip of the castle bluff. Near the tower were the re-mains of a stone bridge. There were no other traces as far as we could see of fortifications on this side of the river, and the purpose of the tower was, presumably, to guard the bridge.

Having completed our tour of the castle, we next turned our attention to the surrounding site. The gorge and the river, respectively, formed the natural eastern and southern boundaries, so we decided to find the northern limits first. About 750 yards from the castle bluff we found the remains of a stone wall on top of a hill and traced its course for about 3 miles. This was, presumably, the outer wall of the site, and could conceivably have been the third wall mentioned by Rawlinson, although it was some distance away from the castle. From here we walked about half a mile down to the western end of the area and our attention was at once attracted by a graceful and slender tower which could have been the minaret of a mosque, but at the same time showed unmistakable signs of having once been fortified. It was built on a slight rise about 50 feet above the river, and from the top there was a fine view to the north-west over the plain to Kurdistan. It was about 30 feet high, and inside there was a double spiral staircase, still quite well preserved. At the foot of the tower there was a small guardroom, 8 feet high by 6 feet wide, the walls of which were pierced with arrow-slits. Below the tower and to the west were the remains of a remarkably fine stone bridge. The river here is quite wide, and the length of the bridge must have been considerable. The bridge as such no longer exists, but some complete arches still stand on both banks, and in the middle of the river can be seen the base of one of the piers. Unfortunately, we could find no traces of the foundations of houses or any other buildings by the bridge, but the ground is marshy here and they may well have disappeared. And it seems unlikely that a second bridge would have been built here unless there was a considerable community near by. If the site of Samiran, as seems likely, did extend from the castle to the bridge, then perhaps Mr Albuyeh's description was not as exaggerated as we had at first thought.

Three other buildings stand out prominently upon the rocky hills. The most prominent is a mausoleum on a hill about 500 yards to the north-west of the castle. It is octagonal in shape and its windows generally face east. It is about 50 feet high, made of brick, and surmounted by the remains of a brick dome, which had probably been about 15 feet high. The mausoleum is in an exceptionally fine state of preservation and is an imposing building. A few steps lead up to the fine arch of the main entrance. Inside it is severely plain, and there are no friezes on the wall. The ground was covered with rubble from the collapsed dome, and after digging down about 4 feet we found the original floor, but, to our disappointment, no signs of mosaics. We walked round the outside, which was decorated with rounded columns, and on the northern wall we came to the remains of an external staircase which led up to the roof. We began to climb up the stairs, but it was clearly unsafe and we abandoned the attempt half-way. Almost due north from the mausoleum and standing on another rise 250 yards away is a mosque. This consists of a central rectangular building 60 by 70 feet. We were told that it contained the tomb of a saint who had died about the year 1410, and the whole building had been converted into a shrine in his honour. Two circular domes surmounted the mosque, and these, we were told, are a sign of royal dignity. Much of the building seemed very old and of the same date as the castle and the mausoleum. The walls are solidly made of stone and plaster and there is a brick roof which looks as though it was restored about a hundred years ago. Inside there are two main rooms, 20 to 25 feet high. One contains the now-empty tomb of the saint, crudely painted and hung with tawdry and tattered trimmings. The second was likewise empty, and its blackened walls indicated that it had been used by the local population as a field kitchen. To the east of the building there is a graveyard littered with recent tombstones and, as if standing apart from the plebs, the ruins of two or three older and more sumptuous tombs. Beside the mosque there is another building which, however, is fairly modern and can be no more than a hundred years old. It has wooden windows carved with fancy latticework, now crumbling away. The smell inside was indescribable, and we hurried away.

Between the mosque and the castle are the ruins of two collapsed towers, and it is reasonable to assume that this was the site of many more houses. We made soundings and were lucky enough to dig up an almost complete plate. It is glazed and coloured brown, yellow, and green. Its date is certainly in the Assassin period and was another indication that Samiran was inhabited by the Assassins after they had taken it.

The last building of note is the eastern mausoleum, which stands on a rise some 300 yards to the north-east of the castle. It is not so large or impressive as the main western one, but scenically it stands out well. It has been badly damaged, and only three walls are left standing. Round the top runs a frieze, which presumably stated the name of the prince buried there. Unfortunately, only the first two letters can be read. This is a great pity, as otherwise we might have been able to date both the mausoleum and the castle with greater accuracy. All that we can say is that Samiran was certainly built well before Assassin times, that it was taken by them, and was probably used as an Assassin base.

While we were there a fierce wind was blowing from the west, whipping up the dust and covering everything. The sun beat mercilessly down. This was one of the hottest places we came across, and it was fittingly called "Death Valley" by the natives. It was difficult to imagine how the site must have looked 700 years ago, as the brown dust gave to everything a feeling of complete decay. There was no green anywhere to take one's thoughts away from the ruins of a long-forgotten era. Although the ruins are certainly among the most impressive to be found in the whole of the Elburz group, we found them less exciting and stimulating to explore than anywhere else we visited. I, for one, was forcibly reminded of Shelley's poem *Ozymandias*:

> Nothing beside remains. Round the decay
> Of that colossal wreck, boundless and bare
> The lone and level sands stretch far away.

In Samiran everything seemed completely lost and forlorn and history dead. It was like digging up the bones of the past: brittle, lifeless, and impossible to revive. Samiran has a sinister influence. Its glories have gone for ever and nothing remains but an outer shell.

It was here that we had our first casualty. On our first morning we split into small groups in order to make a general reconnaissance of the whole site. Ragnar and I went off to try and find the outer city walls while the rest of the party went up to the castle. Robert and Hatemi paired off and slowly walked up the scorching western approach. Hatemi was obviously feeling the heat as he kept on sitting down and maintaining in a loud voice that it was madness to do any work under this burning midday sun. Imagination seemed to be running away with him too, for suddenly he shot to his feet and pointed in the direction of a large rock and whispered, "*Animile.*" Robert was somewhat taken aback and asked him what sort of animals he thought they were. "Dangerous *animile*," said Hatemi, "we must go back quick." Robert took him up to the rock and showed him that there was nothing there, but Hatemi's footsteps became slower and slower until he eventually sat down under a rock saying that he must rest a while and then return to the Land Rover. Robert went on alone, explored the castle, and, feeling very hot and tired, came back to where we had parked the Rover for our midday meal. It was there that Ragnar and I found him an hour or so later gasping for breath and showing signs of heatstroke. We made him as comfortable as we could in the shade of the Land Rover, but as the afternoon wore on the heat became more and more intense. We had little water with us, and we felt it was not safe to drink from the muddy waters of the river. When Sabetian returned he advised us to take Robert back to Menjil as soon as we could. The journey back over the plain was one of the worst we had ever made. We usually came back from work much later, when it was cool. But now the wind seemed to take a malicious pleasure in blowing up a fine dust which got into our ears, mouths, and noses, and almost suffocated us.

By the time we got back Robert was in poor shape. The next day Sabetian called in the local French doctor as a consultant, and after they had taken Robert's blood-pressure and examined him thoroughly they advised that he should return to Teheran in order to acclimatize himself. This must have been a desperate blow for him. He bravely maintained that in no circumstances would he be a burden on the rest of the party, and that if he were not given a clean bill of health in Teheran he would prefer to remain as our agent at base, making occasional trips to see how we were getting on. It was decided that he should stay with us until Ashkavar, then return to Teheran with Bernard Bright, a friend of Mike's who had volunteered to accompany us on the first leg of our journey in his own Land Rover. This event brought home to me forcefully that the expedition was no mere game and that we all bore a heavy responsibility for the welfare and even the lives of each other.

6

Ashkavar

Two days later we left Menjil in the two Land Rovers, both groaning under the weight of the stores we were carrying. If Bernard Bright had not come with his Land Rover, I am not sure how we should have managed.

Our route took us through the mountains, following the course of the Sefid Rud. Just before Rudbar we stopped to have a look at a fort—that may well have been built by the Assassins—on an island in the middle of the Sefid Rud. Not very much was left of it, and it was quite small. It may have housed a small garrison, which could have given warning of any invader attempting to outflank the home valley; or it may have been built after the Assassin expansion as part of the key north-south line of communication. We photographed it, and then stood at the edge of the river wondering if we should attempt to ford it for a closer inspection. But the river looked deep, we didn't really relish the idea of sitting in wet clothes for the rest of the day, and it looked a very insignificant fort. Mike, as so often happened, turned out the bravest of us all. He found a relatively fordable spot and was soon on the island. The rest of us were beginning rather half-heartedly to take off our shoes and trousers when, to our relief, he called back and said that it wasn't worth while anyone else coming over. Time, too, was getting short, and so we piled into the Land Rovers as soon as we could and set off again.

The pass by the western route over the Elburz is not very steep, but as soon as we had crossed the watershed there was a startling change in the scenery. Instead of the bare red rocks, a new lush vegetation began to appear. First there were a few trees and shrubs, and then, as the road wound on down to the coast, we found ourselves travelling through dark-green ricefields, and, to our utter astonishment, it began to rain. Soon we saw houses curiously constructed in slate, and farmsteads which appeared far more prosperous than anything we had seen so far. The peasants were well-dressed, and, when we eventually hit the coast road near Resht, there were even brick houses—for all the world, we might have been motoring along the promenade at Clacton! The Caspian, as we first saw it, was equally banal and disappointing. Somehow one conjures up at the thought of the Caspian a mental image comprised of a dark-blue, mysterious stretch of water, Russians in flat caps and swarthy Persians nervously eyeing one another and fingering the triggers of their machine-carbines across the frontier, highly placed members of the Politburo drinking vodka and eating caviar on the Russian side, fat Persians sunbathing on the sand on the Iranian side, while to and fro flit spies of both sexes.

This is far from the truth. The Caspian is a security area, mainly because of the naval base at Bandar-e-Pahlavi. It is the holiday resort, and almost the Riviera, of Iran, but otherwise it is as nondescript a region as one can imagine. Only two features impressed us—the rain (the average rainfall is 60 inches per annum) and the dark green of the vegetation, rendered more striking by contrast with the prevailing tones of red, brown, and yellow of the rest of Persia.

Any desire we may have had to bathe in the grey waters of this inland sea was stifled rapidly. The dust of the Samiran plain had given way to rather chilling rain, and we sat huddled together listening to the squelch of the tyres on the metalled road. Lunch at the hotel in Resht was miserable, but we were able to stock up with cigarettes and other supplies before proceeding on our way. Richard and I sat on the tailboard and made out a roster of camp-duties, but even this failed to revive our drooping spirits as we realized that we had brought no waterproof coverings at all for ourselves or, far more important, for any of our equipment. The idea that it might rain had just not entered our minds, and so we lapsed into gloomy silence, staring like two disconsolate cows at the dripping landscape.

Roddie was map-reading in front and, with the accuracy that stamped all his actions, soon announced that we had reached the track that led to Rahimabad, our jumping-off point for our journey south into the Elburz mountains. We bumped along this track for 4 or 5 miles until we halted in the middle of the village. Immediately we were surrounded by a crowd of inquisitive, madly gesticulating villagers. They were emphatic that the jeep track went no farther, and a short reconnaissance soon convinced us they were quite right. There were no mules to be had that night, they declared, and so we decided that there was nothing we could do except stay in the village. Rahimabad is quite a prosperous community, being the capital of Upper Gilan.

Fortunately, every one seemed only too ready to help, and there was no need to show the impressive documents, complete with large red seals, which we carried with us from the Ministry of Education and the British Embassy. The local schoolmaster at once offered to lend us the school, and we soon transferred all our kit into the main room. The school was a fairly large, mud-built, one-storeyed building, reasonably clean and ideal for our purposes. It had 480 pupils,

boys and girls, and the schoolmaster told us he had eleven
assistant teachers. Off the main room were smaller class-
rooms, though these did not have any desks or benches.
The pupils sat on the floor as most Persians do everywhere, and they probably received a sound—if rudimentary
—instruction in the three Rs.

We made ourselves supper and then set about reorganizing our equipment for wet-weather conditions.
We had brought a large number of polythene bags with us
to protect our equipment from the dust, but they now had
to do duty as waterproof coverings. In them we wrapped
up everything valuable—photographic and archaeological
equipment, documents and maps, came first, then our
sleeping-bags and camping gear, and finally our personal
effects. This was where Mike's job really began. Each
man was responsible for his own personal equipment,
but Mike had to know in which kitbag the matches or
candles or tins of condensed milk were; no easy matter
when there were at least ten kitbags full of expedition
stores. In addition to our food-supplies we carried spare
parts for the pressure stoves, washing-up powder, lavatory
paper, toothpaste, soap, and all the one-thousand-and-one
oddments and pieces of equipment that were needed to
keep us going. How Mike managed to remember where
everything was we never understood, but he developed an
uncanny ability for unearthing anything we wanted.

That evening we held our first official conference in the
field. Once more we discussed exactly what we hoped to
achieve in Ashkavar, and how we intended to do it. For the
moment we planned to keep together as a group, but in
order to accomplish as much as possible, and to cover the
ground quickly within our limited time, we intended to
split into two groups: a flying squad composed of Richard,
Jah, and myself, and a main party proceeding at a somewhat slower pace. At this stage we had absolutely no idea
what we should find in Ashkavar, although we had four
main objectives.

First, Samuel Stern had suggested that we should look at certain historical sites in the valley. The only information about Ashkavar available up till then had been contained in a book entitled *Les Provinces Caspiennes de la Perse*, published by Dr H. L. Rabino in 1917. Rabino was the son of the first Director of the Imperial Bank of Persia. His father was a British subject (though of Italian origin, as his full name was H. L. Rabino di Borgomale) and the son was British Consul in Resht from 1906 until 1912. He travelled extensively in the three Caspian provinces of Gilan, Mazandaran, and Gurgan in 1908 and 1909, and during his years of office as British Consul collected as much oral information about the villages and their traditions and history as he could. After the war Rabino held consular appointments in Turkey and Morocco. Apart from a number of official reports and articles in learned journals, he wrote two standard works on the Caspian provinces: *Les Provinces Caspiennes de la Perse. Le Gilan*, which was published as a volume of the *Revue du monde musulman* (Paris, 1917), and *Mazandaran and Astarabad* (London, 1928). Rabino had never been to Ashkavar himself, and thus our first object was to check and supplement his account.

Secondly, as far as we knew, no Western traveller had ever penetrated this region before, and thus we hoped to be able to present, on our return to civilization, the only first-hand account of Ashkavar by Europeans.

Our third object was to see if there were any Assassin remains in Ashkavar and to try to determine the extent of Assassin power in this locality.

Lastly, as soon as we reached the confluence of the Chaka Rud and Pul-i-Rud at Sipul, some fifteen miles upstream, we should be on the route Hasan-i-Sabbah had taken in his roundabout journey from Rayy to Alamut in 1090, and we intended to follow this as precisely as we could. Owing to the delay at Samiran we had had to postpone our investigation of the Chaka Rud, but Richard,

Mike, and Ragnar intended to do this after I had left Teheran.

Thus we had a pretty full programme, and in order to keep ourselves within our strict time-limit we decided to spend no more than a fortnight in Ashkavar and, in order to give ourselves a target date, we agreed that if Robert got a good health certificate from the doctors in Teheran he would meet us at Shams Kilaya, the village below Maymun-Diz, in Alamut on August 25.

The date was now August 12, and although we had good reason to be pleased with what we had already accomplished, despite our heartbreaking start, we were always pursued by our chief enemy, lack of time. As far as we could tell from the maps we possessed, Ashkavar was some 30 miles long and seemed to consist of two main groups of villages: one at the northern end clustering around the township of Shuileh, which we later discovered to be the capital of the valley, and the other at the southern extremity, which seemed to have no chief town. The contours showed that most of the villages were situated on the tops of hills at 6000 to 7000 feet. From the southern end of the valley two tracks led over the mountain passes to Alamut, and we estimated that this journey would take us three days or so, but we decided to meet this hurdle when it came. Our maps, which Roddie had obtained, had been compiled from surveys published by the General Staff of the Red Army in November and December 1941. They were supplemented by names from Iranian maps and bore the reliability grading "Fairly reliable." This was a fair estimate of their accuracy.

Having dealt as far as we could with the operational side of the next fortnight's activities, we then drew up a list of duties that we should all have to undertake. This we felt to be vital, as a lot of time could be wasted as well as needless friction caused between the members of the expedition if the administration of the expedition did not work smoothly and efficiently. From our experience in 1959 Richard and I had already drawn up a provisional agenda and, wondering how every one would take this, I read it out. First our proposed timetable: Reveille 5.30; Breakfast 6.0; Move off 6.30; Lunch 12.30; after which we would all spend an hour and a half writing up our notebooks and diaries. Again from our previous experience, we knew that unless we had a period completely sacrosanct for writing this vital part of our programme would get pushed on one side. A second period of work followed from 2.30 to 6.30, and we agreed that during this period Ragnar should be allowed to ask us to pose for photographs and to ask us to repeat actions, as far as this was possible, that he had not been able to film before. Although we would try and co-operate with him in the morning, archaeological investigation would come first. Dinner would be at 7 (the light began to fade soon after) and we piously hoped to be in bed by 8.30. This programme was meant, of course, for the days when we would be in our base-camp, and it would have to be suitably adapted when we were on the move. Whatever else happened, we vowed that we would get up at 5.30 and so work with the sun.

Next came the chores. It was agreed that if the day's work was to be economically and efficiently planned Richard and I must be largely exempt from the morning work in order to draw up the day's programme. Breakfast would therefore be cooked by Jah and Mike, Minou would do the washing-up, Richard would look after the water and supervise the loading of the mules, while Roddie and I would see to the tents and beds. The evening meal would be cooked by Mike and Richard, while Minou and Jah held evening surgery. Finally, Roddie, Jah, and Ragnar would do the evening washing-up. This was agreed to without dispute and remained our standard drill throughout the expedition.

Then we jotted down what results we hoped to be in a position to present after our return. Our somewhat ambitious programme ran like this:

1. The publication of an academic book on the historical topography of the Alamut valley with particular reference to the castles.
2. A paper on the geography of the valley of Ashkavar.
3. A book for the general public on the expedition as a whole.
4. A colour film on the people, country, and expedition for TV and the cinema.
5. The collection of material for a lecture tour.
6. Newspaper articles.
7. A children's book incorporating some of the legends and stories about Hasan-i-Sabbah and this part of the world.

By these we hoped to be able to pay off the cost of the expedition, which had been financed solely by means of a generous bank loan. In addition, of course, we hoped to collect as many specimens as we could of pottery, and possibly manuscripts, to bring back with us.

Our conference lasted far into the night, and when we had finished it was time to go to bed. Mosquitoes abounded, and so for the first and almost only time we suspended our nets from hooks in the walls and climbed wearily into our camp-beds.

When we woke the next morning it was still raining, but not quite so heavily as the day before. We had already decided that it would be pointless to keep three doctors in the party, and so I suggested to Hatemi that he return to Teheran with Bernard Bright and Robert. I pointed out that as well as doctors we needed interpreters and that Kurlu spoke better English than he did. I gave him a letter to hand to the Minister of Health in which I tactfully explained why we were sending Hatemi back, and at the same time expressed our deep gratitude for all he had done. I am sure that Hatemi was secretly relieved at our decision, which he accepted with good grace. He realized that what lay ahead was indeed no picnic and that probably he would not be able to stand up to the rigours of the journey. When we had to put Robert into his care on going sick, Hatemi was able to withdraw with good grace and untarnished honour. We all liked him and felt sorry that he had to go, but there was clearly no other course we could take.

Our first problem after breakfast was to arrange for mules. to carry our equipment to Shuileh, which we had chosen as our first base-camp. This proved much more difficult than we had anticipated. We had just arrived at the harvest season and most of the mules were out working in the fields. So great in fact is the demand for these animals that during the autumn many mule-owners from Alamut send their mules down to Gilan where they can earn good money. In Rahimabad all the mules were owned by one man, who thus had a complete monopoly and could charge what prices he wanted. Sensing a profitable bargain, he had been one of our first visitors the night before, and we had instructed Minou to order as many mules as we needed and at a reasonable price. In 1959 we had paid an average of 10 toman (that is, 10 shillings) a day for a mule and the muleteer, and this was the price we offered now. At first no comment was made, but we were told a lot about the difficulty of producing six or eight mules, the number we required. The morning wore on, and there was no sign of the mules. It began to rain harder, and the mule-owner, a tall, dark man in his twenties, dressed entirely in black, with dark eyes and a hooked nose, told me that conditions up in the mountains would now be so dangerous and slippery that he doubted if we should be able to set out that day at all. All this seemed to us to be part of a big build-up to get as much money out of us as possible, and tempers began to fray. At this moment two scraggy donkeys appeared as the advance guard of our mule-train; the rest would soon be coming, we were told, and with any luck we should be able to leave by tea-time.

By about three o'clock two mules were tethered outside
the school with the donkeys, and then the sombre figure
of the mule-owner appeared in the doorway. He told us
that with the utmost difficulty he had managed to procure
five mules and two donkeys, but that in view of all the
circumstances he would have to charge us 20 toman a day
for each mule. This was daylight robbery, and we at once
protested vociferously. How on earth dared he charge us
£7 a day for the mules, we asked him. Did he think we
were made of money? He merely replied that if we did not
pay his price he was very sorry but we would not be able
to leave Rahimabad, and he made a sign to one of the
muleteers to lead the animals away. We were caught, and
both he and we knew it, but we were determined not to
give in so lightly. We appealed to the schoolmaster to act
as an intermediary, but he said that he had already tried to
get Black Turpin (as we called the owner) to bring down
his prices, but without avail.

At this we played our last card and demanded to be
taken to the gendarmerie, where we would lay an official
complaint. Followed by half the village, we all trooped off
to the gendarmerie, where we were most courteously
received by the resident gendarme. We produced our
impressive credentials, laying heavy stress on our highly-
placed connections in Teheran. But before any business
could be done we must first drink tea. The ever-ready
samovar was produced, and a pile of rather grubby cups
and a few glasses. The tea was handed round, and for a
quarter of an hour the two sides exchanged polite pleasan-
tries through Minou. Black Turpin sat in a corner noisily
sucking his teeth and obviously displeased with the turn
things were taking. When the gendarme had finished
his tea he turned towards me and asked how he could
help the *sarhang*. This word means "colonel": he had
promoted me from my rank of major, and from now on
this was the title by which I was always addressed. It
sounded impressive until Jah told me that there are about

4000 *sarhangs* in Iran! The gendarme, after a good deal of arguing on our part, punctuated with shouts, tears, and wild gesticulations on Black Turpin's, showed in the end the wisdom of Solomon. Would we agree to pay 15 toman, he politely inquired. All parties were so exhausted by the proceedings that we shook hands on the deal, although we made it a condition that we should start within an hour. Black Turpin now showed that he was after all a man of honour. Within the promised hour all our belongings were safely strapped on the mules and donkeys. We said farewell to Robert, Bernard, and Hatemi, who had been patiently waiting all day, and who now would arrive back in Teheran in the small hours of the following morning; then, accompanied by the gendarme, schoolmaster, headman, Black Turpin, and all the village, we left Rahimabad for the mountains.

It was after 5 o'clock in the afternoon. It was still raining intermittently, and the mule-track was a veritable quagmire. We knew that darkness would fall soon after 7.30, and so we tried to push on as quickly as we could for the few remaining hours of daylight. To begin with we had to cross a large number of ricefields, and the track at times seemed to peter out into mere bog. As we were about to cross a particularly soggy morass our accompanying escort prudently decided to return to Rahimabad. The polite handshakes that were exchanged hid the satisfaction that both villagers and expedition felt at being rid of each other, and it was with a sigh of relief that we now resolutely pressed on.

The going was very hard, and after an hour or so we were covered from head to foot with mud kicked up by the mules. As we proceeded signs of civilization began to recede. Whenever we passed a group of houses people would come to their doors, look at us curiously but rather impassively, shrug their shoulders, and then go back to their jobs. In front of us lay the densely wooded foothills of the Elburz mountains. We could not see their summits as they were covered with a thick veil of cloud. Without our guides we should never have found the entrance to the valley of Ashkavar, but gradually the plain narrowed and we found ourselves going up a steep track through the woods. At first it seemed as if we might have been walking somewhere in the Lake District; the scenery appeared no different. Soon we came across a few rocks on top of which were the remains of some old fortifications. We stopped and examined them, but there was very little to go on. Our guide told us that this was Chale Kale, or "Castle of the Neck," as the castle was situated at the extreme neck of the valley. Our maps at this point showed little detail, and we were thrilled when we were later able to pencil in the name Devaz Lat, by which a broad plateau now given up to rice cultivation was called.

For two more hours we climbed up and up. The trees dripped down on us, and very soon we were wet to the skin and exhausted by the slippery climb. At about 8 o'clock we came to a small group of houses, and we decided that there we would stop for the night. We were told that the name of the village was Varabon. The so-called headman came out to greet us and said that we could sleep in his house for the night if we wished. The house was a two-storey building, and it looked extremely dirty. By the time we had unloaded the mules it was completely dark. We were all assigned to an upper room, really a sort of hay-loft, and to get there we had to scramble up a steep ladder with sharp nails sticking out. It was quite impossible to take our kit up this ladder, and so we fumbled about for the next half-hour trying to find our cooking implements and articles we should need for the night. Downstairs there were two small rooms. In one of them sat the rest of our host's family—two wives and about ten children. The wives were cooking supper over an open fire, and, as the room did not contain a chimney, the small space was completely filled with acrid smoke. None of us could spend more than two minutes in it without coming out with streaming eyes and a violent cough. Then the heavens opened again. It was impossible to cook our food outside, and so we had to make a fire ourselves in the other small room, again without a chimney. We had some tepid soup, lukewarm coffee, and bread. It was hopeless to attempt to cook anything else without being suffocated in the process. We then sprayed the whole of our room with DDT and retired for the night. Over our camp-beds we put up mosquito-nets in the hope that they would keep out most of the insects. In this they failed lamentably. Throughout the night each of us woke up in turn, scratching violently, and sprayed more DDT on everything we could think of, then vainly tried to sleep. It was still pouring with rain, and so we were forced to stay in the house. When dawn came we were as miserable a group of explorers as has ever been seen. Our bodies were covered with bites from head to toe, our clothes were wringing wet from the night before, it was still raining, and there seemed no prospect of getting any breakfast. When we showed our bites to our host and asked him if he had slept well he merely said that as he had given us hospitality it was only fair that we should give his insects hospitality in return!

We left the house as soon as we could and continued our climb. After three hours we reached another small village called Palam, and here we stopped for lunch. In the centre of the village was a tea-house and our guides told us that this village would be our last link with the civilization of the plain. The tea-house was small, dark, and smoky, but the cups of hot, sugary tea did us a lot of good. We were able to dry off a little bit, but at the expense of renewing through the heat the excruciating agony of our bites. We hoped that it was not considered impolite in Iran to scratch; and at one moment Roddie let out a cry of "I've got one" and held out in his hand a flea that he had caught off Ragnar's shirt. We asked if we could cook a hot meal for ourselves, and the owner of the tea-house willingly brought out some pots and pans which he lent us. We

made a bully-beef stew and offered some of it to our
guides. They politely refused, and when we asked if they
were not hungry they said they were, but that their
religion forbade them to eat meat prepared by infidels.
After lunch we set out again.

Our destination was Darud, a small village half-way up
the foothills. The valley now began to get narrower and
narrower. We were gradually getting above the treeline,
but the mist and Caspian cloud still hung over everything.
We longed for the sun to come out, not only to dry our
clothes, but also to drive away the mist that now veiled
some of the loveliest views of this part of the Caspian. But
we were disappointed, and, when we eventually arrived at
Darud, morale was low. Darud was a bigger village than
Palam. It consisted of fifty families and was a small
agricultural centre. Our first care was to try to find a clean
house, and we told our chief guide that whatever happened
he must make quite certain that we were given a room
which had recently been disinfected and supplied with
clean straw. To our surprise he found two such rooms in
the centre of the village. We looked at them and they did
seem surprisingly clean. They were small, so that when we
had unloaded all our kit there was hardly room for us to
move. Outside there was a balcony, and this seemed ideal
for use as a kitchen. For the first time we made ourselves a
decent meal and went to bed early, waking up the next
morning feeling much better. After we had eaten breakfast,
a lot of people began to collect outside the house. First
came some sick who wanted Minou to give them drugs or
to have a look at their children, and then a large group of
villagers who had merely come to stare.

We were told that near the village were some ruins,
which we felt we must see. At Darud there is thought to
have been a big battle at the time of the Assassins, and the
inhabitants of Ashkavar are credited with having put up
quite a tough fight. We hoped that these ruins might have
something to do with the battle. We followed our guide

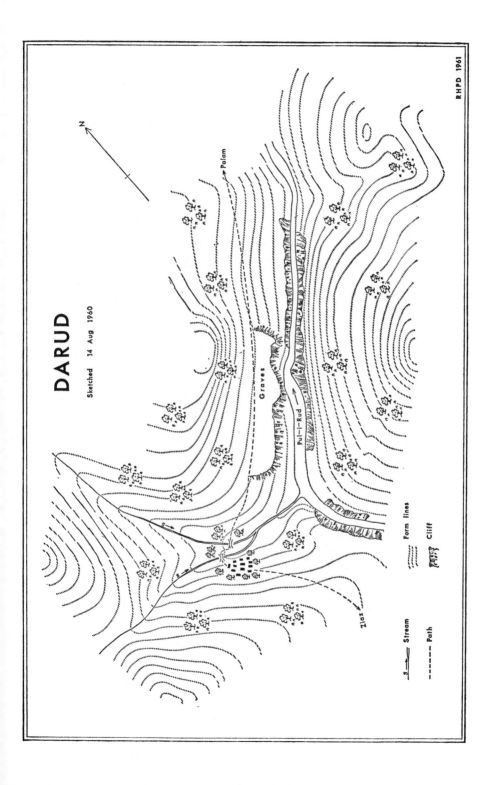

DARUD

Sketched 14 Aug 1960

N

Palam

Graves

Pul-i-Rud

Ziaz

Form lines

Cliff

Stream

Path

RHPD 1961

for half an hour until we came to a small plateau high above a precipice. He then pointed to some graves that he and the villagers had opened. "What was inside them?" we asked. Had they found any gold or silver? "Yes, indeed," was his reply, many precious objects had been dug up. Skeletons had been found, and in one or two places near by coronets and sceptres had been taken out of the graves. This seemed to us to be extremely unlikely, and so we asked if we could see any of the objects that had been recovered. A small boy was sent off to the village and came running back with two or three pots of indeterminate age. They were grey, unglazed, and could really have been made at any time in the last thousand years. Was this all the proof they had, we asked. Our guide then became confidential and said that many wicked men had been trying to find the precious objects, and that the villagers were afraid that we had been sent by the Government. We assured him that we had nothing to do with the Government at all, and entreated him to give us more information. With a wide sweep of his arm he indicated the whole of the plateau and said that here were many graves. If this was in fact the battlefield of Darud, it would seem reasonable that some of the dead would have been buried here. If we excavated a little we might find some interesting Assassin relics.

We therefore decided to stay for at least the rest of that day, and to make one or two soundings. Three or four of the villagers offered to help. We looked carefully at the ground, and it seemed that the stones that littered it were in fact placed in some kind of order. We decided that we should try in the centre, and, with the help of our volunteer labour force, we soon removed two big stones which could have been grave-slabs. We dug down to a depth of 4 or 5 feet and came across some broken bones. We then asked if the graves were laid out in any systematic pattern and if they were bricked. Sometimes they were and sometimes they weren't was the answer, and we dug on. We found nothing else, and we made two other soundings with the same negative results. As this point our guide told us that about 3 miles away was another little village called Aziz, and if we went there we should almost certainly find specimens similar to those recovered from the graves at Darud. By this time it was getting late and so we decided to suspend operations for the night and to move to Aziz the following morning. Meanwhile, Ragnar had been able to get in some shots of our excavations and had spent his time profitably photographing the village.

By the following morning the weather had improved a little. The ground was drier, and so we decided that the expedition should split into two. The main party would push on early and try to make our destination, Shuileh, that night. It would be a hard day's journey, but at least it would save us some money. At Shuileh we could dismiss the muleteers and set up our first main base-camp. We decided that Minou should go with this group and try to hire a house for us in Shuileh, while Richard, Jah, and I would go to Aziz and then make our way to Shuileh by a roundabout route, taking in the village of Rudbarek.

It did not take us long to reach Aziz. This was a nice little village consisting of only ten houses, the principal one belonging to a Mr Hasan Mohammady, a Teheran business man. He was a native of Ashkavar, and at the time was spending his summer holidays at Aziz. He was an educated man and even spoke a little French. When we arrived at his house he invited us in, and in half an hour set a delicious meal in front of us. The main reception room was beautifully carpeted, and on the wall were some magnificent tapestries, which seemed to us to be quite old. We politely explained who we were, and I produced our now rather rain-soaked credentials from the Ministry of Education and the British Embassy.

It was evident that he was delighted to receive European travellers in his house, and he at once set out to make us comfortable and to give us as much information as he

could. He stated that he had never seen any Europeans in
this part of the world, although we were still relatively
close to the Caspian area. His sons soon joined us, and his
eldest boy showed a tact that we had scarcely expected to
find in this remote country district. Noticing our surrepti-
tious scratching, he left the room and came back a few
minutes later with a bottle of eau-de-cologne.

"Help yourselves," he said, "and if you would like to
keep the bottle, please do." We told him that we had spent
the last night but one in Varabon.

"Good heavens," our host exclaimed. "That village is
known for miles around as the dirtiest in the whole of the
Caspian. Your guide should be whipped for allowing you
to stop there."

Although we were not feeling in a particularly charitable
mood towards our guide, we nevertheless thought this
recommendation slightly severe. But, true to his word, Mr
Mohammady sent for our guide, picked up a rhinoceros-
hide whip, and flourished it threateningly. We intervened,
and all was well, but he obviously felt that local honour
had been outraged by our ignorant companion.

Talk now turned to the graves, and we listened, fascinated, while our host told us of the excavations and finds
that had been made during the previous twelve months. Mr
Mohammady began by saying that the original village had
been called Ziaz, not Aziz, and it had been situated about
half a mile higher up the mountain. There had always been
a legend that a considerable treasure had been buried at
Ziaz in the distant past at the time of the Persian
"heraldic" kings. We continually heard about the Persian
"heraldic" kings, but no one could quite tell us who they
were or when they had lived. They seemed to be part of
Persian mythology and in a vague way connected with the
legends of Rustum. Anyway, this treasure, as happens with
all the best treasures, was guarded by a dragon or snake,
and whoever found it would acquire the riches of ancient
Persia. This legend, rather like the Niebelungen saga, had

been handed down through the centuries, and every now and then a small digging party would scrape away on the barren mountainside and find nothing.

In 1958 the attention of some landlords had been attracted by the regular mounds near Darud, and they had decided to investigate. They came across the graves and found bronze swords and grey pottery similar to the examples we had seen. On a journey to a village called Diarzan some 11 miles to the west, one landlord had noticed mounds of similar shape. Being a man of education, he concluded that the mounds at Darud and Diarzan must be Zoroastrian graves. He decided first to dig up as many of the graves at Darud as he could, and approached the headman of the village for permission. The headman refused, and so the landlord decided to take the law into his own hands. He rounded up a posse of some thirty able-bodied men from his own village, armed two or three of them with shotguns, and, at night, after posting sentries around the grave-area, had proceeded to dig. Any villager from Darud who approached was roughly told to mind his own business and a warning shot fired over his head. This procedure seemed to us rather high-handed, but in these parts of the Elburz mountains it was apparently quite normal practice. Ten graves were opened at Darud, and then the landlord had transferred his activities to Diarzan. Here the haul was much richer. The first treasure brought to light was a silver statuette of a woman, about 7 inches high and weighing about 7 pounds. Mr Mohammady told us that the proportions of this statue were perfect, that the face showed features very akin to those of Kurdish tribesmen (that is, with salient cheekbones and Mongol eyes), and that there were bangles round her arms and legs. In some of the other graves gold and silver brace-lets were found as well as bronze swords and daggers. One mass grave contained about 500 skeletons, males and females having been buried together. Soldiers could easily be recognized, as they had their swords either at their

sides or behind their heads. A gold image of a snake en-
crusted with a hundred rubies had been found, and a big
silver plate adorned with precious stones and embossed
with figures of gods and goddesses.

After listening to all this we asked Mr Mohammady
what had been done with these treasures. He replied that
they had been sold one by one through a private agency in
Teheran—the "Statue of Diarzan," as he called it, being
sold to an American for £10,000. We asked him to be
more specific, but it was difficult to get much more detail
out of him as he was obviously afraid that we would tell
the Government in Teheran and his fellow-landlords
would get into trouble. Naturally enough, all excavated
works of art are considered treasure trove and belong to the
Crown, and a full report of finds should be made to the
competent Iranian authorities: but some landlords had
not done this. Later, in other houses, we saw some of these
relics, and one of the excavators presented us with a bronze
dagger which has since been identified by the British
Museum as being of the Luristan variety and dating back
to about 1500 B.C.

After we had left the house Richard and I discussed at
length what he had told us. At first, of course, we were
inclined to be sceptical. The Persians' love of exaggeration
is well-known, and, although the control of the Ministry
of Education over works of art is pretty loose, we felt
that if all that Mr Mohammady had told us had been true,
some inkling would have filtered through to Teheran, and
the Government would certainly have taken steps to
investigate this area for themselves. When we returned to
Teheran we found that the Government did in fact know
all about the finds, and had prohibited any further excavation by the local inhabitants, but it was quite powerless to
enforce this order. Neither did it have sufficient means,
and possibly interest, to equip an expedition of its own to
send to this area. It was also true that unidentified precious
objects and statues had been coming down to Teheran and

been sold at exorbitant prices to tourists, mostly Americans. So far it has not been possible to run any of these treasures to earth so that they may be scientifically examined. All of this we suspected at the time, and we decided to keep our eyes wide open for any further graves.

Mr Mohammady gave us one other valuable piece of information. He had not seen any Zoroastrian fire-altars, which would have supported his theory of a Zoroastrian civilization in these parts, but he did know that at the confluence of the Chaka Rud and the Pul-i-Rud there were the remains of three or four large castles. He knew very little about the Assassins, but we decided that these castles must be investigated.

We hurried on that afternoon in order to reach the village of Rudbarek where we had decided to spend the night. The track was now steeper, and we were climbing, according to our maps, over ridges of 3000 or 4000 feet. In the middle of the afternoon we reached the junction of the two rivers at a place called Sipul, which means "Three Bridges." Sipul was not marked on the map, but it was here that Hasan-i-Sabbah turned south-east on the final stage of his journey from Rayy to Alamut, and so we once more linked up with his route. Legend relates that even in his day there were three bridges here, and that he stood on the central one attended by only one servant, stretched out his arms towards the south, and said, "This is the boundary of my kingdom. From now on all the territory that I shall cross belongs to me."

The site is magnificent. The Pul-i-Rud here flows through a narrow, wild gorge. The track clings to the mountainside, 500 feet above a sheer drop to the valley beneath. There is a similar gorge to the west, and just before the Chaka Rud joins the Pul-i-Rud there is a most impressive waterfall about 200 feet high. The water comes tumbling down, green from the mountain snow, and foams over great, jagged rocks. At the junction of the two tracks it is dark and cold, as the sun hardly penetrates through the thick undergrowth that lines the sides of both gorges.

To our surprise, two teams of mules were resting there, and tucked under one of the rocks was a little tea-house. We stopped and asked for tea from an old, toothless woman who evidently owned the tea-house. We sat there, sipping our tea, for half an hour, and Jah chatted with the muleteers, asking them for further information. One of them showed us an old rock on which was carved, still quite distinctly, drawings of warriors dressed in medieval armour. This rock is still known as Hasan's Stone. We tried to photograph it, but the light was so bad that unfortunately nothing came out. We took a rubbing, but this was lost when one of our mules was washed downstream in the Alamut river.

The light was now fading, and it was beginning to get cold. We were told that the village of Rudbarek was at least 15 miles away, and it looked to us as if we should have a very unpleasant walk along the side of the gorge at night. Fortunately, after we had been travelling for two hours, we rounded a corner and there was our village lying by the stream. A group of people were gathered just outside, looking along the mountain path, and when they saw us coming they began waving excitedly, pointing in our direction. This was a pity because just at this spot there was a lovely, deep pool in which we had hoped to have a bathe. By now we were extremely tired and dusty, and this seemed our only opportunity of a dip. We decided to ignore what was obviously a reception-committee and walked down to the pool. We threw off our clothes, and a moment later we were sitting in the beautifully cool, clear, running water. Just then the reception-committee rounded the corner. They saw us and made straight for the pool. To our horror we noticed that among them were two women, and this posed a very difficult problem. We sat up and waved our arms, shouting salaams. Were we the *sarhang's* party, they inquired. Jah replied that we were, and that if they would have the goodness to go round the corner we

would soon come up and greet them. At this they roared
with laughter and sat down at the edge of the pool. There
was nothing for us to do but to put a brave face on things,
climb out of the pool hastily, wrap towels round ourselves,
and then dress as quickly as we could. Meanwhile, a great
knot of village children had also collected, and they were all
laughing madly and finding the whole incident a great joke.

When we had dressed, the headman came forward and
shook my hand with grave courtesy. He had been informed
by the Ashkavar authorities that the honourable *sarhang*
would be coming through his village, and he had already
put his house at our disposal. We followed him into the
village, which was very small, and the usual ceremony of
tea-drinking at once began. We were taken to a very
pleasant house, given a meal, and then the whole village
was allowed to enter. I always found these receptions a
little trying. My own store of Persian was always
exhausted after two minutes, and then there was nothing
to do except sit back looking rather silly while all the
village gaped and stared. We asked our usual questions
about castles, and the headman of Rudbarek confirmed
what Mr Mohammady had already told us. He offered to
lend us a guide the following day, and this we gratefully
accepted. We also asked him about the poisoned well of
Rudbarek. Legend says that here was an extremely
dangerous well, and anyone approaching too close to it
would at once be overwhelmed by the fumes and die
shortly afterwards. It had, supposedly, had its political
uses too, as dissident members of the royal family and
disloyal governors and nobles could be escorted to
Rudbarek and then pushed down the well. This story put
more than a strain on our credulity. It seemed unnecessarily
troublesome to take a fractious noble to such a remote spot
when simpler methods for disposal were at hand.

However, the headman solemnly assured us that the
well was still there, though it had been filled in for safety's
sake, and he promised to show it to us the next morning.

It turned out to be much smaller than we had expected. Nevertheless, we approached it gingerly, up-wind, and kept at a respectful distance of some 15 feet. On the top of it lay two dead chickens and one or two field-mice. The headman promptly put his hand round his nose and dashed in and took the two chickens, which he said he would have for lunch, and this seemed rather a convenient way of supplying the larder. We could not make any scientific investigation of what caused the poisonous gases, but there was certainly a smell of sulphur. The headman must have noticed our disappointment, because he at once proceeded to tell us some highly unlikely tales about the people who had met their deaths here, and then, as our expressions became more and more incredulous, he hastily broke off and offered to lend us a guide to take us to the castles we wanted to see.

Richard, Jah, and I had already decided to send a note to the main party, which, by that time, should be firmly established at Shuileh, telling them that our arrival would be delayed by forty-eight hours. I tore a page out of my notebook, wrote on the top "On Her Britannic Majesty's Service" to give it an air of importance, and in it asked Roddie if he would lead a subsidiary expedition to the following places: (*a*) Wagul Khani, where we hoped they would find an old shrine; (*b*) Laspu, where, according to the accounts of Rabino, they should find the site of the old city of Kocht; and (*c*) Chaka, which was also the site of an old town. I asked them if they would take photographs and make plans and sketches of these places and in particular look out for old coins and manuscripts. In Rudbarek we had met a priest who said that he was quite sure that an old manuscript of Zahir-ad-Din was still in existence as he had seen a copy of it at the village of Laspu. He had also heard about an old history book called simply "The History of Gilan and Daylaman" and I asked Roddie to keep an eye open for these two. The headman promised that this message would get to Shuileh within six hours, and, escorted by our own guide, we set off to climb to the castle of Lima.

We soon found that the route to Lima was going to be much steeper and much longer than we had anticipated, and in order to save time I asked Richard if he would go with our guide, whom we now found was a local school-master, across the hills to the village of Poramkuh where Jah and I would join him that night. At Poramkuh, we were told, we should find a large Assassin castle. In fact it turned out to be a heap of rubble on top of a sheer cliff 2000 feet high.

Jah and I reached the castle of Lima after a four-hour climb. There was a little village quite near where we stopped and had tea, and once more we heard the usual tale of Zoroastrian graves, and were shown pottery and some rather poor examples of arrow-heads and short daggers. The castle itself was half a mile from the village and stood on a promontory overlooking the whole of the valley. The outer walls and buttresses were still quite well preserved, and there was a big central block rather like a keep, 15 feet high and 20 feet square. The central doorway had collapsed, but the local inhabitants had made a tunnel as a means of entrance. The ground was littered with shards of pottery.

One most interesting feature was a long water-pipe, which emerged from a wall about 150 feet from the top of the castle and which was still in a fine state of preservation. The guide told us that the inhabitants of Lima had found a whole series of these pipes in the hills round the village. We explored farther along the crest on which the castle was built and came across foundations of houses and more water-pipes, suggesting that Lima must have been quite an important town. The villagers could give us no valuable information, but from the structure of the brickwork and the condition of the mortar it looked very much as though this castle did in fact date from Assassin times. Strategic-ally, it would have dominated the entrance to the valley of

the Pul-i-Rud as well as being an important outpost on the
trading route to the Caspian sea. We again asked if any
Europeans had been seen in this area, and we were told
the only people they had seen were a party of Russian
surveyors during the war. The Russians had explored the
castle and had made plans of it and had apparently set up
their main camp there. But then they had quarrelled with
the good townsfolk of Lima, and, because taxes had not
been paid at the time due, they had shot two of the
inhabitants. This had so enraged the villagers of Lima that
they decided to take reprisals on their own, and one night
they stormed the Russian camp and killed every one there.
Of course, there was no evidence for the authenticity of this
story, but we could well believe it to be true. We asked if
the Russians had taken any further reprisals, and were told
that they had never been seen again. When we asked for a
description of the Russians, we were told that most of them
were fair-skinned and had fair hair. When we told Richard
about this, he at once said that he must dye his hair with
henna in the manner of some of the villagers so as not to be
mistaken for a Russian!

When we left Lima it was about 5 o'clock, and we
decided to retrace our steps along the river up to Sipul, and
then follow the course of the Chaka Rud until we got to the
village of Poramkuh. By the time we arrived at Sipul, it
was dark. Our guide said that he knew the way, but it
soon became clear that he did not. We now had to go a
distance of some 5 miles over extremely rough and steep
country, and the narrow twisting mule-track ran right
along the edge of a steep trough. We had no light, and it
began to rain. Once I missed my footing and fell down the
side of the hill for about 100 feet till my fall was stopped
by a bush. The rocks were extremely slippery and I had
twisted my ankle quite badly in my fall, but I managed
somehow to scramble to the top again. Jah bound it up as
best he could, and I hobbled on. We asked if we were
likely to come upon any villages before Poramkuh, and

we were told that there were none. Gradually my foot-steps became slower and slower, and I found it very difficult to move at all. Our guide, who was a strongly built man, seeing that I was in pain, picked me up like a sack of potatoes and threw me over his shoulder, and it was in this way that we managed to cover the last 2 miles or so. When we at last got to the village we found an extremely worried Richard. He was trying to get a search party out to look for us, but as the villagers had not the least idea what he was talking about, they thought that he must be trying to say that he was hungry and insisted on bringing him more and more food. He gave a gasp of horror when he saw me dumped unceremoniously down in one corner. My face was covered in blood from some cuts on my forehead, but these were not particularly severe, and Jah was able to patch me up without great difficulty.

The next morning I felt better but not up to walking a great distance. Richard had reported that the castle of Poramkuh was certainly not worth visiting, and so we decided to go and see another castle at Tulah. I went on a mule, and the rest of the party followed on foot. Tulah itself turned out to have a rather fine watch-tower. It was obviously extremely old and had probably been in existence for a long time before the Assassins came. The villagers said that their ancestors had lived there and that it was haunted. The walls were about 30 feet high and it had clearly never been destroyed but, judging by the large heap of rubble at the side, the walls had fallen down of their own accord. Again we found water-pipes, but this time no pottery. This was interesting, especially as the villagers told us that they had never come across any shards either. We dug a little round the castle, but we did not excavate anything at all significant.

That night we went back to Poramkuh, where we opened two new graves. In them we found three vases about 6 inches high and two interesting daggers. The hilts were carved as animals' heads—probably bulls' heads, although it was difficult to tell exactly. The blades were triangular, short, and stubby, and, altogether, they were wicked-looking instruments. The inhabitants had not heard of the digging that had been going on elsewhere, and so here was a place where we should be able to test for the first time the truth of all that we had heard. We did not have time to stay long, but if further excavations are made here it is likely that some valuable objects will be recovered.

On the following morning we set out across the hills to Shuileh. This was a pleasant journey. The path was not too steep and the sun soon cleared the Caspian cloud, but it took us a whole day, and we did not arrive at the town until evening. We found that Roddie had been given the upper part of some stables as his headquarters, but that sickness had already struck hard at the party.

Shuileh, a town of about 200 families, is built on the side of the mountain, but the atmosphere is dank and most of the wooden houses drip continually with moisture. For some reason the Caspian cloud seems to hang in a heavy, thick pall over the town, and it is only very rarely that the sun manages to shine through. I think it must have been the dampness, as well as fatigue and strain, that brought on the first serious bout of sickness in the expedition. When Richard, Jah, and I arrived, the only person still on his feet was Minou. All round the two rooms that Roddie had made his headquarters there seemed to be groaning bodies lying under piles of damp blankets. We asked Minou what had happened, and he said that Roddie, Ragnar, and Mike all had fairly high temperatures, ranging from 101° to 104°. Ragnar was most severely hit, and Minou had been giving him injections of penicillin in order to bring down the fever. It seemed that shortly after their arrival Roddie and Mike had complained of headaches and stomach pains, and at first Minou thought this was dysentery. However, he took their temperatures and found these were well above normal, so he ordered them to bed

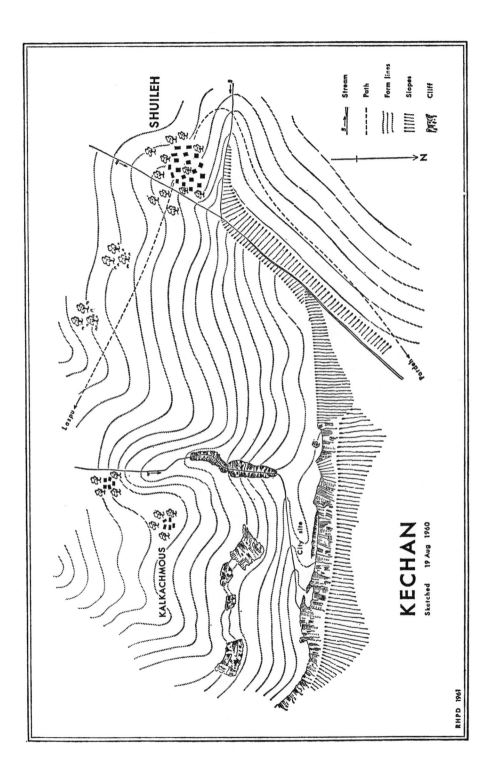

KECHAN

Sketched   19 Aug 1960

SHUILEH

KALKACHMOUS

City site

Laspu

Poldah

Stream
Path
Form lines
Slopes
Cliff

N

RHPD 1961

and hoped that they would sweat it out. Unfortunately this had not happened, and Ragnar was almost delirious. Minou proposed to use even stronger drugs if the penicillin did not work, and Richard and I sat up for the rest of the evening beside Ragnar's bed. By the morning his temperature had dropped a little and in two or three days he had completely recovered, but still felt very weak. This applied to our other sick as well, and it was not until we had left Shuileh that they completely recovered. Minou seemed to keep reasonably well all the time that we stayed there, and so did I, but after our third day Richard developed a temperature too. It could not have been the water that was causing this sickness, as we were particularly careful to boil it all, and we took special precautions over all the food we bought.

Our finds at Shuileh were on the whole fairly extensive. Our main object here was to try and find the site of two lost cities, one of which is called Kashan and the other Kalkachmous. The name Kashan seemed to be fairly familiar to the inhabitants of Shuileh, and it did not take us long to identify it with the present-day hamlet called Kechan about a mile to the east of Shuileh and overlooking the Pul-i-Rud. The site is a magnificent one right on the edge of a very steep precipice. Just behind is a range of granite hills called alternatively the "City of Dervishes" or the "Place of Kings." We were told that there had been a village on the top of these hills, but, fifty years before, the spring had dried up and the houses had been destroyed. We were informed also that this particular rock formation was well known as being a haunt of vipers, and in fact we did see two or three snakes sunning themselves on the rocks. We gave them a wide berth, and it was clear that the inhabitants were terrified of them. They maintained that their bite was deadly, and that two or three people died each year from snakebite.

The Place of Kings gave way to a plateau, and at the very edge of the plateau we could see the remains of the

foundations of the old city. Rabino mentions it in his book
on the provinces of the Caspian. It is difficult to give an
exact date to the city, but it probably dated back to about
1000 B.C. Like most of the old towns in Ashkavar, Kashan
was built in terraces ascending almost to the foot of the
Place of Kings. In the centre were the foundations of
what could well have been an old temple. The forecourt
stood out clearly, and measured some 20 feet by 35
feet. We could still see some of the original paving-
stones and mosaics. At the northern end of this forecourt
were the remains of pillars rather in the form of a Greek
temple. Around the temple were signs that many houses
made of brick and stone had once stood there. Little
remained, but we were able to map the area and to make
an approximate sketch of the layout of the town. More
recently a holy man was buried here, and there is a rather
dilapidated shrine.

Apart from the interest of the town itself, the landscape,
and in particular the view over the vast chasm of the river,
was the main attraction. When we had finished our day's
work on the site, we would sit with our legs dangling over
the edge, looking down at eagles and vultures wheeling
above the floor of the valley hundreds of feet below. The
other advantage of this site was that it enabled the sick
members of the expedition to come and join us for a few
hours at a time. It was within easy reach of our headquarters, and so everybody was able to take some share in
the excavation, which kept up morale and prevented people
from being too absorbed in their own illnesses.

Kalkachmous was not quite so interesting. A very small
hamlet here consisted of just two or three houses, and the
ancient town must have been much smaller than the one at
Kashan. Our most interesting find was a stone that looked
very much as though it might have been a Zoroastrian
fire-altar. It was smooth, some 5 feet high, and the top
measured 3 feet by 18 inches.

Near Kalkachmous more graves had been excavated.
C.A.—I.

We looked at some of them, and the same pattern as that at Ziaz and Darud emerged. As we started to turn up the ground around the fire-altar, we came across the brown, glazed pottery which resembled that of the Assassins. This, apart from Lima, was the only place in Upper Ashkavar where we found such remains, and so it is reasonable to assume that this was an Assassin settlement.

We were told that in olden times two kings lived at Kalkachmous; one was called Kikavas Shah and the other Sharivah Shah. The two quarrelled. Sharivah Shah was defeated and banished. Kikavas took over his territory and gave his name to the city, which became known in its corrupted form as Kalkachmous. The local people said that this had happened 5000 years ago. All this was supposedly written down in a book which, we were told, was eight inches thick. Unfortunately, the book had recently disappeared, and so we were unable, despite our pressing inquiries, to examine it. The last objects of interest that we were able to excavate were two long water-pipes, both originating in the Place of Kings, one going to the village of Kalkachmous and the other to Kashan. Both these watercourses were obviously extremely old, and the pipes we saw were probably the original ones. It seemed odd, however, that these two cities should have existed side by side and have been contemporary. We tried to find out more precise information about them, but in this we failed. In the neighbourhood of Shuileh there are reputed to be many sites of old cities going back 2000 to 3000 years, some of which we were able to visit, but time prevented us from making more than purely superficial investigations.

In Shuileh, as well as the usual village shop, there is a dentist, and one afternoon we took time off to go and visit him. Ragnar had sufficiently recovered by now to take photographs, and we asked the dentist if he would object to his surgery being filmed. The dentist was delighted, and we spent an hour or so filming the filling of teeth, extractions, and so forth. We were really rather impressed with the standard of hygiene in the dentist's surgery. It was a modern wooden hut open on two sides. In the centre was a chair for the patient, and beside it an old-fashioned drill worked by a foot-pedal. Beside the drill there were two cabinets containing all the various equipment of a dentist. We asked him if he ever gave a local anaesthetic, and he said that he did from time to time. Ragnar thought that it would be a very good idea for the film if I pretended to have toothache and was filmed sitting in the dentist's chair. I was rather reluctant to agree to this, but in the end gave way. I told the dentist that in no circumstances was he to touch my teeth at all, and that the drill must be empty. He promised this and was in fact a very good actor. The village thought that I really did have toothache and crowded round in great numbers to watch what they hoped would be a painful extraction. Their faces were delightful to watch, and Ragnar was able to get in some extremely good shots of their curiosity and surprise.

Towards the end of our stay Roddie had sufficiently recovered to go with Minou to examine the shrine at Wagul Khani and the ruins at Laspu. They were away for two days, and when they returned Minou at once sat down at a dilapidated typewriter and produced his report, which I think deserves to be quoted in full. As a Persian doctor he was naturally more interested in the local manners and customs than in archaeology.

On the night of August 15, amidst the dust and debris, pots, pans, shovels, cameras, and medicine boxes, the "Colonel" [*i.e.*, P.R.E.W.] was planning the next offensive. Richard and Ragnar were lying sick. As usual we had a large audience: local children, curious adults, peasants in rags, and sick people demanding attention. To Dugmore and myself was delegated the work of exploring villages and settlements in the vicinity of Shuileh.

We set out early next day. Jaafar the muleteer came

up with two pack-horses, and we moved off on foot, travelling downhill at first and soon uphill north-north-westward. We had been told there was a shrine of some importance in the vicinity of Samat-abad.

As one of the pack animals was entirely unloaded I gave in to Jaafar's persistent persuasions and mounted. On the whole it was a matter of great concern to our muleteers that we always insisted on going about our business on foot, even when, at the end of a day's climbing and marching, we slackened and could do with a ride. It did not occur to our friends that our funds were limited and the journeys long. Some of them protested that we lost prestige by travelling on foot. Others thought we were mean; more so as they were sure we could always dig up an old treasure pot with the aid of our instruments.

The animal was an old grey, big-hoofed and not very sure-footed either. When going over precipitous ridges into the misty mountains it occurred to me that the old beast was more frightened than I. I let it have its own way of negotiating the terrain.

On the way up we bumped into "the Chief." He and his aide-de-camp, another gendarme, were the only representatives of the law in these remote mountain climes. When Mike, Roddie, and I had first arrived on a chilly evening at Shuileh we met the Chief sipping tea at the local grocer's. He looked at us with dark suspicion, and kept asking me irrelevant questions, while Mike indulged in the aqueous delight of a fresh melon. I dealt with him correctly and told him that we were the *avant-garde* of a party of British archaeologists. Of course he was not satisfied. Like all the other people either in authority or under it whom we met during our long, arduous marches in this mountainous hinterland, he suspected that we had come to unearth some large *ganj* or hidden treasure of the ancients. However, when he discovered that I was the doctor he was all charm

and said that although he was fit and fighting he would
not mind having a complete medical check-up by so
eminent a healer as myself. There not being many
contestants to my eminence at 9000 feet above sea-
level, I agreed to give him a clean bill of health duly
signed and witnessed. I soon realized that our gendarme,
although only a private in rank, enjoyed great authority.
He was, in fact, universally known as the *Aghaye Rais*
or the 'Mr Chief.' Meanwhile, my reputation as the
doctor to the party had penetrated far and wide and
travelled ahead of us. I had already earned the revered
name of *Aghaye Docteur*—Mr Doctor, to be exact. This
name travelled with or ahead of me from the Caspian
shore to the Kazwin motor road uninterruptedly,
although our other Persian medico, Dr Jah Kurlu,
worked harder and dealt more efficiently with the local
populace than I.

Anyway, on this misty morning, the Mr Chief and
the Mr Doctor met atop a ridge overlooking Wagul
Khani. The Chief saluted Dugmore and me. He was on
horseback, proud and perky and clearly pepped up in
expectation of rewards to be had on this constabulary
mission.

We both talked inquiringly. It transpired that he was
on his way to a place to the north of Wagul Khani to
settle a local brawl in which some one had inflicted
physical injuries on a second party. With him was his
gendarme, on foot and armed with a rifle and wearing
several menacing rounds of cartridges round his waist.
There was yet another man, small in stature, hugging a
folded case to his chest and panting uphill. He was the
local scribe, who would take statements from witnesses
and compile a dossier about the belligerents. The Chief
said that he rather liked these missions as they gave him
a chance to look over his flock, inspect the villages on
the way, and drop in on old friends for food and
drink.

The little scribe told our muleteer that he should run
ahead and spread the word that *Aghaye Docteur* was on
his way. The least claim he could then have on the land
would be barley for his horses and rice for the distinguished riders. I overheard this and promptly forebade
the man to take such counsel.

By this time we could see in the distant heights overlooking the helmet of Samat-abad, the shrine, Astaneh
Suri, perched on a desolate peak. I asked the Chief if he
thought the shrine was worth inspecting, and whether
it was in fact the resting-place of some important local
saint. He shrugged his shoulders, laughing. "They have
probably dug the ground and put a dead goat in it and
called the place a shrine." This sardonic reference to
saints and shrines is probably fairly typical of the
Persian, although he manages to appear irreproachably
religious. And this attitude extends to other observable
phenomena. After a long history punctuated remorse-
lessly by unpredictable men and events, the Persian has
come to symbolize the history of his land. His beliefs
and loyalties are ephemeral. The ecology of the land
itself betrays a multiplicity of peoples and places. Those
who, from motives of political expediency, advocate a
passionate nationalism in Persia invariably find the
realities to be disheartening. Yet any constructive
design must needs have recourse to reality. From the
times of the Achaemenian king of kings, the Persian
armies were organized on a regional or ethnological
basis. There were Persians, Medes, Scythians, Lurs,
Kurds, Baluchis, Turkomans, Caspians, Caucasians, and
a whole host of others. These made up the seventy
nations to which Xenophon alludes. Right up to modern
times, although the country is but a tenth of its former
expanse, the ethnological divisions persist and are
officially recognized. Indeed, the continued recognition
of the distinctive character of the numerous Persian
tribes and peoples could help to build and sustain a

representative federal government having the interest of all in mind.

Dugmore and I parted company with the Chief and his retinue on a humorous note of warning from the Chief that we should let him know of any treasures we found. We proceeded to inspect the shrine. It was situated on a lonely peak, 7500 feet high. The village of Wagul Khani was to the west, and the hamlet of Samat-abad to the south-west down in the valley. The shrine consisted of a stone-and-mud construction with a wooden door and two side windows. Inside, a wooden pyramid was the centrepiece. There were several banners of *Panj Tan* (the five holy persons) arranged neatly round the sepulchre. To these were tied many dozen pieces of variegated cloth, scarves, kerchiefs, strings, and threads. These characteristic adornments are to be found in most Persian shrines. They are placed there by the faithful and represent a form of talisman for the fulfilment of a wish. Jaafar the muleteer suggested that every one should utter the name of God, Ya Allah, whenever entering or coming out of the shrine. We obliged, although the expression is liberally used on diverse occasions utterly unconnected with religion. Jaafar said this was not much of a shrine. He knew of one in Safidab to which no infidel could ever gain entry as an invisible seal bars the way. He said no human force could break the seal.

Towards lunch-time we descended into Samat-abad. We were offered food and tea, which we had on top of a roof, watched as usual by the handful of villagers.

After lunch we hastened southward along the western slopes of Sawad-Kuh range and arrived in Laspu. Here we made searching inquiries to locate any site likely to be of interest. A man who lived in Chamtu and had been in Shuileh to see me as a patient told us about the existence of many *gabr ghabre* (Zoroastrian graves) near Laspu. He said the local *galesh* (strictly speaking,

shepherd-folk, but used generally to refer to all poor
tenants) had dug up innumerable bronze weapons and
pots from these graves.

We proceeded uphill for about a quarter of a mile
east of Laspu to a place called Kashka-Dar. Here we saw
a great expanse of land with numerous ancient graves—
all dug up as usual for treasure! Every foot of land here
abounded in shards of pottery. It was clear that the old
and ancient city of Laspu had been, in fact, situated here
in Kashka-Dar. Although most of the land had gone
under the plough, vestiges of walls, dug-outs with
walled interiors, and similar architectural remnants
were plentiful. The shards were either thick and
unglazed, characteristic of older periods, or glazed with
distinctive features of the Assassin times. Overlooking
this expanse, on a mountain ridge to the north, we
were told of the existence of a castle. We climbed up.
The remnants of old fortifications were apparent, but
the most interesting find here was a huge cistern on the
top of a peak on the east side of the castle. This measured
some 40 feet across and was clearly designed as a
reservoir. Cut stone and old bricks lined the walls. The
aneroid reading here was 7500. Our guide said that in
olden times this cistern was connected to Kiram-Kuh by
means of clay piping. It is true that about $1\frac{1}{2}$ miles
south of Laspu the mighty mountain of Kiram-Kuh is to
be found. It is also true that a pass named Gardan Ab-
Ambarkash, the Col of Connecting Cisterns, exists
there. We, however, could not find any piping elements
or tunnels associated with this cistern. We concluded
that the fortifications and the reservoir were designed
to serve the large city settlement of Laspu in ancient
times, and probably during the Assassin period as well.
Thus the site of the old city of Laspu can be claimed to
have been located with reasonable accuracy. In the
whole periphery of Shuileh for a radius of 4 or 5 miles
covering Wagul Khani, Kiaseh, Ir-Mahalleh, Balkot,

Chamtu, Tukas, and Purdeh no vestige of ruins as extensive as these found at Kashka-Dar could be found —hence our conclusion.

Towards evening we passed through Balkot, there to find the Chief sitting imperiously among the village notables sipping tea. A message was delivered to us that the local landlord's nephew would like to extend his hospitality to us at his country seat in Ir-Mahalleh. We were by now exhausted, and accepted the offer with gratitude. Good mules were offered to us, but once again we declined to ride, sticking to our principle of "exploration on foot." By nightfall we were in Ir-Mahalleh with the young landlord. We were ushered into a large, clean house with a beautiful veranda. Large, expensive carpets were to be seen everywhere—on the floors and walls. Tea was served while we talked. The landlord was a young man of about twenty-four, fair-complexioned, with short, curly, red hair. He had small, penetrating eyes, but was jovial and easygoing. While we were having tea, from small glasses with silver holders, he kept up an intelligent conversation. At the same time he delivered a stream of orders right, left, and centre in the local patois, which I had difficulty in understanding.

Presently two of his tenants, an old man and his son, were ushered in. They remained standing although our host made a gesture to them to sit (on the floor, like the rest of us). When he dismissed them, Dugmore was curious to know what it was all about. Our host said that the boy had been rather wild recently. He thought the time had come to get him married to a girl he had in mind. The boy's father needed his son in the fields and was unwilling to let him go to another village to settle down with the prospective bride. He could not afford the cost either. I was interested to find that whenever a marriage takes place among the local *galesh* both parties to the marriage are obliged to offer presents to the

landlord according to their status, the smallest accept-
able present being a ram. As marriage was the topic of
our conversation our host said that he had heard a lot
about eager and willing maidens in Europe and had
thought of making a pilgrimage to those plentiful
shores. I asked if he was married. He said with a chuckle
that he had two wives and intended to marry a third. I
saw his third prospective bride later on at our base at
Shuileh. She was a young girl of twelve, very self-
conscious, and clearly forcing herself to behave as an
eligible girl should.

Our host said that most of the land in these regions of
Upper Ashkavar belonged to his uncle the Great Hajji.
He was, however, old, and did not fancy the summer
heights. They had large houses in Gilan and Shahsawar
where they spent most of the spring and winter. He
begged our indulgence for the humble surroundings
and accommodation here. This was clearly said hypo-
critically, as he added that it had cost 400,000 rials to
carpet the house here.

We had a sumptuous meal of kebabs, rice with various
dressings, home-made cookies, and melons. Our host
again apologized for the inadequacy of preparations as
our visit was unexpected.

Later in the evening a messenger arrived from another
big landowner whose domain extended to Gilan and
Lower Ashkavar. Our host and the messenger talked in
standard Persian, presumably for my benefit. The
purport of the messages and discussions was the
imminent general elections in Iran. They discussed
the arrangements for movement of *galesh* voters to the
polling-booths. It transpired that here, as in most other
parts of Persia, the big landowners make most of the
voting arrangements. They mobilize their tenant folk,
who are illiterate and obedient, tell them where to go to
vote, and give them the ballot-papers already marked
with the name of the candidate of the landowner's

pul, or "Three Bridges," in Ashkavar. Legend says Hasan-i-Sabbah crossed the
ver at this point on his way to occupy Alamut and said, "This is the boundary of
y kingdom."

A modern Assassin?
Or a hashish smoker?

EXPEDITION FINDS

Above: Shards of Assassin pottery at Samiran.
Below: Decorated fragments of Assassin pottery from Lammassar.

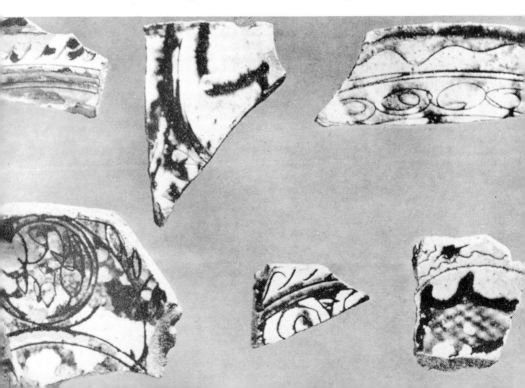

Entrance to one of the galleries at Maymun-Diz. The cat-walk along which we climbed runs off to the right. Author in the centre.

Half-way up the rock-face there is an Assassin arch. The tree-trunks with which we attempted the ascent can just be seen at the foot of the rock-face.

THE ASCENT OF MAYMUN-DIZ

Villagers haul one of the tree-trunks over the scree towards the castle.

Mike Oliver points out plaster-covered brickwork which was part of the Assassin internal structure of the castle.

INSIDE MAYMUN-DIZ

the entrance to the highest lery of the castle one of guides sits among the ble of the fortifications.

Roddie Dugmore
surveying at Samiran.

Qanat at
Lammassar. The
cistern is more
than 30 feet deep.

PERSIAN GLAZED POTTERY OF THE ISLAMIC PERIOD

ove: Fragment of bowl with carved and pierced decoration: twelfth century. Dia-
ter: 8·2 inches. *Below:* Bowl decorated in lustre on white glaze. Kashan: dated
09. Diameter: 11·3 inches.

By kind permission of the Trustees of the British Museum

Interior of bowl with undergla decoration in black and bl Kashan: dated 1214. Diamete 8·4 inches.

PERSIAN GLAZED POTTERY OF THE ISLAMIC PERIOD

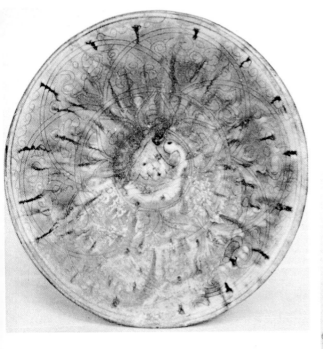

Bowl with incised decoration und splashed glaze of green, oran and brown. Nishapur: ninth–te century. Diameter: 12·75 inch

By kind permission of the Trustees of the British Museum

Bowl with moulded decoration under turquoise glaze: thirteenth century. Height: 9·6 inches.

choice. I was told with a knowing chuckle that at election times many ballot-papers are obtained on production of birth certificates whose owners have long been extinct. These are bought or variously obtained from ignorant relatives and are stamped when a vote is cast. This revelation did not come to me as a surprise as I already had an inkling of the electioneering process in Persia. To be sure, exactly the same story was told me in the village of Garmrud in the Alamut Valley later by the headman. This particularly rumbustious headman said there was really nothing immoral about this kind of voting, as the dead men are thus able to fulfil their duties as good voting citizens even as they are lying in their graves! The fact that they do not elect a candidate of their own choosing is immaterial. After all, some ninety per cent. of the living in Iran do not do their own choosing either!

Next morning I found a large queue outside the house. These were my patients. The morning clinic, it seemed, had to be attended to wherever I went. Our young host intervened to say that he thought they all needed penicillin. To this counsel I paid no attention, and proceeded to examine the patients and dispense from my small medicine case.

We took our leave at about 10 A.M. and headed back towards Shuileh.

When we had all finished our work at Kashan and Kalkachmous we felt that we must push on without any further delay because camp lassitude, probably an aftermath of the sickness, was beginning to spread over the party. Each day we tended to find some excuse for putting off our departure, and in the end it was necessary for me to take a firm hand and to say categorically that we would leave in two days' time. Mike and Richard were not really fit to walk long distances, and so it was agreed that they should ride on the mules. There were then further infuriating delays about getting the mules. They had gone off to Gilan to help with the harvest, or else were required for urgent jobs around the town, but by a mixture of threats and coaxing we managed to get together an ill-assorted mule-team of eight animals, and, having loaded up our gear, left Shuileh for Karkarud.

7

Lotosan

KARKARUD IS only about three hours' walk from Shuileh. We first descended once more into the valley of the Pul-i-Rud, and then climbed the opposite slope. The village is a small one and quite new. It is 3 miles away from the ancient town of Karkarud whose history goes back at least 1000 years. We visited it and were shown old graves which, by the shape of the tombstones, certainly looked as though they dated from the thirteenth or fourteenth centuries. The villagers seemed independent and proud of their historical past. In conversation they continually referred to the kingdom of Karkarud and to their ancient kings. We were shown several graves just outside the old village and one or two interesting silver coins which had been found there. One coin had the image of a king or chieftain wearing a crown stamped on it. We tried to buy this, but the villagers refused to sell. The villagers cultivate wheat and hazel-nuts, and seemed to be rather more prosperous than those of other villages in the area. We gathered that Karakud is a trading-post and that caravans pass through it on the way to Oman and Soman

higher up in the mountains. The standard of living was
better there too. When we asked the headman if he had
much contact with the people of Alamut, he said no, and
that most of the inhabitants of Ashkavar regarded Alamut
as a very primitive, undeveloped spot. It certainly seemed
to us that Ashkavar was a much gentler place than Alamut
both in its climate, its landscape, and in the manners and
looks of the inhabitants. They do not look like a warlike
people at all. Their faces lack the strongly marked features
that are found in Alamut. They are gentler and kinder,
too, and seemed to treat their womenfolk with more
consideration. From time to time, we were told, the
rugged inhabitants of the Alamut valley still make raids
into Ashkavar and carry off sheep, cows, and goats.
Ashkavar is afraid of taking reprisals, and so they tolerate
these outrages with considerable patience.

We spent only one night in Karkarud and then pushed
on along the mountain-tops in the direction of a village
called Orkum. This was a lovely walk, and we met several
teams of cattle descending from the *yaylak*, or high,
summer grazing-land, down to Gilan and the coast for
winter. The cattle all appeared well nourished and cared
for. As we walked along we saw in the distance the first
mountains of Alamut. When Hasan-i-Sabbah came this
way, he, too, must have had his first glimpse of his future
kingdom from about this point. The contrast is most
impressive. All around is the green, lush vegetation of the
uplands, and in the distance there are sharp, jagged, bare
hills marking the boundary between the two valleys. We
stopped for lunch at a tea-house surrounded by a delightful
garden, and there we had tea to the accompaniment of the
tinkling of goats' bells.

Our chief muleteer went by the romantic name of Ali
Baba, and he waited on us hand and foot. His face as well
as his hair was dyed with henna, which gave him a most
ferocious appearance, belying his soft, gentle nature. When
we asked him why he used this adornment he said it was

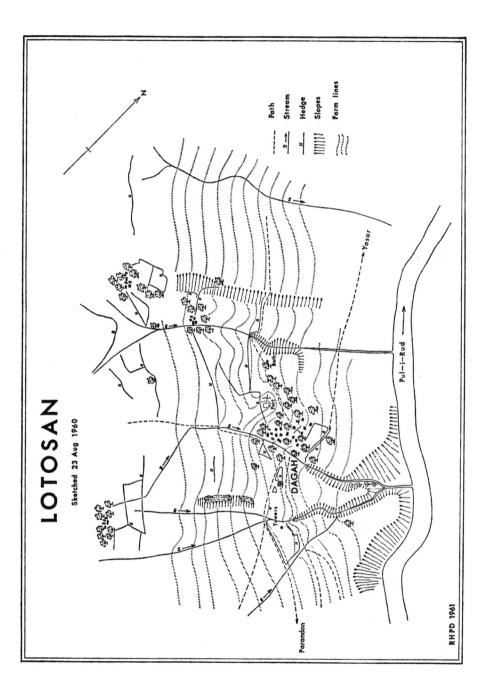

LOTOSAN

Sketched 23 Aug 1960

N

Path
Stream
Hedge
Slopes
Form lines

Yasar

Pul-i-Rud

DAGAH

Bath

Towers

Parandon

RHPD 1961

because henna makes the skin soft, and is apparently frequently used as a soothing ointment as well as a dye.

From Orkum the path descended into the valley, crossed the Pul-i-Rud and ran along the other side of the mountain. The landscape was barer, and there was less water in the river. Hazel-bushes were planted round any waterhole and there were a few plantations of French beans. The next village we came to was called Yasar. It was rather dirty, and the people seemed unfriendly and sly. For instance, they deliberately pointed out the wrong road to us, merely out of spite so it seemed, as they had nothing to gain by misdirecting us. That night we stopped at Sangisarud, or Stony River. The name symbolized the changing scenery. Stones and boulders were strewn everywhere, and the paths leading all round the village were extremely difficult to negotiate. It was a very small place and contained only fifteen or sixteen families. It, too, seemed to have had better times in the past, and was the ancient capital of a small tribe.

On the next day we arrived at our destination of Parandon, a small town at the head of the valley. Here we were invited to stay in a private house, and two rooms were given over to us as our headquarters. We were entertained on our first night by the headman, who had a local land-owner from Teheran staying with him. As usual we first asked about the old names of the villages and were told that near Parandon was the ancient site of Lotosan or Losan, which we had read about in Rabino's book. We asked if the villagers had excavated on the site and were told that they had not touched Losan, although digging had been going on in other areas. As soon as the sun rose on the following day, which was now August 22, we went out to have a look at the site, about two miles to the north of Parandon and near the village of Dagah. Just here was the last fertile patch in Ashkavar, extending for some fifteen square miles. As well as the river there were innumerable springs, and the countryside appeared once more clad in the deep green that is typical of the region. Some of the slopes were wooded, others were planted with hazel-nuts, rice, and wheat. Quite often the angle of slope was about 45° and the earth was held in place only by rocks jutting out from the mountainside.

The old city of Losan must have been about a mile long. The terraces on which it is built are not natural, for there is nothing similar to them in the immediate neighbourhood. To begin with we walked round the whole site, and at once came across shards of pottery, mainly blue, although some were brown and yellow. At each end of the terraces we could see the remains of a tower, which presumably marked the corners of the city walls. In the middle of the site there was a well. It was blocked, and we excavated it to a depth of about 8 feet. Inside we found pottery and two bronze daggers of the type that we had seen elsewhere. By now we were extremely interested in our discovery, and in the evening we invited to our headquarters old men of the village and questioned them about the legends and stories they had to tell. When we were finally able to put the whole account together it seemed that some 1500 years ago there had been two towns here. One was called Balaturk, named after the Turkish general who had founded it. This town was built a little higher up the mountain and soon became prosperous and rich. Shortly after the founding of Balaturk, Losan itself was built, being called after its founder-king. It was famed for its seven mosques. The people of Losan were more industrious than the inhabitants of Balaturk and soon had far outstripped their rivals in the magnificence of their buildings and in military prowess. A war broke out and Losan was victorious. Now the city was able to expand over quite a large area, and the various chieftains paid homage and taxes to Losan. No one could tell us how or why it was destroyed, and even the date remained a mystery.

We were very much intrigued by this story and decided to take a day off to visit Balaturk. I don't know that "day

C.A.—K.

off" is really the right expression, because the climb up to the village was just as difficult as any we had undertaken up to now. To get there we had to leave early in the morning, at about 5.30, and did not return to our base-camp at Parandon until about nine in the evening.

Ragnar and Michael were suffering from septic blisters and so stayed behind to do some much-needed washing of our own personal gear and to give the cameras and survey instruments a thorough clean. Jah said he thought he had sufficient directions about the way to be able to do without a guide, and in fact there was only one steep mountain-track leading up to the village.

Balaturk itself proved disappointing. There was certainly no trace of the ancient city. It was just a small hamlet of some fifteen to twenty families and there was nothing really to distinguish it from any other small Ashkavar village, but while we were having tea with the headman he suggested that we ought to push on farther up the mountain and visit a town called Liasi. We should not find any historical ruins there, he said, but Liasi was the rich man's village, and the so-called Teheran of Ashkavar. It seemed pointless to return to Parandon, as the day was wasted anyhow, so we followed his advice. From Balaturk to Liasi was only about an hour's walk, and when we reached the plateau on which Liasi is built we were startled at the layout of the village. Instead of the usual mud houses with wooden roofs we saw stretched out in front of us well-built brick and stone houses with corrugated-iron roofs all neatly laid out around regular squares, which were planted with small trees. It looked like a specially designed model village, and, to our surprise, we found that this was what it was. The only things that were obviously missing were television aerials!

As was our custom, we made our way to the headman's house, and he directed us to the house of the richest land-owner of the village. Here we were courteously received and invited to lunch. Our host, Dr Zahidy, explained that in the last two or three years several landowners had built new houses in Liasi and had now taken to spending their summer holidays there because of the relatively cool climate and the complete contrast with Teheran, where most of them lived for the rest of the year. Dr Zahidy spoke quite a passable French, and so for once we did not have to rely on the services of our interpreter and could put questions directly to him. After chatting for a while we were ushered into the dining-room. This was a handsomely furnished room with old and very valuable rugs on the floor and some exquisite miniatures decorating the walls. Mrs Zahidy had lunch with us. Although she was dressed in the native costume she told us she had visited Paris, London, and New York, and even seemed familiar with the latest shows being played in London at the time. She had seen *My Fair Lady* twice and was thrilled by it. Dr Zahidy produced a transistor wireless set and we spent a few minutes trying to tune in to London, but did not succeed. We plied him with questions about the economy of the valley and his replies confirmed our own impressions. Ashkavar is still very remote and its people poor, although not as poor as the inhabitants of Alamut. The landowners have some vague plans for improving the irrigation of Ashkavar, and are pressing the Government in Teheran for money grants, but they realize that this will take a long time. Meanwhile they are attempting to persuade the peasants to do as much for themselves as possible, and also to take up once more the ancient craft of weaving. Dr Zahidy seemed to be a progressive man and showed us with some pride a beetroot plantation that he had just laid out. Over a number of years he had found that the climate of Ashkavar suited this root vegetable very well, and he hoped that it would later be possible to establish a flourishing sugar-beet industry.

We tactfully introduced the subject of archaeological finds and the so-called Zoroastrian graves; but at this his manner quickly changed from one of open friendliness to

cool reserve. He was obviously not prepared to say anything at all. He would admit only that he had heard stories
of digging and of discovered easure, but he hastily
assured us that this had not been on his land and that in any
case he was sure all accounts were highly exaggerated.
Politeness forbade us to press the point, but we could not
help uneasily suspecting that perhaps our worthy doctor
knew far more than he was prepared to say.

After lunch, over which we lingered for two or three
hours, he produced some vodka, and then insisted on
showing us round the village with his wife, who by now
had changed into a rather startling pair of tartan jeans.
This seemed to us to be very emancipated, and we
wondered how the villagers would take it. But no one
appeared to bat an eyelid, so they were obviously used to
Mrs Zahidy's sartorial tastes. Our tour lasted a good two
hours, and it was interesting to see how a completely new
village life had developed under the stimulus of modern
ideas and equipment. For instance, in the centre of the
village there was a perfectly respectable well, complete
with bucket and chain, and this was fenced off to prevent
pollution by animals. The peasants' houses were im-
measurably better than any others we had seen. There
were decent stables for the cattle, the streets were clean,
or relatively so, and even the little children seemed to be
well dressed. We asked our host if all these improvements
had made any difference to the essential life of the people,
and he proudly replied that his was the most respectable
and moral village in the area. From what we heard later
on from other villagers this was not really so, and in fact
the inhabitants of Liasi were now regarded as rather a
strange and almost alien race. If this is true it is a pity,
because Dr Zahidy's intentions were obviously beyond
reproach. When we left we congratulated the doctor on his
brave experiment and hoped that it would spread to other
villages. His reply took a little of the gilt off the ginger-
bread, as he said that progress could only be slow, and for

some time would probably be confined to the areas in which the landowners themselves lived. This made us feel that perhaps the motive behind some of these improvements was more self-centred than we had originally thought, and that the landowners were mainly concerned with making a clean and agreeable centre for their own holidays.

When we got back to Parandon we were astonished by the change that Ragnar and Mike had made in our head-quarters. When we had left, the floor had been littered with mess-tins, cups, and equipment of all kinds. Now everything was carefully arranged and put tidily on one side, and even our drinking mugs had our names boldly painted on them. Over the door was a large sheet of paper which said in striking letters: "Wipe your feet before you come in." We hardly dared move, and Ragnar watched with an eagle eye to see that we put everything back in its right place. He had obviously not wasted his day, and as well as tidying up our house he had cleaned and polished the photographic and surveying equipment. The only thing he had not thought of was that none of our evening visitors could read his notice, and very shortly after our return the room was filled with the usual crowd of villagers who certainly had not wiped their feet, and who left behind them all the usual, rather disagreeable traces of their visit. However, we did make an effort for the remaining three or four days that we spent at Parandon to live up to the high standard that Ragnar had set.

After our 'holiday' we started our excavations of the city of Losan in earnest. Our attention had been drawn to about 20 feet of clay pipes that had been dug up by the inhabitants. These were in the middle of one of the terraces, and we thought we could do no better than to follow their course. We employed ten villagers to dig the topsoil for us, and carefully staked out the line along which they were to work. The pipes lay 5 feet under the surface, and soon we had a trench some 200 yards long. By this time we were approaching the edge of the terrace, and we realized that the angle of the pipes was becoming sharper. After some further excavation it became clear that the pipes were running into a kind of bath. This was very exciting, so we cleared the topsoil away from an area of 50 square yards. When we had dug 2 feet, Richard came across a blue tile. This had some cement on the back, and it was then that we realized that we were obviously on the track of a bath-house. Gradually we were able to clear away all the refuse under which it had been buried and expose its complete outline. We first found that the pipes ran into a heating-chamber measuring some 6 feet square and about 18 inches high. The chamber was formed by solid blocks of stone, some of which were still blackened by the fires. Inside were remains of charcoal and also an iron shovel, which had been used for stoking the furnace. Above the heating-chamber was a room 12 feet long by 7 feet wide. Around the sides ran a stone slab or bench at a right-angle to the edge of the bath on which the bathers could sit and dangle their feet in the water. The back of the bench was 18 inches high and mostly covered with blue tiles. These were octagonal in shape and ranged from very dark turquoise-blue to a light grey-blue. The bath itself was 3 feet deep, and the floor was made of stone. It looked as though it had originally been covered with some fine mosaics, but most of them had either crumbled away or been destroyed. The entrance to the bath-house was on the fourth side, where we uncovered three steps, 2 feet deep.

Beside the bath-house was a second, smaller room, presumably intended for cold baths, for, as far as we could see, there was no heating-chamber underneath. This room was 10 feet long by 6 feet wide. On one side there was a plain, small stone bench, and in a corner stood a big slab covered with blue tiles on which a man could lie full length. This might have been used as a sort of masseur's table. In the side of the chamber opposite the bench we found some pottery and one bronze dagger, quite plain and unadorned, about 8 inches long.

Naturally the excavation of this bath-house was carried out with extreme care, and when we had finally completed our work we spent a lot of time measuring and photographing. The villagers carried out their part of the work with tremendous gusto, and in fact often had to be restrained from driving a pick through a tile. It was difficult to put an exact date to the building, but it seemed reasonable to suppose that it belonged to the same civilization and era as the other pottery and bronzes that we had unearthed—that is to say, about 1500 B.C. It was a most important find and we were naturally extremely thrilled with it.

Then came tragedy. We took the last photograph of the bath at about 4 o'clock one afternoon, and then decided to walk down to the stream to have a bathe. When we came back we could hardly believe our eyes. Everything had gone. The villagers had taken advantage of our temporary absence to loot and plunder this priceless relic of a long-lost age. They had stripped the tiles from both rooms, and had used our picks to hack up a large part of the floor to see if there was anything underneath. At first we were so angry that we were almost speechless. As far as our investigations were concerned it did not matter too much as we had everything down on paper or on film, but the sheer wanton destruction of it all made us almost want to cry. Gradually, however, we regained our sense of proportion and realized that for the villagers the archaeological value of this find was less than nothing. They thought we had completed our work. In fact we had said so, and had taken away two or three of the best tiles. They reasoned that this bath was scarcely our property, and if it belonged to anybody it belonged to them, and so they felt fully justified in taking away as much as they could to decorate their own houses. Nevertheless, we could never quite forgive them for what they did, although, looking back, it is difficult to see how we could have stopped them.

We spent two more days in Parandon, but we were now

suffering from a sense of anticlimax caused both by disappointment at the looting of the bath-house and by
the knowledge that we did not really have time to carry
out any more detailed work. So we confined ourselves to
tracing the full extent of the city and making soundings by
the outer walls. Here we excavated two stretches of wall
made of dressed stone 10 feet long and 3 feet deep. At one
point we came across a semi-circular wall and at another
the foundations of what must have been a large house.
There is no doubt that the site of Losan is extremely rich
and interesting and that it would be rewarding for a full-
scale archaeological expedition to examine it in detail. We
should like to make a second visit there in the not too
distant future.

Before we left Ashkavar we wanted to investigate the
site of two castles called Kale Konti and Giri. These two
castles are situated opposite each other at the narrow,
southern end of the valley. We had heard about them
during our stay at Parandon, and Richard and Minou had
spent one day finding their exact location. This was one of
the few times that any serious quarrel arose between
members of the expedition. I should not like to pretend
that our relationships were entirely harmonious all the
time. This would be too much to expect of any large-scale
expedition that remains out in the field for some weeks or
months. It would be interesting for a psychologist to
analyse all the different factors that influence the actions of
individuals in a group such as ours. Although a leader
obviously takes the temperament of the different members
of the expedition into account when he chooses them, there
are bound to be divergent opinions and aims which may
well lead to friction. Individuals react quite differently to
difficulties and frustrations, and quite often, unless one is
very careful, a trifling incident can develop into a serious
quarrel, particularly when people are feeling tired and have
not had sufficient relaxation. In this case there was a silly
row about which of two paths to follow. Richard and Minou

were each convinced that he was right and obstinately refused to give in to the other. Both paths led to the castles and so the quarrel was harmoniously composed. I merely mention this incident as a small example of what can happen. On the other side of the picture there were plenty of examples of complete unselfishness and sometimes very gallant behaviour. I think that I can truthfully say that I was always extremely proud to be the leader of this expedition, and that I could not have chosen a finer or more loyal body of men.

We eventually decided that we would make a detour on our way out of the valley to visit these two castles. Richard and Minou said that they were now fed up with Kale Konti and would much prefer to go to Giri, and to this we all laughingly agreed. The history of both these castles is obscure, but according to local legend they were both built by Kia, one of the names of the founder of Losan. There was a third castle at a village called Kashayah, but tradition says that it was destroyed by the Assassins and that nothing remains. The castle of Giri stands on a great spur overlooking the valley. We climbed up to it on a misty day, and when we eventually reached it we found that it consisted of a circular outer wall enclosing an area of some 200 square yards. There were also remains of the central tower and some out-buildings. The tower itself was very unsafe, and although there was a spiral staircase inside we were able to climb up only about 30 feet. The tower commanded a view of the approach to the valley from the south. Looking towards the north, we could clearly make out the villages from which we had just come. On the other side of the pass we could see the remains of Kale Konti. These were not very extensive and, in fact, the site of the castle was marked only by a few piles of rubble and stone. The line of the southern curtain-wall could be traced, but apart from this it was impossible to reconstruct any kind of ground-plan.

It had been agreed between us that both parties would

meet that night at the village of Savardeh, but Richard's party had much farther to go than ours. Accordingly, when we got to Savardeh, we had to wait two or three hours before the others joined us. Now we had to decide the route that we would take to the valley of Alamut. There was a choice. We could either go directly over the mountains, which would be a long and very steep climb, or we could take a gentler route over one of the passes to the south. Our muleteers, who had transported all our kit from Parandon, were obviously all against our taking the direct route. It was dangerous, they said, and there were a lot of snakes and scorpions. In the end we were persuaded to travel along a pass that would bring us to the western end of the valley of Alamut. We were sorry in one respect as we should have liked to see the magnificent scenery of the central mountain range. On the other hand, apart from considerations of physical comfort, it was much more likely that Hasan-i-Sabbah had taken this route, so we felt justified in accepting the recommendations of our guides, which satisfied both historical and personal requirements.

In order to save time, once more it was agreed that Richard, Jah, and I should push on ahead of the main party and establish our base-camp at Shams Kilaya (the site of Maymun-Diz). By this time we had collected a considerable number of specimens—pottery, bronzes, tiles, and other relics from the bath at Losan and elsewhere. These we had carefully packed into two crates, but they slowed our progress, as it was necessary for the mule that carried them to be accompanied the whole time and carefully watched. This was to avoid any possible theft, and also to make sure that nothing happened to the mule. For instance, when going down a steep slope, we did not much mind if a mule slipped and our camp kit went into a river, which happened on more than one occasion, but we always insisted that the number one mule, as we called the bearer of our precious load, should be given preferential treatment, even if it meant going much slower. Getting the crates to pack up the specimens took us some time. Wood for any purpose was difficult to come by, and we had to pay the equivalent of £5 for each crate, and they were very crudely constructed at that.

The three of us, then, hurried on ahead. The mule-track climbed steadily upward, and we soon left the last villages of Ashkavar behind us. The vegetation now consisted of grass and sparse scrub only, and water was very scarce. At about 9000 feet we came to a spring on a small plateau, and we were glad to wash and refill our water-bottles. It was on this plateau that the main party who were following us camped for the night. When they awoke the following morning, they found the valleys below them filled with the Caspian cloud like fluffy cotton-wool. It was quite a remarkable sight, just like some fairy scene—the cloud and mountain-tops tinged a deep pink by the rays of the rising sun. The cloud stretched out to the horizon, unbroken except for the peaks of mountains rising up like islands. Unfortunately, Richard, Jah, and I missed this view as we hurried on over the pass at 10,000 feet and began the descent down the other side. In front of us lay the first of the Alamut valleys, barren and bare and still shimmering with the heat-haze. It was like being on a bridge between two worlds of quite different character, the one which we had just left soft and gentle, and the other into which we were now descending harsh and strident. Darkness was falling, and we were glad when we reached the village of Safidab, where we spent the night in a small hut in the centre of the village.

The next morning we continued our descent. The landscape was now completely desolate and resembled a scene from a Western film—sparse scrub, sand, great rocks and boulders, and no water. It was on this journey that we suffered most from thirst. At the beginning of each day we filled up our water-bottles and sterilized the water with "Halizone" tablets; then we had to use iron discipline in

rationing ourselves. By midday the temperature was un-
endurably hot, and often there was no shade at all to rest in.
As we descended, the countryside unrolled before us. In
the distance we could see the broad band of the Shah Rud
running like a silver girdle through the foothills on either
side. On the horizon towered the jagged ridges of the
Chala range. We stopped and took it all in. It felt rather
like coming home again. We exchanged reminiscences of
the previous year's expedition and felt that the wheel had
now turned full circle.

Some 10 miles farther on, at Wastah, there was a
veritable crossroads guarded by a fort. Along the east-
west axis lay the road from Lammassar in the west through
Shams Kilaya, Alamut, and on to Nevisar Shah in the east.
From the south another road came up from the Shah Rud
and continued on over the mountains into Ashkavar and to
the Caspian. This point must have seen many a caravan
from the time of Hasan-i-Sabbah and far earlier threading
its way along its dusty surface. It was a historic meeting-
place and it must have been at this precise spot that Hasan,
like ourselves, really entered the territories of Alamut. To
us, too, it had a special and exciting significance. Here, as
we had always suspected, was the road that linked the
fortresses, and here was Wastah, which is mentioned in
the chronicles of the twelfth and thirteenth centuries, and
which no European traveller had yet described.

The fort at Wastah was a pleasant, almost cosy, place.
Its architecture seemed domestic rather than military,
although its strategic importance was clear at first glance.
It was circular, built of good stone, which was still well
preserved. The walls were 4 feet thick, and at regular
intervals there were four windows pointing to each
cardinal point. The entrance was through a narrow archway and led into a vaulted room 12 feet high. The roof had
caved in and the floor was littered with rubble. Between
the main windows there were little peepholes and, looking out, we could see Lammassar and Shir Kuh. This

building must be one of the best preserved of the Assassin forts. Possibly it lay too far away from the main Alamut valley to have been destroyed by the Mongols, or they may have found it useful for preserving their own lines of communication.

We rested inside and slept for about two hours, and then moved on. It was still as hot as a furnace but the going was a little easier, and, at about 5 o'clock, we reached the township of Dikin—the last village before Alamut. As we entered it, we saw what looked like fine, golden rain slanting down from the top of a near-by hill. We went up to see what it was, and came across a harvest scene that must have been repeated for hundreds of years. The sheaves of corn were spread out on a big threshing-floor made of baked mud bricks and clay, and over the corn fierce, dark-skinned villagers were driving little carts with wheels like small paddles which acted as flails. Then the corn was taken to another place where it was winnowed by being thrown high into the air—the grain falling into wickerwork baskets. All the village was there, shouting, happy, and excited. Here were the fruits of the earth which were to provide life for them during the coming winter months. Old and young stood side by side, the old staring at this familiar sight with dull eyes in wizened, bronze faces, and the young staring too, fascinated by the colour and movement of the scene. But we did not stop long as we were very anxious to complete our journey that day. The path now wound upward. We felt tired, but we kept going. Another two hours and the sun was beginning to sink, casting great shadows over the hills. As we rounded a corner a sudden gust of wind nearly bowled us over, but there before us lay the valley of Alamut.

8

The Conquest of Maymun-Diz

WE ARRIVED in the valley of Alamut on the evening of August 27 after our long trek over the mountains. This time we had approached it from the west over the old road that led from Lammassar to Shams Kilaya, thus avoiding travelling along the rather dull bed of the Shah Rud. And in addition we wanted to explore the road that must have been the main route between the castles. After we had crossed the last peak we saw the whole of Alamut laid out in profile, so to speak, before us. Although this entrance lacked the atmosphere of mystery and terror of the narrow gorge at Shir Kuh, we had the advantage of seeing in one breathtaking sweep the broad panorama of Alamut. It was evening, about 6 o'clock; there were some clouds in the sky and the shadows were sweeping across the hills. Far in the background the prospect was closed in by the mighty peak of Solomon's Throne. To the left stood out sharply against the setting sun the smaller but still high peak on which lay Nevisar Shah. To our right, or south, lay the river-bed with the silver stream of the Alamut Rud twisting and turning like some monstrous snake. On each side of the river the small valleys rose up precipitously until they reached the heights of the Taliqan range in the south and the Hawdeqan in the north. It was from the point where we were standing that we first realized the extent of the valley and the care that the Assassins had taken to establish their intricate system of intercommunication between the different castles. Just at our feet was a pile of stones that could well have been the remains of some fort or watch-tower guarding the track along which we had travelled. To the north-east we could already see the monstrous bulk of Maymun-Diz, its contours softened in the evening light, its sandstone rock suffused with a gentle pink. To the south-west, half-way up the Taliqan range, we could, through field-glasses, see the site of the castle of Shir Kuh. Straight ahead, but tucked in one of the side valleys, lay the castle of Alamut, but between us and it we could again discern a watch-tower. When we later visited Nevisar Shah the same pattern could be discerned at the eastern end of the valley.

We lingered for about half an hour taking in the majesty and serenity of this scene. The valley has many different moods, ranging from the glaring harshness of midday to the softness and serenity of night and the freshness of the early dawn. We always found that evening and early morning were the pleasantest times, but not only because they were comparatively cool: then the dust seemed to have settled, the green of the trees and the ricefields seemed to stand out in darker, cleaner tones, and the sky had lost its harsh brilliance. We could even hear the tinkling of cow bells, and the distant murmur of the river reminded us of gentler scenes that might almost have been set in Switzerland.

After resting, Richard, Jah, and I hastened onward. The evening light was deceptive, and we knew that we had a good two hours' walk before we reached the capital of Mu'allim Kilaya. The road was quite broad at this stage and could easily have been used as a jeep track. We walked on in silence for about an hour and then saw three men coming towards us. As we approached them they recognized us at once from our visit of last year and came up and kissed us on our cheeks. "Welcome," they said, and at once talked exuberantly without allowing us to get a word in edgeways. When we had told them the purpose of our return visit they insisted on running ahead and telling the headman of our arrival. We reached the village about three-quarters of an hour later, and there to our astonishment we received a heroes' welcome. The head-man was there, surrounded by all the elders, and, keeping a respectful distance behind them, the rest of the village had collected. Gravely the headman came forward, took off his hat, and bowed low. I went up to him, took both of his hands, and kissed him on both cheeks. The villagers burst into a roar of applause, and we were soon surrounded by a milling, jostling crowd, all of them wanting to touch us and kiss us. In a trice we were hoisted on to their shoulders and carried in triumph along the steep path to the centre of the village. There we were gently lowered to the ground. Tea and fruit were brought, and we were made to sit down and tell of all our adventures. A tricky moment came when the headman asked us about the photographs we had promised to send him after our last visit. Thinking quickly, I replied that the photographs had not come out very well, and one of our principal objects this time was to take pictures that would really be worthy of our brave and courteous hosts. This seemed to satisfy and please them, but they at once demanded that photographs be taken of our reunion. Although it was quite dark and we knew that no photographs would come out, we proceeded to oblige them, making certain that we did not turn the camera on, and so spoilt only one shot. We then gravely asked the headman's permission to camp on the same site as before, and this was granted with alacrity. Although I have no doubt that the villagers were very pleased to see us again, they also knew that our arrival heralded a short economic boom, and very soon we had offers of services as guides, porters, cooks, and everything else. However, we put off all these decisions until the next morning, saying that we must await the arrival of the rest of the party. It was now getting a little late, and we were beginning to wonder why the others had not yet arrived when, shortly afterwards, to the tinkling of bells and to the accompaniment of more merriment and laughter, the rest of the mule-train came up. Mike had again suffered from septic blisters, and so the journey had taken them much longer than they had expected. Once more the ceremony of welcome began, and it was not until well past midnight that we were able to disentangle our camp-beds from our gear and go wearily to bed. We had, however, a feeling of great happiness and satisfaction that the first part of the expedition had been successfully accomplished and that the second part was now to begin, and if the unexpected success of our finds in Ashkavar was any sort of omen for the future, we felt that here in Alamut we should not be disappointed. Moreover, we ascertained that no one had visited the site of Maymun-Diz since our discovery last year and therefore we were still alone in the field.

We got up late the next day and spent two or three hours sorting our kit and establishing a base-camp. We noticed that the Caspian cloud, which had followed us all our journey, had still not been left behind, so that for the first two hours of the morning the top of the rock was invisible. An early visitor was the local gendarme, the only one in the valley, and we presented our credentials to him, including our permission to dig and to take photographs, and he told us we must not be afraid to ask him for anything we wanted. He had received a message from the central Government in Teheran telling him to help us as much as lay in his power. Then, of course, there were a large number of people to be treated, and the two doctors spent an hour dealing with the most urgent cases.

After we had set up our camp we spent a little time

C.A.–L

reading over again Juvayni's account of the capture of Maymun-Diz and refreshing our minds on the problems that we were there to solve. At this point it may be useful to remind the reader of the significance of the castle and its problems.

It will be remembered that Hulagu Khan had decided to extend his conquest into the Elburz mountains during the spring of the year 1256. Up to this date he had been successful in subduing most of the southern part of Persia and Turkey, but the Assassins, with their reputation— somewhat tarnished by then—as hard-fighting, strong warriors, still prevented him from accomplishing his dream of complete domination over the Middle East. The Syrian branch also still stood firm and he realized that they must be subdued later. If the "World Conqueror" could subdue the Assassins in their home valleys and destroy the source of their power and wealth he would have little difficulty in invading Syria. He knew the castles were well fortified and amply provisioned, and that, in all probability, the fanatical core of the Assassins would fight to the death; also, that he did not have much time; even the tough Mongols would not be able to penetrate the high mountain passes or maintain supply-lines once winter had set in.

Hulagu seems to have spent a long time feasting and drinking in Rayy, while the inconclusive negotiations for the submission of Rukn-ad-Din, the Grand Master of the Assassins, which had been going on for some time now, pursued their tortuous course. Sensing that Hulagu's patience was becoming exhausted, Rukn-ad-Din sent his seven-year-old son to the Mongol ruler as an earnest of his intentions to submit, but the wily Hulagu had the boy returned to his father, maintaining that he was too young to act as a hostage and secretly doubting whether he was Rukn-ad-Din's son at all. Rukn-ad-Din now sent his brother, accompanied by several important members of the Assassin hierarchy to parley with Hulagu. It was evidently the Grand Master's intention to gain as much time as possible and so prevent Hulagu from attacking before the winter set in. But it was now too late. Hulagu's patience was exhausted. He sent a final message to the Grand Master telling him to destroy his fortress of Maymun-Diz and come and submit himself before ill-fortune inevitably overtook him. Then Hulagu set out with his armies to settle the matter by force. His army divided into two, one half approaching Maymun-Diz from the west along the Alamut valley, while Hulagu himself, after a series of dashing forced marches, burst over the Taliqan range from the south and suddenly appeared at the fort of Maymun-Diz, almost catching the garrison napping.

Juvayni gives a graphic description of the advance of the army and the taking of Maymun-Diz, which is worth quoting in full from Dr Boyle's translation:

> They set out by way of Talaqan with the speed of the wind, like a flood in their onrush and like a flame of fire in their ascent; and their horses' hooves kicked dust into the eyes of Time. And on the very day of departure they came midway upon a mountain ram. Some of the young men, eager for fame, at once filled it with their arrows. The King took this as an omen and knew that the butting ram would be a victim in the oven of calamity and the faith of Hasan-i-Sabbah would be without followers.
>
> That day the World-King's forces encamped in the district of Talaqan and he ordered the armies of Kerman and Yezd to besiege the local castles such as Aluh-Nishin, Mansuriya and several others; and he strengthened the hand of these troops with a force of Mongols who were their mainstay.
>
> The next day when the bright-faced Sun thrust his head out of the collar of the horizon they beat the drum of departure and [advanced] by way of Hazar-Cham, which was as twisted as the curls of a sweetheart, nay as narrow as the *sirat-i-qiyamat* and as dark as the road to Hell. There was no room to place one's feet, how then could one go forward? An the chamois could not easily keep their footing, what then could men do? To tread on the level parts was no simple matter; on the rugged parts what could one do but come to grief?

[Yet] the King passed over and chose toil and pain rather than the road of ease. And the tongue of Destiny sang this song:

> Give ear to thyself, because the self is the soul of a
> world bound up in that dear soul which thou hast.

The next day the troops and squadrons arrived at the foot of the castle and at noon

> That parasol to which the heavens are inferior, [which]
> is a cloud shading the sun,

was opened up on a hilltop opposite the castle.

And from the direction of Ustundar, which lay on the right, there came Buqa-Temür and Köke-Ilgei with armies all fire and fury along steep roads as crooked as the covenant of the wicked, with hilltops twisted around them, full of defiles.

And from Alamut, which lay on the left, came the princes Balaghai and Tutar with a great body of men, all clamouring for vengeance. And behind them came Ked-Buqa Noyan with a host like a mountain of iron. The valleys and mountains billowed with the great masses of men. The hills which had held their heads so high and had such strong hearts now lay trampled with broken necks under the hooves of horses and camels. And from the din of the braying of those camels and the noise of pipe and kettle-drum the ears of the world were deafened, and from the neighing of the horses and the flashing of the lances the hearts and eyes of the foe were blinded. *'For God's behest is a fixed decree.'*

After describing the advance of the Mongol army Juvayni goes on to describe in the following words the building of Maymun-Diz:

Now the history of that castle is as follows. At the time when that people were at the height of their power, his father [*i.e.*, Rukn-ad-Din's] 'Ala-ad-Din, in accordance with [the words of Pharaoh:] *"O Haman, build for me a tower that I may reach the avenues, the avenues of the heavens,"* had instructed his officials and ministers to survey the heights and summits of those mountains for the space of 12 years until they chose that lofty peak which confided secrets to the star Capella; and on its summit, which had a spring of water on its top and three others on its side, they began to build the castle of Maimun-Diz making the ramparts out of plaster and gravel. And from a parasang away they brought a stream like the Juy-i-Arziz and caused the water to flow into the castle. And because of the extreme cold it was impossible for beasts to find a home or live in that place from the beginning of autumn till the middle of spring. On this account Rukn-ad-Din thought it impossible for human beings to penetrate to the castle and lay siege to it, since the mountains intertwined and the very eagles shrank back from the passes whilst the game animals at the foot sought some other way around. Nay, because of its great elevation that lofty place applied to itself the words [of 'Ali] : *"The flood rusheth down from me, and the birds rise not up to me."*

After this description Juvayni gives a long and detailed account of the battle, so I shall quote only the passages that are relevant to our story. The Mongol army first set up on the tops of the surrounding hills mangonels, or catapults, with which to bombard the castle. This must have been a formidable operation, as we are told that the best athletes in the Mongol armies were chosen to transport the heavy poles and pillars. On the next day Hulagu "ordered his bodyguard to climb to the top of the highest peak and pitch the Royal encampment there." The garrison in the castle meanwhile set up their own mangonels and, as Juvayni says, "In the middle of Shavval [November 1256] commenced a brisk discharge of stones." He goes on to describe the course of the battle in these words: "and on this [*i.e.*, Mongol] side also the young men were splitting hairs with lances like arrows and themselves flinching before neither stone nor arrow. Arrows, which were the shaft of Doom discharged by the Angel of Death, were let fly against those wretches, passing like hail through the sieve-like clouds."

This preliminary bombardment lasted for three days, causing considerable casualties on both sides. On the fourth day the Mongols attempted a direct assault, but this was repulsed. They brought up more siege-engines, and then their secret weapon, which was called a *kaman-i-qav* and had the astonishing range of 2500 paces. It was apparently a large version of a cross-bow, which hurled javelins, some of them dipped in burning pitch, instead of quarrels. These projectiles wrought considerable havoc amongst the defenders, and Juvayni relates "of the devil-like Heretics many soldiers were burnt by those meteoric shafts." The defenders replied by pouring stones down like leaves, but "not more than one person was hurt thereby"—a remarkable statement.

After this first display of force on Hulagu's part Rukn-ad-Din appears to have hesitated and then decided that discretion was the better part of valour and, in Juvayni's words, "to knock at the door of peace." Quite why he did so is rather obscure, but he must have lost his nerve. He pretended that all along he had meant to surrender and was preparing gifts to propitiate the World Conqueror, but that some of the garrison were angry when they had heard this and had tried to assassinate him. Hulagu merely replied that it was up to Rukn-ad-Din "to guard his own person," and gave orders for the erection of more mangonels all round the circumference of the castle. Later that same day he ordered a thorough bombardment and

. . . from the whole circumference of the castle, a distance of a parasang [*i.e.*, 4 miles] or more, the battle-cry was blended with its echo; and from the rolling of boulders hurled from above a trembling fell upon the limbs and members of the mountains. From the clashing together of the rocks the level ground between with its core of hard stone became mere dust, and from the frequent assaults the collar of the ninth sphere was rent open.

As for the mangonels that had been erected it was as though their poles were made of pine-trees a hundred years old

(as for their fruit, *"their fruit is as it were the heads of Satans"*);
and with the first stone that sprang up from them the
enemy's mangonel was broken and many were crushed under
it. And great fear of the quarrels from the crossbows over-
came them so that they were utterly distraught and everyone
in the corner of a stone made a shield out of a veil, whilst
some who were standing on a tower crept in their fright like
mice into a hole or fled like lizards into crannies in the rocks.
Some were left wounded and some lifeless and all that day
they struggled but feebly and bestirred themselves like mere
women. And when the heavens doffed the cap of the sun and
the earth raised the curtain of night from the soil up to the
Pleiades, they withdrew from battle.

Rukn-ad-Din now decided to capitulate. It is obvious
that he had been hoping that snow would fall at any
moment and force the Mongols to break off the siege, but
through some extraordinary freak of nature the sun
continued to shine, and Juvayni says in his account that
old men of 100 could not remember such a mild winter.

In these circumstances Rukn-ad-Din decided to throw
himself upon Hulagu's mercy, and he dispatched a messenger once more, begging forgiveness for his past crimes.
Juvayni praises Hulagu's utter compassion, and says that
he followed to the full the command of the Koran *"Forgive
with kindly forgiveness."*

It is worth recalling here that Juvayni's task as official
historian to the Mongol conqueror was to present all his
master's deeds in the best possible light. As an orthodox
Moslem he readily identified himself with Hulagu's avowed
intention to extirpate the Ismaili heresy. When reading
Juvayni, we must, therefore, take all his comments with a
pinch of salt. There is no doubt that he himself was a kind-
hearted enough man and a scholar into the bargain, but
there is equally no doubt that Hulagu was as black-hearted
a ruffian as ever existed in the long line of Mongol warrior-
kings, as his subsequent treatment of Rukn-ad-Din and the
Assassins was to show.

On November 19 Rukn-ad-Din, accompanied by his family and followers, hastened down from Maymun-Diz and, "in an attitude of shame and contrition, confessed to the crimes and sins that he had committed in former days and in the preceding months. And since the King united in his person all the graces of kingly beneficence and all the wonders of royal kindness, he changed Rukn-ad-Din's feelings of loneliness and foreboding into a mood of ease and happiness and conveyed to his soul the glad tidings that he and his family who had been dead were alive again."

The evacuation of the castle was completed the following day, and although the Mongols were content to spare the lives of the garrison for the moment, they certainly had no intention of allowing the castle to stand. Accordingly, they entered it and began to destroy all the buildings, "brushing away the dust thereof with the broom of annihilation." We can certainly testify that the broom swept pretty clean.

Some of Rukn-ad-Din's bodyguard were made of sterner stuff than their lord and master and, perhaps foreseeing what their real end was likely to be, determined to take up arms again and resist to the very last. They went to the topmost tower of the palace, taking with them some mangonels, and proceeded to open fire on the Mongol camp. This fanatical resistance met with an equally fanatical desire to annihilate the *fida'is* whom Juvayni calls "pur-blind, crooked-hearted unbelievers." On the fourth day of this epilogue "the snake-like warriors and valiant stalwarts of the army scaled that lofty and majestic peak and utterly crushed those serpent-like miscreants and hacked the limbs of those wretches to pieces." The treasury of Maymun-Diz was ransacked and distributed, and, having made sure of the central Assassin castle and taken the Grand Master with a large part of his army, Hulagu now set about sub-duing the other main forces in the valley. He first sent an *elchi* (messenger) to the commander of Alamut calling on him to surrender and follow his royal master's example. The commander hesitated, and a substantial portion of the

Mongol army was sent to surround Alamut. The mere size of this force struck such panic into the defenders that they, too, sued for quarter and begged for favourable treatment. Rukn-ad-Din interceded on their behalf and for the moment at any rate "the King [Hulagu] was pleased to pass over their crimes." Alamut and "all the inmates of that seminary of iniquity and nest of Satan came down with all their goods and belongings." Three days later the Mongol army entered the castle, set fire to the buildings, and razed them to the ground. Rukn-ad-Din himself was allowed to linger in a state of uncertainty as to his fate. He seems to have been treated fairly kindly, taken to Kazwin, and was there instructed to send messengers to the castles in Syria ordering them to surrender. The Syrian branch, however, realized that Rukn-ad-Din was acting under pressure and took no notice.

It is evident that Hulagu was merely sparing the Grand Master's life in order to use him to the full. As soon as this usefulness was at an end he would have no scruples about putting him to death. But before this happened it seems that Rukn-ad-Din fell in love with a Mongol girl, who was bestowed upon him in marriage by the King. His mind must steadily have become more and more clouded, for he developed a passion for Bactrian camels and would talk about them for hours with anybody who had the patience to listen. He even asked Hulagu Khan for thirty stallion camels because he wanted to watch them fighting. He rather enjoyed the role of a distinguished prisoner and was glad to be rid of responsibilities and decisions he was neither fitted by nature nor willing by temperament to undertake. He asked to be allowed to go to Mongolia to visit the Great Khan, promising that on the way he would endeavour to persuade the outlying Assassin fortresses, such as Gird Kuh, which still held out, to surrender. In this he failed, and as he no longer fulfilled any useful purpose as far as the Mongols were concerned, it was decided he should be put to death. One version of the end of this weak ruler, which Juvayni also relates, states that the Great Khan told him he must return to Lammassar, which was still holding out after a year, and tell the garrison to surrender. As he set out on the long journey back from distant Transoxania with a strong escort of Mongol *elchis*, he was led away from the road on the pretext that a feast had been prepared for him. Then "he and his followers were kicked to a pulp and then put to the sword" (Juvayni). Meanwhile orders had been issued that Rukn-ad-Din's family, who had stayed on in Kazwin, should suffer the same fate and that the captured garrisons of the Assassin fortresses should also be killed. Estimates of the number of victims of this ruthless purge vary, but it is likely that well over a hundred thousand Ismaili followers perished. Well could Juvayni say: "Of him [Rukn-ad-Din] and his stock no trace was left, and he and his kindred became but a tale on men's lips and a tradition in the world."

Despite the dimensions of this massacre, Hulagu had not managed to kill every Assassin, and he issued orders that any Assassin who was found lingering in any city or on the corner of any street should either be enslaved forthwith or be put to death. Juvayni, in a rather self-satisfied way, sums up the results of the campaign in the following words:

> The propagators of Isma'ilism have fallen victims to the swordsmen of Islam. . . . Their governors have lost their power and their rulers their honour. The greatest among them have become as vile as dogs. Every commander of a fortress has been deemed fit for the gallows and every warden of a castle has forfeited his head and his mace. They have been degraded amongst mankind like the Jews and like the highways are level with the dust.

He ends his panegyric with a quotation from the Koran:

> *And the uttermost part of that impious people was cut off.*
> *All praise be to God, the Lord of the Worlds!*

MAYMUN-DIZ

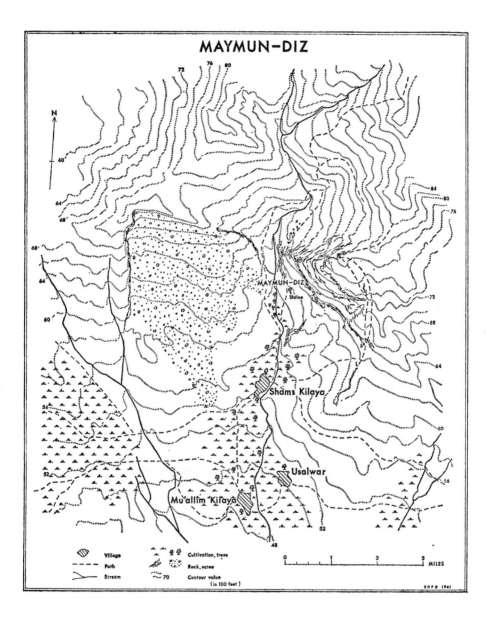

72 76 80

N

60'

64'
68'

68'

64'

60'

MAYMUN-DIZ
Shrine

64'
80
76

72

68

64

56'

52'

Shāms Kilāya

60'

Usalwar

56

Mu'allim Kilāya

52

48

	Village		Cultivation, trees
	Path		Rock, scree
	Stream	70	Contour value
			(in 100 feet)

0   1   2   3
MILES

RHPD 1961

In order to establish that the castle of Shams Kilaya was in fact that of Maymun-Diz, the expedition had to prove that the site and local topography fitted in as closely as possible with the description given by Juvayni. We made a list of the main points that we had to prove, and they are as follows. First of all there must be a hill-top *overlooking* the castle on which the World Conqueror could have set up his parasol of war. Secondly, there must be sufficient space around the foot of the castle for the considerable Mongol armies to encamp and to set up their mangonels. Juvayni mentions that the circumference of the castle was a *parasang*, and although we need not literally expect this to be 4 miles, it must be something of that order. Thirdly, the castle itself must be built on top of a lofty peak, and the climate in winter must be sufficiently severe for it to merit the description which Juvayni gives. Its battlements must be made of gravel and plaster, and we must search for the remains of a large central tower at the top on which the Assassin stalwarts made their last stand. Fourthly, and perhaps most important, it must be well supplied with water. Juvayni is fairly explicit about this, and states categorically that on its summit was a spring of water and three others on its side. In addition, a stream was diverted from a *parasang* away and made to flow into the castle. Fifthly, Juvayni mentions a near-by "town of heresy" in his descriptions of the building of Maymun-Diz, and although absence of the remains of such a town would not disprove the claims of the site—Juvayni frequently lets his imagination have a free rein—signs of the existence of such a town would be another indication that this was Maymun-Diz. Finally, Maymun-Diz must lie to the west of the castle of Alamut as Hulagu stopped at Shahrak after he had captured Maymun-Diz in order to rest and regroup his forces before proceeding to besiege Alamut.

We had established this last condition in the 1959 expedition, and it had seemed from our preliminary exploration that all the other conditions for positive identification could be fulfilled. However, it was now our task to prove beyond doubt that this was Maymun-Diz, and, even more important, to explore the inside of the castle. We decided that we should spend our first day in a general reconnaissance of the castle and should try to walk all the way round it. This would give Roddie an opportunity to see exactly what he was in for as far as the survey work was concerned, and enable Ragnar to choose the best vantage points from which to photograph the rock. Roddie's job was to make an accurate sketch-map of the outside of the castle and a ground-plan of the gallery-system inside the rock itself. The summit of the rock is about 2000 feet above the floor of the valley, and to reach its base you have to scramble up 600 feet over steep scree. The top of the rock is about 1500 feet long by 300 feet wide, but it broadens out considerably at its base, and with the adjoining foothills has a circumference of about a *parasang*. It thus rises gradually above a great saucer-shaped moat of a sufficient size to contain the Mongol armies. Most of the fortifications are in the south-west corner—that is, facing down towards the main valley and the river. The fact that there were no visible fortifications on the northern side worried us at first. The answer probably is that the Assassins expected to be attacked from the south, and therefore contented themselves with posting a few sentries on the northern side. The pass from Alamut to Shams Kilaya was extremely difficult to negotiate, and was most unlikely to be used as an approach route by an invading force in an attempt to encircle the position. With their backs to the mountains, a resolute garrison could concentrate on defending the southern approach and preventing any enemy from establishing a position on the mountains to the north. And, in fact, Hulagu did enter the valley from the south.

As we studied the topography of the ground we felt that it was curious that the garrison at Alamut made no attempt to relieve Maymun-Diz, as geographically they were well placed to carry out sorties and raids on the encircling armies, but evidently the garrison commander was not prepared to take the risk.

The first thing that struck us on this preliminary reconnaissance was how much more masonry existed than we had thought the previous year. Practically the whole of the south-west face of the rock was covered with well-preserved squares of stone cemented together with plaster and gravel, extending 50 feet up the side of the mountain over a distance of some 200 yards. This stone was covered with a brown plaster which blended very well with the natural colour of the rock-face, thus forming the perfect camouflage. In the centre of this fortified front we saw a well-formed semicircular bastion reaching right down to the ground. On each side, to the right and left, there were three brick bridges spanning small crevices. They undoubtedly formed part of the main defence works and had somehow survived the destruction of the castle. We could not understand how we had missed all this last year, and the answer probably is that by the time we had reached Maymun-Diz we were all so weak with fatigue, dysentery, and jaundice that our powers of observation had been considerably reduced. In addition, it is often difficult to distinguish man-made brick from the natural conglomerate rock, but this time there was no mistake. Taking a closer look at this face, we saw a great crevice about 60 feet high and no more than 3 feet wide leading up to a cave-like opening in the castle wall, which formed, we had been told in 1959, the entrance to the "stables," so called because, according to local tradition, horse-manure had been found there a long time ago. We decided that we would first force an entrance into the stables on the following day and see exactly where they led. Continuing our walk around the castle, we noticed next at least three separate springs. The previous year we had located one of these springs two or three miles away, and had seen that its course had been diverted and now ran into the foot of the castle. We were not able to follow how far it went.

On the western side there was a deep but fairly narrow valley which separated the main rock from a spur on which, we were told, there used to stand another castle, called, rather attractively, the "Castle of the Moon." A landslide has obliterated all traces of this castle, and all that remains is a mass of tumbled rocks and boulders, some of considerable size. The headman of the village said that Mu'allim Kilaya stood at the foot of this hill until the landslide came and swept it away, but this story was probably based on hearsay passed down from one generation to another, and there is no way of checking it. Certainly this hill was there in Assassin times and on its slope the Mongol armies could have set up their mangonels. The shots would have reached the top of the semicircular bastion, which, we later discovered, contained the main staircase. Such fire would have been most effective in preventing communication between the different galleries inside the castle. This western valley runs for about a mile until it joins a hill immediately to the north of Maymun-Diz.

At the north-west corner the natural cave-system seemed to peter out, although the faulting in the rock was heavily outlined in dark-blue streaks, which were sometimes almost black. Just here were the remains of a quarry, and it is reasonable to suppose that the Assassins used it to procure the stone for building the outer walls. To the north of the castle was a narrow neck of land that joined Maymun-Diz to a big hill immediately to the north in the Hawdeqan range. This hill overlooked the main rock by some 300 or 400 feet, and, although it was difficult to climb, it was probably here that Hulagu, after forcing his way past the dispirited and cowed garrison manning the main south-western defensive positions, set up his parasol of war. From the top of this hill we were able to get a very good idea of the natural defences of the rock, and also to see the courses of the three streams.

On the eastern side of the rock there were many openings and some of them we later explored. There was no particular evidence that these had ever been fortified, although we did come across one or two shards of pottery, but as the grey Caspian ware has been used in this part of the world since time immemorial the shards could have belonged to almost any day. It is also very likely that shepherds have been continually using these caves during the past century and that some of the debris belonged to them.

With difficulty we made our way back along the southern face. As well as the openings of the caves we could see big patches of plaster on the natural rock as we approached the south-western corner. The fortifications must have extended a considerable way along the southern face, and the patches would have been the scarring left after the destruction of the ramparts. We rounded off this reconnaissance by a visit to the top. The only path up, if path it can be called, is a twisting goat-track that often got completely lost among the boulders and rocks and wound its way up from the eastern face. It was a very stiff climb indeed and our guide was almost as exhausted as we were when we got to the top. We had hoped that there would be some signs of fortification, but although we came across bits of brick and plaster there were no foundations that we could be certain belonged to the thirteenth century. This did not surprise us too much because, as I have said, the defence of Maymun-Diz must have been planned on the same principle as the fortifications inside the Rock of Gibraltar. If in the worst event an enemy did get on top of the castle there was very little he could do and it would be perfectly possible for him to be driven off again by the garrisons at Alamut or Shir Kuh, provided again that they were made up of men of metal. And, judging by the thoroughness of the Mongol destruction of the inside of the castle, there is every reason to assume that no trace of any external fortifications would remain.

It had now become abundantly clear that if the Assassins had been led by a man of the calibre of Hasan-i-Sabbah, the castle could have held out more or less indefinitely. The strategic position of the castle could not be faulted. But, as is so often the case in war, the factors that finally determine victory or defeat are human.

The next day we decided to make our first attempt to get into the stables. We set off fairly early, accompanied by the headman and our chief guide from 1959, Shukrallah, or Ape-man. He went on ahead with the rope and tried to find a passage up the crevice that would not be too difficult for us. We scrambled up the scree, always an agonizing process, and then passed a little shrine some 300 feet above our base-camp. This shrine went by the name of Damagah and was dedicated to some long-forgotten saint. It had been kept up quite well and was a small wooden building flanked on either side by two enormous elm-trees. The elm-trees, according to the local legend, were once two of the saint's bodyguard. Just before he died, the saint had requested that he be buried near the village of his birth, and charged his two faithful retainers to see that his last wishes were respected. They carried their dead master back into the mountains, dug his grave, and erected a shrine over it. But such was their devotion that they determined to spend the rest of their days as guardians of the shrine. When they died, each was turned into an elm-tree. Every time we went up to Maymun-Diz we passed by this shrine and by a little rivulet with extraordinarily clear water running round the shrine. Here we would pause, look up at the vast bulk of the castle, drink, and then go on our way refreshed.

Shukrallah found the climb into the stables more difficult than he had imagined. It took him a good hour to get into the entrance himself, and while he was climbing a shower of stones came pouring down. This was extremely unnerving, and we moved back a good distance to see

C.A.–M

exactly what we were in for. At last he had cut sufficient steps to enable us to squeeze up inside the crevice, but at one stage we would have to be hauled up a distance of about 30 feet. The headman was the next to climb to the entrance, so that he and Shukrallah together could haul us up. The rope was sent down again, and we were pulled up one by one, first of all Mike, as he was the most agile, then Roddie, Richard, Ragnar, Jah, Minou, and finally myself. I thought it just as well to be the last so that the whole party could turn to hauling me up! The rope was slipped under our shoulders, pulled tight (far too tight), and up we went. Once inside the stables, the outer wall of which had been destroyed, we got a better look at the external structure. The remains of a staircase twisted up outside the wall. The blocks of stone that formed the steps were evenly hewn, but although some of them were loose, it was just safe to scramble up. At the top, the staircase led to a very narrow outer ledge, no more than 18 inches wide, with a sheer drop to the foot of the castle. It seemed madness to attempt to traverse this ledge, so we returned to have a good look round the stables.

The roof of the stables was 15 feet high, and parts of it had caved in, so there was a good deal of rubble on the floor. A passage on the left led to an interesting water-cistern. It had been hollowed out of the rock and its sides were covered with some kind of greyish cement. It was hard and did not flake. Leading into this water-cistern were three pipes made of earthenware and joined together with plaster. Two must have led to the outside of the castle and the other one went straight up into the roof: it was impossible to see exactly how far.

Our first job in the stables was to try and find the original floor-level. After an hour of strenuous digging we came to solid stone covered with plaster, and there were, in fact, traces of manure. We concluded that this vast cavern was probably the main guardroom of the castle. Before the ground around the castle had eroded, the original track must have come up to the south-west face of the rock, and we could in fact still see parts of the track on the lower slopes.

At the back of the stables a gallery ran for about 300 yards into the rock. At head height there were holes lined with plaster. Since the floor-level was once much lower, these were almost certainly beam-sockets for roof-beams, a surmise supported by fragments of charred wood in the sockets. The walls were covered with plaster to a height of 2 or 3 feet, mostly scorched, and on the plaster were faint graffiti, but these were too indistinct to decipher. This gallery led to a vault, and mounted troops could have entered the castle through the guardroom, passed along the gallery, and stabled their horses in the great vault.

Leading off from the vault there was a narrow passage filled with rubble, which led farther into the rock. Mike, Richard, and I decided to explore this, although our guides refused to come with us, maintaining that evil spirits lived at the end of the passage. We crawled along on hands and knees for about 100 yards in pitch blackness, being careful not to dislodge more stones. Gradually the roof became lower and lower, until we found ourselves inching our way along more or less on our stomachs, and with the air becoming more and more foul. After a further quarter of an hour we emerged into a series of three rooms, each of them 25 feet long, 12 feet wide, and 10 feet high. By the flickering light of our torches we saw roof-beams and plastered walls similar to those in the gallery. As we were looking around there was an ominous rumbling behind us, and so we decided to move back as quickly as we could. We found that there had been a small fall of rock half-way along the narrow passage, but we were able without too great difficulty to squeeze our way through. We wondered whether we should go back and try to photograph the rooms, but when we suggested this to the rest of the party and to our guides, they said it would be madness, and so, to our utmost regret, we had to abandon the idea of further investigation of these rooms. As it was, we had taken a very considerable risk indeed, and might well have been buried alive. Sobered by this unpleasant thought, we decided to call it a day and return to our base-camp, especially as the sun was beginning to set, and we had to negotiate the steep climb down to the floor of the valley. We were extremely pleased with what we had achieved on this our first real day of exploration at Maymun-Diz, as we had proved beyond any doubt that there were large rooms right in the heart of the rock.

The next day, August 30, we were up early. Over supper the night before we had worked out our main plan of campaign for entering the central chambers on the western face. We thought that it would be possible to build a ladder out of trees, and, using it to scale the rock-face, climb up with the Ape-man into the holes. It was a very complicated arrangement. First two trees, young poplars, which were not plentiful in the valley, had to be felled, and there was a good deal of arguing over the price. Wood is mostly used for building houses and is quite expensive. We eventually bought each tree for £2. Then nails had to be found. There were no nails in the village, and a special messenger had to bring them from a village called Asalbar, some five miles away. The smith at Asalbar had spent most of the preceding night forging them from old bits of iron. Lugging the trees up the steep scree leading to the foot of the mountain was very difficult, and it needed five men to each tree. We went ahead, so as to explore a different route to the foot of the castle, and Richard and I grazed ourselves badly, but by 8 A.M. we were all assembled at the foot of Maymun-Diz complete with torches, "Tilley" lamps, and ropes. The trees arrived about an hour later and each had to be manoeuvred into position. They were about 60 feet long and very heavy, but we all set to, and with cries of *"Yek, do, sey"* ("One, two, three") we managed to hoist the trees up against the rock. We were rather annoyed to discover that our best climbing rope was being used for hauling the trees up, and we examined it carefully to see if it was in any way strained. One or two strands were badly grazed and so we thought it better to discard it for climbing and to keep it for hoisting gear. The next job was to nail cross-slats on the two trees. This was done by the Ape-man, starting at the bottom. The slats consisted of narrow bits of wood cut from the branches of our trees and crudely hammered into the trunks.

By 1 o'clock this makeshift ladder had been completed. It looked an extremely rickety affair. The cross-slats were very thin in some places, and it was obvious that they had been badly hammered home. We decided to take a rest, and bread, onions, and cheese were handed round. In the middle of our meal we heard a great shout and a cry of agony. We rushed over to see what had happened and saw one of the workers lying on the ground holding his foot and obviously in great pain. We were told that he had been stung by a rock-scorpion. These are little grey scorpions, which hide under the rocks and have a very poisonous sting. Fortunately Minou was at hand. He lanced the foot, injected some anti-scorpion serum near the wound, and the man was escorted back to the village. Although the pain continued for forty-eight hours or so, he then recovered completely, but this episode made us all very nervous. We had killed the scorpion, but were not very cheered when one of the villagers told us that it was a male scorpion and that whenever a male was killed a female came out on the warpath. This reminded us of Dr Hatemi's fears at Samiran, and we hoped that this story would be equally groundless. We actually did see two more scorpions, one of which was caught by the villagers, who then proceeded to torment it. They first of all teased it with a pencil, which it stung violently. Then, seeing that this produced no reaction, it moved slowly round in a circle while Ragnar tried to photograph it. Tiring of this sport, one of the guides eventually killed it with a stone.

Lunch over, we decided to start the next stage of the assault on Maymun-Diz. The Ape-man, carrying with him all the climbing rope we possessed, was the first to go up. The ladder swayed alarmingly under his weight, but he reached one of the holes in the rock-face, and started looking for a way up from there. Every one then looked round expectantly at me. I suggested that Richard should go up next as he was the lightest, but Minou said emphatically that this was a question of prestige, and that if I was not the first of our party to climb the ladder I should lose a considerable amount of face. I gingerly inquired if it would not be a good thing if I were roped, and was told that this was quite unnecessary. Slowly I started up the ladder. Although not very tall, I am heavily built, and the ladder began to creak under my weight. The Ape-man had placed the slats about 2 feet apart, and so climbing it was very difficult. I had to put my hands above my head, reach for a slat a long way up, and then haul myself up by my arms. Also, the two tree-trunks had been nailed so closely together, it was possible to put one foot only on the middle of each rung. The other had to be placed on the little piece of cross-slat projecting from the side of the tree-trunks. Occasionally there was a sinister, cracking sound, but after what seemed an age I got to the top. There the ladder was swaying in the breeze, and there was a nasty overhang to be climbed before I could join the Ape-man. I asked him to sling down a rope, which I then tied round my waist, and I half climbed and was half dragged up the remaining slope. There was just room for the two of us to stand inside the hole, and it was perfectly obvious to me that it would need an extremely skilled mountaineer to climb the remaining 50 feet or so up to this south-western entrance to the castle. It looked far too hazardous, and so I decided that it was an unjustifiable risk. I shouted down to Mike and Richard to ask if either of them wanted to come up, but they said they would rely on what I thought. I then started the descent, being gently lowered down to the ladder by the Ape-man. Coming down was even worse than going up. The Ape-man had told me that I must take off my shoes, but this I had rather unwisely refused to do. Cautiously I descended, and had come down about five rungs when there was a loud crack. The rung split under my weight, and down the ladder I slipped. I fell for about 15 feet, with rungs tearing away from the nails under the impact of my falling body, until I came to a full stop. This was a terrifying moment as I really thought that I was bound to fall right down to the ground. The others had seen what was happening and had run to the bottom of the ladder to hold it steady, and when I glanced down they were looking up with frightened faces. Only Ragnar, who had been photographing my descent, went on calmly in his professional way. He seemed almost disappointed that I had stopped where I had, although he said this was bound to be a very dramatic part of the film. I got down to the foot of the ladder as best I could, and then felt blood running down my leg. During my fall I had received a gash along my thigh from the projecting nails. Again the wisdom of having a doctor continually at hand with a first-aid kit proved itself. Minou put disinfectant on the wound and bound it up in a trice.

We were disappointed at the failure of this first attempt. Even if we could repair the ladder and insist on its being made safe, we still could not negotiate the 50 feet of rock-face above. The only thing to do now was to return to the entrance to the stables, which we had explored the day before, and cross the very narrow ledge at the top of the staircase. After resting, we went up into the stables once more. I climbed out on to the beginning of the ledge, then crawled along as far as I could on my hands and knees, but after about 15 yards it became so narrow that one foot was almost hanging over the side, and there was a sheer drop of 100 feet to the foot of the castle. My leg was beginning to hurt and it felt rather stiff; so I returned and asked the Ape-man if he thought he could get across.

He said that he could. We put a rope round him and anchored it firmly to a boulder inside the stables. He took off his shoes, and in ten minutes he was across to the other side. Mike then asked if he could go across, and with some misgivings I agreed. We all held our breath while he gingerly felt his way across this dangerous traverse. Half-way across he dislodged some stones, and one fell on the hand of a guide who was down below. Minou returned to the foot of the castle and treated him, giving orders at the same time that all the spectators from the village who had come up to watch the fun were to keep well away. All this made a spectacular subject for filming for Ragnar. When Mike had safely reached the other side, the rest of us descended to the foot of the castle. We asked Mike to explore as much as he could inside, and he shouted down to us an account of all that he could see. He said that here was another series of rooms with plaster-covered walls, and that he could clearly distinguish the outline of the battle-ments and the brickwork. He spent about an hour inside the castle, and thus earned the distinction of being the first European ever to enter the main apartments of Maymun-Diz since it fell to the Mongols 700 years ago.

Dusk was now falling, so we decided to abandon operations for the day and return to our base-camp. It was very obvious from Mike's preliminary report that further investigations must be carried out the following day, and we then had to consider who would be in the party to cross the 'cat-walk,' as we called it. The final choice rested with me, and I suppose that picking the party for this operation was one of the most difficult decisions I had to make as leader. There was very real danger. Mike, being the most athletic and nimble, was an obvious choice. Although Ragnar had hurt his knee two days before, and had grazed it badly by falling on some scree, he begged to be allowed to go, saying that there must be a photographic record of the inside. I admired his courage, but wondered if he would ever make the traverse. In the end, I yielded to his pleadings, as photographs of this part of the castle would, of course, be of inestimable value. Naturally Minou wanted to come too, and so did Jah. I also wanted to see these apartments, not because I distrusted Mike's ability to report correctly, but because he did not yet have sufficient knowledge of Assassin archaeology to be able to assess the true value of any finds. Finally I decided that the party would consist of Mike, Jah, Ragnar, and myself. The others loyally accepted this decision, and so we turned into bed to get as much sleep as possible.

We got up early the next day to avoid the midday heat, and once more climbed the by now well-known route into the stables. There we were, a rather solemn group, as I think we all realized that the next hour might bring tragedy or great reward. We decided that each man should be securely roped, and that as an additional precaution another rope would be stretched along the inside of the cat-walk to act as a sort of safety-rail. If anyone slipped he could still grab the rope. The Ape-man was to go along first and secure the safety-rope and the other end of the individual ropes. He went across with his usual dexterity. Minou was laying out his surgical kit—bandages, anaesthetics, and a whole array of fearsome-looking instruments—just in case. Mike was the next to go, and we watched him with bated breath. When he got to the other side, he shouted back that he had dislodged some stones again, and that I must proceed with extreme care. The traverse had become even more dangerous.

Then my turn came, and I climbed to the top of the steps leading to the cat-walk feeling rather like a prisoner walking to execution. The headman, who was standing beside me, turned with a smile and said (with Minou translating), "Go in the name of Allah." The rope was tied around my waist, and I groped my way gingerly forward, then past the point that I had reached the day before. Just at the spot where Mike had told me to be particularly careful there was a rumbling sound and some of the rock beneath me collapsed. I grabbed for the safety-rope, and then realized that the rope that had been tied round my waist had come loose and the end was entwined round my feet. One leg hung over the precipice, and I was supported only by one foot on the ledge and my hands grasping the safety-rope. With what felt like superhuman effort I pulled myself back on to the cat-walk. I was shaking all over, and had to pause for a minute to pull myself together. Then I moved slowly on, and eventually rounded the corner to safety. The Ape-man gave me a huge grin and a pat on the back that felt like a sledge-hammer. Ragnar gave the thumbs-up sign from down below—and no wonder! I had again provided him with dramatic film material! I sat down and lit a cigarette. Never in all my life have I known a cigarette to taste so good.

The next task was to bring Ragnar across. We threw down ropes to haul up his cameras, which were securely packed in metal boxes to soften the effects of jarring. Richard stood below, and, with his own camera, photographed the gear being hauled up by the Ape-man, Mike, and myself. The operation was simpler than I had anticipated, and only once did the rope stick, but the whole time there was great danger from falling rock. Ragnar had the same difficulty as I did in crossing, but this time the ropes were tied far more securely, and although he slipped once, the rope tautened immediately and he was held in position. Jah also crossed safely. Then we hauled up our lamps and torches, also packed in metal boxes. All this had taken about three hours.

We unpacked the gear and proceeded to explore the inside of this part of the castle. Mike acted as our guide and led us up a narrow, twisting staircase inside the battlements, pointing out several small rooms on the way. These had been destroyed by the Mongols, and only about 2 feet of the walls had been left standing. This was enough, however, to give us a good idea of the plan of this part of the castle. The staircase led up some 20 feet. Parts of it had fallen away, and there were some tricky gaps to traverse. Eventually we crossed a huge boulder blocking the entrance to the main apartments and went down a narrow passage. This opened out into a series of impressive rooms, which in all probability were the staterooms of the castle. It was easy to imagine Rukn-ad-Din holding court here. The rooms had high ceilings carved out of the natural rock, and the walls were again covered with plaster. A lot of it had been defaced, and there were great black scorch-marks, reminders that the Mongols had set fire to the castle. It was an eerie sight. The rooms were lit by two "Tilley" lamps casting their flickering shadows on the walls. We put candles in niches to give more light, and photographed the window embrasures and the plaster hollows where the roof-beams had fitted. Some of these still survived—blackened and scorched by fire. We looked carefully to see if there were any pieces of pottery under the rubble that littered the floor, and found the same kind as those in the guardroom. We measured the proportions of the rooms and photographed everything that could be of the slightest scientific or archaeological interest. By night-fall we had explored only about half the rooms, and we had to recross the cat-walk to get back to safety. This seemed a little easier on the second occasion. In fact, Mike became reckless and ran across it, dislodging a shower of stones as he went.

When we returned to camp, we decided to celebrate with a special meal. So we made a tasty stew and sat up very late into the night talking about our discovery. At last we had accomplished something tremendously worth while: the veil of mystery that had surrounded Maymun-Diz had been at least partly lifted.

It is always difficult to assess the importance of one's own achievements, particularly at the time. Looking back, I suppose that the greatest hazards lay in the nature of the rock itself. Being conglomerate, no part of it was safe.

There were no secure holds for hands or feet, so we were liable to slip and fall. There was also the constant risk of falling stones and rocks.

Once inside the castle there was a different menace. The Mongol destruction and time had loosened the stones in the roofs of rooms and passages and in the vaults. Evidence of recent rock-falls abounded, and we dared not speak above a whisper. The deeper we penetrated into the castle, the greater were the chances of falling rock. Our original idea of using explosives to clear some of the blocked galleries certainly could not have been put into operation without suicidal consequences. We should all have been buried under tons of falling rock. So Roddie's task was largely confined to drawing plans of the inside of the castle and making a detailed map of the immediate surrounding area to show how its position corresponded to Juvayni's account. There was another danger. So complex and twisting were some of the passages and rooms that we were often nearly lost. Frequently, we had to squeeze through very narrow openings, which were very easy to miss on our return journey. The farther we went, the colder it got; water dripped from the walls, and the air was foul. Fortunately, none of us suffered from claustrophobia, but there were many occasions when the eerie, oppressive atmosphere was most uncomfortable.

In August 1961 I returned to Maymun-Diz with an expedition led by Tom Stobart and Ralph Izzard. The purpose of the expedition was to make a series of films about unusual aspects of Persia and the Middle East, and the valley of the Assassins was one of the areas chosen for filming. Joe Brown, that distinguished and likeable mountaineer, was also in the party, and I watched, fascinated, as he climbed the chimney that had defeated us, and where we had attempted to set up our ladder of trees. Even this experienced climber found it an extremely difficult task, but in the end he succeeded. He then let down a light pot-holing ladder so that the rest of the expedition could enter. But even with this aid it was certainly no joy-ride. It took half an hour's gruelling climb up the ladder—which twisted and turned like a thing demented—before the opening of the gallery was reached. Inside we found another series of tunnels, and these we explored. Here, unfortunately, there was far less plaster and brick-work and no evidence of rooms. There was a lot of broken pottery on the ground, most of it plain, but we did find one almost complete, cobalt-blue ewer, probably dating back to the twelfth century, and a large, slim, grey jug, which may well have been used for storing grain.

The 1961 expedition provides a useful yardstick against which to measure our own achievements in 1960. Firstly, I think we can congratulate ourselves on being able to enter so much of the castle with so little climbing equipment and no professional help. Secondly, the later expedition made me acutely aware of the grave risks we had taken on the earlier. We were not excessively rash or foolhardy, but we had certainly pushed our luck to the limit. Thirdly, this 1961 expedition showed that we had investigated nearly all the important parts of the castle in 1960, which in itself was no mean achievement.

It may perhaps be appropriate at this point to summarize our findings at Maymun-Diz. Roddie's detailed survey shows that the topography in the locality of the castle at Shams Kilaya matched the description given by Juvayni of Maymun-Diz. We had located the hill-top overlooking the castle where Hulagu Khan could have set up his parasol of war. The surrounding valleys were ideal for the Mongol armies to encamp and invest the castle. The total circumference of the rock was about a *parasang*. If there was a near-by "town of heresy" it could have been Shams Kilaya. The rock in which the castle was built was certainly high and formidable enough to justify Juvayni's description. The battlements were indeed made of gravel and plaster. The tower on which the Assassin stalwarts made their last stand was there, and we could see where the fortifications had been, although there was no direct way of approaching it. We had located, too, the three springs on the side and the one on the summit and the diverted stream. And finally its geographical situation in relation to Alamut was correct. In our imaginations we reconstructed the castle as Juvayni saw it.

'Ala-ad-Din's advisers must have chosen the site because of its fine strategic position and the advantages of the natural cave-system. To enlarge and develop the caves would be quite an easy matter, since the conglomerate at Maymun-Diz is very coarse: the matrix does not bind the pebbles very solidly, and the tunnels and rooms could well have been made by any simple tool that would extract the pebbles from the matrix. Deeper caves cut out in this way would have provided useful strongrooms, as well as a safe and secure supply of drinking water in time of siege. With the utter destruction of the castle by the Mongols, the caves were thereafter left to underground water erosion. Much of the original layout can no longer be discerned, for streams have cut down through floors and caused the collapse of ceilings. The construction of the fortifications on the outside of the castle was quite a different matter, and this must have necessitated a great deal of hard work as well as engineering ingenuity.

On the lowest level of the castle were the guardroom and storerooms (the so-called stables), and these were approached by a track leading from the foot of the rock round the south-western corner. From here two staircases led up to the large staterooms, which we entered in 1960. Continuing upward, there were probably the soldiers' quarters (the galleries we entered by rope-ladder in 1961 with the Stobart-Izzard expedition), and finally there were more fortifications higher up the western wall, into which we had "climbed" in 1959. Here, too, was a secret exit by a trap-door, which we saw. Thus, Maymun-Diz was at the same time a large castle, amply provisioned and stocked, a well-fortified garrison, and a royal palace.

When we awoke the next morning, feeling somewhat refreshed, we held a full expedition-meeting to review the results that we had achieved so far and to assess what we still had to do in the time that was available to us. We felt that we had achieved quite impressive results in the valley of Ashkavar, at Samiran, and at Maymun-Diz, but we still had to investigate the sites of Nevisar Shah and Shir Kuh, believed by some authorities to have been the site of Maymun-Diz. There was also a lot more work to be done at Alamut. In the 1959 expedition the party had split after we had visited Maymun-Diz, one half under myself going to visit Lammassar, and the other half led by Digby Brindle-Wood-Williams making their way out of the valley through the eastern exit over the mountains past Garmrud. Their route took them past Nevisar Shah, but unfortunately they were too weak to climb up to the castle.

We only had a fortnight left, and if we were to try and investigate some of the other castles it was clear that we must separate once more. So it was agreed that Richard, Ragnar, Roddie, Mike, and Jah should go to Gazur Khan and spend four or five days surveying, photographing, and exploring Alamut, in particular the northern face, which Ivanow had said (when we had met him at Teheran University) would be well worth detailed investigation. Meanwhile Minou and I would proceed on foot with our own cameras down the valley to Nevisar Shah. We intended to examine it closely to see whether or not the topography would fit in with Juvayni's description and justify Ivanow's theory that Nevisar Shah was Maymun-Diz. Minou and I then planned to look at the castle of Ilan, which lay back in the mountains to the south-east, to investigate the question of communications and intervisibility between Nevisar Shah and Alamut, and then go directly to the castle of Shir Kuh, which was the third possible location of Maymun-Diz. Richard would leave Alamut and join us in Shahrak in five days' time. From there we would go to the extreme western end of the valley and explore two other forts at Shir Kuh thoroughly before I left for Teheran and home.

We were very sad at having to part, as I should not see Jah again; nor would I see Roddie, Mike, and Ragnar until they returned to England. However, this plan was accepted by all members of the expedition as inevitable. We drew up a dispatch for the *Daily Mail* and arranged for this to be sent by special messenger to the Press attaché at the British Embassy in Teheran. It had been agreed with him earlier on that he would transmit it to London as an exclusive feature article. In point of fact the diplomatic bag was delayed and this dispatch with two or three photographs of the expedition posing beneath the rock of Maymun-Diz did not reach London until after I had returned home. Ragnar said that he wanted to spend a few more hours inside the caves of Maymun-Diz, as he was not satisfied that the photographs he had taken the day before were of a sufficiently high standard. Mike volunteered to accompany him, and so Minou and I said farewell to them as they set off. There then came the business of sorting out our provisions between the two parties. This took a good two hours. We ordered our mules. I paid the headman and the muleteers for their services, and we all bade one another an affectionate farewell.

9

Base-camp

I THINK we might pause here for a moment to describe our life in base-camp. When we were not on the move, base-camp was the one fixed point of stability, safety, and rest, and as the days wore on we came to regard it affectionately as our home. When, after a gruelling day at Maymun-Diz or Shir Kuh, we would say, "Let's go back now," our thoughts would turn to the shady green patch that contained all our belongings and was, for the time being, the centre of our lives. The complete expedition stayed for the longest time at Maymun-Diz and so I will describe this as being typical of any major base-camp.

There are many factors to be considered when choosing the site for a base-camp. The first is that, although it must be near a village, it should also be well outside it. This will ensure at least some privacy, although a base-camp inevitably becomes a centre of attraction for the local villagers. We told the headman of Shams Kilaya that we were prepared to be "at home" to the villagers at certain hours, and that for the rest of the time we should like to be left severely alone. This request met with a certain success, but unless an expedition is prepared to be rather ruthless and brutal in its dealings with the local inhabitants, complete privacy is never possible.

Next, a base-camp must have some shade, not only for the comfort of the members of the expedition, but also because the equipment and tinned food should be kept as cool as possible. We therefore always looked for a patch of trees, although we suffered in the evenings when swarms of mosquitoes came in to the attack. We smeared insect-repellant on our hands, faces, and necks, but however much we put on we could be quite sure that there would still be some spot left exposed to the merciless attacks of all sorts of stinging and biting things. A base-camp must also be near water, if possible above the supply used by the village. There were always cattle or shepherds' huts above the camp, but the essential thing was to be well away from the main supply used by the villagers. Finally, the camp had to be as near the site of operations as possible in order to reduce the amount of carrying, and so spare the members of the expedition unnecessary fatigue.

At Shams Kilaya we found an almost ideal spot just above the village. It was situated at the edge of a clover field, and there were five or six trees to give shade and a spring with good water coming directly out of the ground near by. Although this spring was also used by the villagers, there was little risk of contamination because it was covered. We took the precaution of sterilizing our drinking water with "Halizone" tablets, and for our meals all the water was boiled. It was important, too, that we should see some green. Out on the sandstone rocks our eyes became tired and strained with the continual glare. I do not like wearing sun-glasses because I feel I can see more sharply without them. One of the nicest things about the return to camp at night was the restful green of the ricefields and clover fields, which reminded me of the countryside at home.

Our camp-beds were set up in a long line by a low stone

wall, each bed with a label to indicate the owner. The beds were the light safari type, very strong and quite comfortable to sleep on. They had been supplied to us by the Army, and however much the struts were battered or bent, it always seemed possible to push them back into shape again. At times the canvas tore, and that created a problem because among all the one-thousand-and-one things we had taken with us we had neglected to bring large, strong needles for mending canvas. Some of the expedition used mosquito-nets, but we found that once we had gone to bed we were very seldom bothered by mosquitoes. They seemed to be attracted mostly in the evening when we were sitting round our campfire and then, as I have said, they were a perfect pest. Beside our camp-beds we had our personal kitbags and rucksacks. It was a point of honour that no one should ever look into anybody else's kitbag or rucksack, or borrow anything without first asking. This was a very valuable rule as I am sure it saved a lot of needless friction.

In the centre of the site we put up three medium-sized tents. The first contained our food neatly stacked according to type and variety; the second, photographic, archaeological, and survey equipment; and the third, surgical and medical stores. Of course, it never rained in the valley, but the tents gave some protection from the sun, dust, and flies as well as from pilfering hands. There were no means of securing the tents, and all we could do was to lace them up in front and put up notices with skulls-and-crossbones saying: "DANGER. KEEP OUT." We knew that hardly any of the villagers could read, but we hoped that at least the skulls-and-crossbones would convey a warning. By the stone wall we also built our kitchen. This was really a hollow, lined with stones. We cooked by pressure stoves, and found that unless they were protected from the wind it was impossible to keep them alight. Near by we dug a pit for rubbish, which we sprayed every day with a strong disinfectant, and over on the side of the hill we

built a latrine. Camp headquarters consisted of two
packing-cases in the centre of the camp and a crudely
constructed table. Whenever we had a conference most
people would bring up their beds and sit on these. Between
the trees we had suspended rope, which we used as lines
for drying our clothes. It was very important to have our
clothes washed as often as possible, as otherwise unpleasant skin infections would have developed. We hired a
woman from the village to do our washing for us, and
every day she came to collect what we had put out
together with some bars of local soap, and bring it back in
the evening. In this way we were able to have a change of
clothes more or less every other day, and this was a great
morale booster.

The camp commandant was Mike, and he had undisputed
sway in his capacity as quartermaster over anything
connected with base-camp. In the beginning I had been
doubtful about agreeing to his joining the expedition.
I wondered if he had had sufficient experience for such
a job and if he was mature enough for the responsibilities
with which he would be faced. I need have had no doubts.
The job of quartermaster proved to be immense, for
not only did he have to know the exact quantities of
food and other necessities that we were likely to use over
the next stretch of our travels, and so arrange for the most
efficient and economical splitting of the stores, but he also
had to know where everything was. This was a task that
might have defeated even a quartermaster in the Regular
Army, but whenever we pitched camp at night he seemed
to know instinctively which kitbag contained the matches
and which the soap or the bully beef. He looked after our
comforts with a thoughtfulness and care that we all
appreciated. I remember, for instance, on one boiling hot
day, returning to base-camp at Maymun-Diz to find that
Mike had put some cans of beer in the stream to keep
cool for us. He cooked more meals than the rest of us. He
was usually the first up and the last to go to bed. His

culinary skill was something to be envied, and he was a genius at producing different varieties of stews from our limited rations. When Robert Moss had to return to Teheran, Mike filled the breach as mountaineer—no ridge, chimney, or escarpment seemed too difficult for him to negotiate. Fit, agile, and light, he was the first to attempt a climb, and only once—at Maymun-Diz—was he defeated. He was also in charge of all our tape-recordings, and he seemed to have the happy knack of knowing just which sounds we needed and which we did not. He got on with everybody—the rest of the expedition, the local villagers, and especially the children, who adored him.

In our daily routine we managed to keep more or less to the timetable and the list of camp duties we had drawn up at our first conference at Rahimabad in Ashkavar. Reveille was between 5 and 5.30, when it was still dark and rather cold. All of us had heavy, Army sleeping-bags, and when we first went to bed we were usually far too hot. The temperature dropped rapidly at about 1 A.M., and we would invariably wake up then, sleepily search for a heavy pullover, slip this on, and snuggle back into our sleeping-bags again. (Since there was always a heavy dew during the night we usually put our clothes under our pillows to keep them dry.) Most of us slept like logs, but strangely enough we had little difficulty in waking up early. Mike, being normally the first person to get up, would give Jah and me a shake, and while I smoked the first of innumerable cigarettes, pondering over the programme for that day, Mike and Jah would set about cooking breakfast. This meal was a pretty substantial one, consisting of fried eggs, sausages, bacon, and baked beans (all, except the eggs, out of tins), followed by the local bread and, as a special treat, "Rose's" marmalade. The local bread is dark and unleavened. When it is fresh it is good, but it very soon acquires the consistency of rubber and after twenty-four hours is almost inedible, but it is nourishing. We had with us a great many tins of margarine

but naturally after they had been open for a time they
became slightly rancid and the only way of eating the
bread when it was at all stale was to pile the marmalade
thickly upon it. To drink, we had coffee or tea. Breakfast
was over by 6 A.M., and plates and dishes were then
washed up by Minou and Richard.

Immediately afterwards came sick parade for the
members of the expedition, and Minou would then give
me a report. Fortunately, we avoided serious illness or
injury, but often we came very near to exhaustion through
the intense heat and the sweat and strain of our daily life.
All of us had dysentery, and at times this was severe, but
we just had to make the best of it and force ourselves to
keep going. The tenacity and endurance shown by the
younger members of the expedition was amazing, for
there were moments when life was complete hell and
breaking-point was nearly reached, but somehow the last
reserve of energy was tapped and the crisis was overcome.
Anyone injured or feeling unwell would stay behind to act
as camp guard for the day.

Following the sick parade, we had a conference around
our table in which I outlined the programme for the day.
This was usually a very democratic affair. Everybody was
keen to get on with the job and often had useful suggestions
to make. It was important that not a minute was wasted by
unnecessary duplication of effort, and so we used to work
things out to an approximate time-schedule, which we did
our best to keep to. When this was over, the villagers
would arrive with the provisions that we had ordered the
day before. Mike would check them and see that we had
sufficient for lunch. Lunch normally consisted of bread,
onions, grapes, two or three tins of luncheon meat, and—
for those who liked it—*mast*, a kind of local yoghourt.
Lunch was carried up to the site on which we were working
by one of our guides.

Meanwhile, Minou and Jah attended to emergency
surgery for the villagers. The main surgery-hours were

always in the evenings, but inevitably there would be two or three patients who had to be seen straight away or who had been told by our doctors to report back. At this stage the headman always came to say good morning to me, and I would have to spend ten minutes in fruitless gesticulations—hoping that I was being polite—because our interpreters were engaged in their alternative occupation as doctors. Roddie and I would then sterilize the camp and see that everything that could be was covered, while Richard saw to the filling and sterilizing of our water-bottles. Ragnar was meanwhile checking his photographic equipment, which demanded a great deal of attention.

We usually wore long trousers, open-necked shirts (not white), and broad-brimmed hats. It was essential for continuity in the film that everybody should wear the same clothes when they were in front of the camera, and as white often appears rather blurred on colour film we avoided it. It would often have been pleasanter and cooler to wear shorts, but long trousers gave us some protection against thorn-bushes, or if we fell on scree or sharp rocks when climbing. Minou and Jah were most conscientious about taking emergency first-aid kit wherever we went so that any injury could be dealt with at once. At base-camp, ready to be brought up by a guide at a moment's notice, was a more extensive medical outfit, which included anaesthetics, surgical needles, and a breathing-tube.

We found it easier not to shave in the valleys and so we sported beards of different colours and textures. Ragnar gained first prize for a black, silky beard of which he was inordinately proud. Most of us wore ordinary suede chukka boots, which were very light and gripped the rocks well. They gave our ankles some support so there was less chance of a painful twist or sprain, and also afforded some protection against scorpions and snakes. Our guides either went barefoot, because they assured us they found this the best way to grip the rock, or else wore sandals, which they called *gives*. *Gives* have a flat, rubber sole with no heel and the uppers are made of cord. They are very strong, but take a lot of breaking in. Mike and Roddie tried a pair (they are quite expensive as they cost £1) but soon gave them up. Proper footwear was, of course, very important as we could not carry more than two pairs of shoes each. We often had to wade through a stream or river up to our waists and then climb a steep, slippery scree or rock. This meant that our shoes had to dry out quickly. We all got blisters in the first few days, but very soon our feet became as hard as leather.

By 8.30 we were usually ready to set out. If Roddie had an independent task he would often go ahead. After myself he was the oldest man in the party. Tall, dark, and tough, he seemed to stride away over the hills with seven-league boots. He quickly grew a long, dark beard, and even in ragged clothes he looked the most impressive figure in our party. As one would expect from a captain in Military Survey, he had an intensely practical and methodical outlook. His job was in some ways the most exacting of all; while the rest of us were able to explore to our hearts' content inside the castles and to have the thrill of realizing that with each new discovery we were adding something significant to man's knowledge of this part of the world, he had to stay outside the atmosphere of glamour and excitement, methodically plotting the position and noting the measurements of the sites we were investigating. This must have appeared at times a tedious, thankless task, and incidentally it meant too that he had to walk much farther than anybody else. But much of the final evaluation of our findings would depend on the accuracy of his calculations and drawings. He often had to test the probability of our own surmises by applying to them the yardstick of scientific investigation, and we came to place implicit faith in his judgment and reasoning powers. In his daily life he was quiet and unassuming, but tenacious and generous. His dry flashes of humour often cheered us up when we were feeling tired or depressed. His Army training in camping was invaluable: whenever the pressure stove failed to work or there was a problem in the mechanics of a crudely constructed winch or hoist, we instantly turned to Roddie for advice.

Roddie suffered more than the rest of us from the heat and the ravages of insects, but each morning he would be the first to leave camp, followed by some little boy helping him to carry his gear, and at evening when we returned we would see his gaunt, tall figure still silhouetted against the skyline behind his survey-board. I only once knew him lose his patience. He had carefully constructed piles of stones to act as markers, and then saw some little boys gaily knocking them down. This was too much, even for Roddie —he went up to the boys, glowered at them, and pointed towards the village, looking for all the world like Hasan-i-Sabbah himself. The boys stared for a moment at this frightening figure, then turned tail and fled.

The morning was spent working, and we had lunch when we could find a spare moment. We always tried to collect together at lunch-time—except perhaps Roddie, who might be some distance away—so as to discuss the results of our work so far. It was at about this time that we began to suffer most from thirst. Our water was limited to one small water-bottle each, and this had to last us until we returned to the camp. We could, I suppose, have sent one of our guides back for more, but this would have taken time, which we could ill afford. It was surprising how quickly we were able to discipline ourselves to a small quantity of water, and we took salt pills in order to make up for the loss of salt in our bodies through excessive sweating. By the time we gathered for lunch we were dirty, grimy, and dripping with sweat, and it was good to have a short rest.

At about 4 o'clock the tireless Ragnar, who up to that time had been photographing our labours without interrupting us at all, now demanded his pound of flesh and made us pose or re-enact some activity for his benefit. This was a welcome change, and his wisecracks and jokes cheered us up after our long, tiring day. Mike and Richard left shortly afterwards for the base-camp to prepare the supper, and I used the time in making field-sketches in my notebook. We returned to base-camp at about 6.30, loaded with gear and equipment, and this return was often the worst part of the day. Running down from Maymun-Diz there was a steep scree slope. We could either come down it walking diagonally, digging our heels firmly into the ground to stop ourselves from slipping, which was an agonizingly slow way of travelling, or else take it at one fell swoop, running from the top and hoping that we would stay upright until we reached the bottom. I never seemed to manage this, although for the younger and more athletic members of the expedition it was easy meat. I would normally get about half-way, trip over a stone or boulder, and then go flying head-over-heels for the last 50 yards, ending up in a thorn-bush. Our guides thought this was great fun, and stood at the bottom of the slope waiting to see the *sarhang* falling, as they said, like a thunderbolt from the blue.

When we got home there was usually a cup of cocoa ready to cheer us up. The light was beginning to fade, but we could not rest just yet. First the equipment that had been used had to be checked for damage and cleaned. At the end of the day it was covered with a fine film of reddish dust that seemed to penetrate everything. There were queues of people waiting to be treated, and Minou and Jah had to attend to evening surgery, which often ended in the flickering light of candles or hurricane lamps. I would spend the time writing, because unless our results were written up at the end of each day, when they were fresh in my mind, they would soon be forgotten and confused. Forcing myself to concentrate when I was tired and surrounded by a noisy, bustling crowd of people waiting to see Minou or Jah or Mike was a trying experience, but I soon got used to it and became impervious to any outside noise. Supper was always a good meal. If Minou had finished surgery early he would often take a hand and prepare an exotic Persian dish, which tasted delicious, or we would have a big stew, using our own tinned meat and adding potatoes, onions, beans, and any local vegetables we had bought. After supper there was more washing-up, and then the final conference to review the day's work. At this we all tended to romanticize a little, and quite unlikely theories about Hasan and the castles came like quicksilver from our vivid imaginations. At 10 we had our last brew of the evening, usually a hot drink of cocoa, chocolate, or coffee, and then we would sit and talk. By now it was cool, and we talked about anything and everything that came into our minds. Often, one or two of the villagers would come and sit in the background, patiently, silently watching us. They seemed glad that we were happy, and when we offered them a glass of tea or a mug of cocoa they would willingly accept. If some one had been injured or hurt they were full of solicitude and brought along herbs which, they said, would make him better. Often they pleaded with us to give up our searches, because, they said, we ran too many risks, and they did not want to see any of us killed or even hurt. We tried to reassure them as best we could, and always turned to the laughing Shukrallah to back us up. Sometimes, Shukrallah would speak to us of his life and experiences: he had a pleasant, rather naïve way of expressing himself, and it was easy to understand how hard his life had been—and yet he did not wish it otherwise. It was always an effort to make ourselves go to bed, but this we did at about 11. The last cigarette, and gradually the subdued mutter of conversation died away and we were asleep, the great vault of the sky set with the sparkling jewels of myriads of golden stars.

10

Alamut

EARLY ON the morning after we had finished at Maymun-
Diz, Richard, who was in charge of the Alamut party,
ordered the necessary mules, but as usual they did not
arrive until four or five hours later. There was also another
delay, owing to the fact that the headman of Shams Kilaya
insisted that I had not paid him for his services before I had
left with Minou for Nevisar Shah. This was quite incorrect
and Richard knew it. When Richard later told me about
this incident I was very surprised, as the headman had
struck me as being an honest enough man. However, bitter
experience taught us that we were always regarded by the
inhabitants of the valleys as being fair game. This was
understandable from their point of view. Our equipment
was obviously valuable, and from this they concluded that
we must be rich. They probably considered that the prices
and wages we offered were fairly low, and that it was therefore quite justifiable for them to make money out of us in
any way they could. If we allowed ourselves to be taken in,
this was our fault and not theirs. In this case, after Richard
had firmly told the headman that he had already been

amply paid, he did not press his claim and he bade farewell
with a good grace and obvious sincerity.

At this point I might perhaps just say a word about the
ethical standards of the inhabitants of Alamut. We always
found that they kept their word once they had given it, and
they never let us down. On the other hand, we continually
found that things had been 'borrowed,' and it was sometimes with great difficulty that we managed to get them
back. Sir Claude Auchinleck had lent me his field-glasses,
and these were invaluable in distinguishing the brickwork
of castles from the natural conglomerate rock formation,
and often saved us two or three hours of what would have
been a fruitless climb. On one occasion when we returned to
camp, I found that the field-glasses were missing. I asked
what had become of them, but none of the villagers
seemed able to give any information. I then let it be known
that unless the glasses were produced within twenty-four
hours I would inform the local gendarmerie as well as the
authorities in Teheran. This again produced no result.
Finally, I gave out that I was sure the glasses had been
taken by mistake, and that I would be very happy to give a
reward of 20 toman to the person who recovered them for
me. Within a quarter of an hour the field-glasses were
back. Normally, we left a guard in camp, either one of
ourselves or a native guide, but even he could not prevent
petty pilfering. The things that seemed to be most
attractive were small domestic items like spoons, knives,
mugs, and mirrors. Once when we were paying a courtesy
visit to a house in Ashkavar, we found one of our camp
mirrors stuck up on the wall, but we felt it would be only
tactful to say nothing about this.

The Alamut party set off eventually in the late afternoon, after Ragnar and Mike had completed their work in
Maymun-Diz, and decided to camp at the small village of
Andij for the night. It was to Andij that Hasan-i-Sabbah
had sent his *fida'is* before he arrived in Alamut himself, and
it was there that he had set up his headquarters before he

managed to get possession of the castle of Alamut by trickery.

Andij is an attractive village lying on both banks of the Andij Rud, a small tributary of the main river. All around the hills rise steeply. The same conglomerate formation as at Shams Kilaya can be observed here. In 1959 we had been told that just north of the village there was a large castle, but no one had been able to scale it. All our attempts to find its exact site proved fruitless, and I personally doubt whether this castle does exist. There were, however, some very interesting caves near by, and these ran for 500 to 600 yards back into the hill. They were probably used as a hideout in times of trouble and as a secret storehouse. In them Richard and his party found the usual pieces of broken pottery, animal bones, and traces of charcoal, but it was impossible to draw any conclusions from these remains.

From Andij the track rises steeply over two ranges of mountains and passes through a small village with a shining white mosque, which can be seen from a long way off. In 1961 I was told that this mosque possibly contained the tomb of Hasan-i-Sabbah. Although I knew that this could only be the fancy of the local inhabitants, I decided to make a special journey to see it. The most important of the big landowners of the valley, Mr Alamuti, was there to meet me and to take me into the mosque. There I met the guardian, an old, wizened man, wearing a long black cloak. I asked him to tell me what he knew, and he related that about 150 years ago some workmen had discovered a plaque engraved with letters which the villagers could not translate. It had been taken to Teheran, and a scholar there had deciphered the ancient writing. The inscription said that here was the tomb of Hasan the Great. I asked if the inhabitants had excavated, and was told that they had not dared to do this. I was then shown the site of the alleged tomb, and Mr Alamuti promised that if I wished to dig he would get me the necessary permits. I felt, however, that

excavations here might lead to very complicated consequences—especially if we found a tomb—and so I declined
Mr Alamuti's offer. Moreover, it is highly improbable
that this is in fact Hasan's tomb, as most evidence suggests
that he was buried in Kazwin.

About five miles beyond the mosque the path drops
steeply, and shortly afterwards the village of Gazur Khan
can be seen. It nestles at the foot of the Rock of Alamut,
and, to the south, a broad plateau slopes gently away
towards the main river-bed. The village is a large one for
this part of the world and consists of some 500 families.
Most of the houses are built of mud bricks and have an
attractive veranda facing north in order to be shaded from
the sun. In the centre is a large village square. It is on the
site of an old cemetery, and the children run happily
among the small tombstones that mark the ancient
Moslem graves. At the southern end are two great elm-
trees, which must have stood here for over 500 years at
least. Tradition says that they were planted by Hasan
himself, but it is unlikely that they are as old as this.

It was here that the Alamut party set up their new base-
camp. I, too, know the village well, as I have stayed there
on three separate occasions; and perhaps this is a good time
to describe the way of life of its inhabitants, as it is typical
of the whole valley. Although their standard of living is
very primitive, every one seems remarkably content
and happy. The family spirit is very strong, and forms the
basis of social life. The houses are one-storeyed and have
an open veranda in the front. The focal point of each house
is the main living-room, about 15 feet square, which also
serves as a bedroom. It is usually kept immaculately clean
—in marked contrast to the rest of the house—and is
replastered each year. In the centre there is a hole in the
ground, covered by rugs in the summer, which serves as a
fireplace. In the long winter evenings the family groups
round the fire, and it is here that local legends and traditions are handed on from father to son. Whenever

strangers are present, the women are relegated to the
kitchens, dark and noisome holes whose walls are covered
with soot and grime. The smoke from the kitchen fire
escapes as best it can through a hole in the roof, but if the
wind is blowing the wrong way the occupants are almost
suffocated. I inquired how long such houses lasted, and was
told that they usually stood for sixty years. Some of the
bigger houses have an upper storey containing two guest-
rooms. Repairs are easy, for if a piece of wall falls down it
is a very simple job to build it up again with fresh mud.
The mud stays remarkably hard and is proof against the
severe storms that often sweep the valley in January and
February.

Household possessions usually consist of some hand-
some quilts and eiderdowns (there are no beds and everybody sleeps on the floor at night), an oil lamp, a German
alarm clock, and a few cooking pots and spoons. Spoons
are rather a luxury and are usually offered only to
distinguished visitors. Their gay clothes are kept in
wooden chests, which are usually made out of old packing
crates and covered with tins that have been flattened. It
was odd to see on some of these chests labels taken from
cans of beer, baked beans, and other well-known com-
modities stolen from our rubbish-pits! We soon learnt
the great value that is attached to tins, so we never threw
ours away. When we had finished with them, we always
gave them to the children, who eagerly seized them and
took them home.

Most of the inhabitants are, of course, illiterate. One or
two have been to Teheran, either on business or for
national service. Most are fairly content with their way
of life and would not exchange their primitive dwellings
for the bright lights of Kazwin or Teheran. Even national
service does not seem to make the young men discontented
although, of course, there are exceptions. The system of
selection for national service seemed to us to be very
haphazard. A party of soldiers, usually consisting of a

lance-corporal and two privates, tours the valleys once a year. Each village is supposed to provide its quota, fixed in advance between the Government and the local landowner. However, as soon as the recruiting squad appears, the young men take to the mountains, and only those who have been slow off the mark are taken back to Teheran to enlist.

Each family has a small plot of land and tries to be as self-supporting as possible. We found that, in effect, each village specializes in cultivating one or two principal crops apart from rice, which is grown almost everywhere. Thus, for instance, the best melons and grapes could be bought at Gazur Khan, but there were no tomatoes. These could be obtained at the village of Shutur Khan, about three miles away. Gazur Khan also went in for beans, potatoes, and onions, and very good they were too. Surplus produce is bartered for other goods. Money as such plays little part, and is used only for buying special things at the village shop. Not every village has got a shop, and there are only about four or five in the whole of the valley. These are stocked with a rather crude kind of brown soap, tea (mostly imported from India or Ceylon), nails, cigarettes, matches, and bales of cloth, all of which have to be brought in from Kazwin by mule. The villagers make everything else for themselves, including their household utensils and agricultural implements, which have been made according to the same design for years.

In each village there are two or three specialists— carpenter, builder, shoemaker, bath-keeper—who have a higher social status than the farmers. Gazur Khan is fortunate in having a bath. It is situated near the village square and is open every afternoon, Monday and Friday being reserved for the women. In the low, dark entrance-hall there is a small pool of running water where the bather first washes his feet. He is then taken to the dressing-room, a kind of cell with a barred window set high in a corner. An iron door leads from the dressing-room to

C.A.–O

the hot-water chamber. The smell is nauseating, and the room is filled with stifling steam. In the middle there is a tank filled with very hot and rather dirty water. The walls and floor are slimy and slippery, and breathing is difficult. Two or three people use the bath at the same time, and when they have finished they go into the last room, where they plunge into a tank of cold water. Bathing in these conditions is an experience that even a hardened traveller does not care to repeat.

Each village is governed by a headman and a council of elders. In some villages the headman is appointed by the landowner; in some he is elected by the villagers, in which case he is likely to be the richest man; and in others the office of headman may be hereditary. Families who often provide a headman are very proud of their tradition. The headman has considerable powers, even of justice. Minor crimes, such as theft, are normally dealt with by him summarily, the punishment usually being a fine or, less commonly, a whipping. More serious crimes are reported to the gendarmerie at Mu'allim Kilaya, the capital of the valley, and the transgressor may then be taken to Teheran for trial. The headman appoints his elders. These are normally four or five experienced villagers who help in administration and in settling disputes. The central Government leaves the villagers very much to their own devices and interferes only when it has to. On the whole this system seems to work well.

Apart from the crops grown on the acre or two owned by a family, the other sources of income are sheep and chickens. Some flocks are communally owned, but in most cases each family rears three or four sheep or goats. Sheep are fattened and killed on special occasions, such as weddings. The goats are milked, and we found the milk sweet and good, although we always took the precaution of boiling it. A sheep can be bought for as little as 25 toman (25 shillings)—ridiculously cheap by Western standards, but expensive in relation to the economy of the valley. Eggs are reasonably plentiful, and these formed a large part of our diet. The villagers eat eggs only occasionally, and a lot of them are wasted. For breakfast the modern Assassin has boiled potatoes, unleavened bread, and tea. His midday meal consists of bread, onions, and goat's cheese, and for supper he will content himself with a vegetable stew and tea. A poor family will not eat meat more than two or three times a year. Despite this, they are, on the whole, a healthy people, although rheumatism and arthritis are common complaints. Flies breed everywhere, and we were surprised that they did not cause more sickness. Other pests are hornets and wasps, which sometimes made our lives a misery.

Water in the villages is surprisingly plentiful. There is sufficient for irrigation, and each village has its own well. The local well is one of the centres of the village social life, and around it at any hour of the day, groups of men, women, and children are to be seen idly chatting. In fact, it often seemed to us that no serious work was done during the day at all. Most families get up at sunrise—at least the women do; the men stay in bed until breakfast is ready.

Meals take a long time as friends and relations often drop in for a chat. Then, while the women clean up the house and fetch water, the men may do a little work—perhaps out in the fields or repairing their houses. As they have very little sense of time it does not matter whether a job is done to-day or to-morrow. They eat their lunch at midday and then take a siesta for four or five hours. In the middle of summer the temperature will often rise to over 100° in the shade, and in the sun it is unbearably hot, even for the villagers. When the temperature drops, between 4 and 5 in the evening, more work is done. The women do their washing in the streams, stamping on the clothes with bare feet to get the dirt out. The men go once more into the fields, but as it begins to get dark at 7 there is not much time for work. More chat in the evening, and then most people are in bed by 10. The most energetic people in the community are the muleteers. If they have loads to carry they will get up early in the morning and plod patiently on with their animals throughout the day, resting only during the very hot hours in the early afternoon. They are hardy people, tough and wiry.

A coarse grass, which is used for cattle fodder, is usually grown on common land just outside the village, and in the evenings we often saw men bringing back great loads of dry grass and hay to the villages. They carry these on their backs, and, to prevent themselves falling headlong down the steep tracks and paths, they steady themselves with a stick between their legs. Quite often they run at full tilt down a steep scree slope, but they never fall over or lose their balance. The hay is kept on the roofs of the houses, just as it was in Hasan's time.

The girls marry young, at about fourteen years of age, but the men seem to treat their womenfolk well, although, as in most Oriental countries, the women do most of the work. Wherever a woman goes the children go too, and there is usually a baby strapped to her back.

Some villages have their own mosque, which is kept clean and in good repair. From time to time itinerant dervishes come round, and they are always treated with great respect by the local population. Most dervishes possess a fine voice and it is a delight to hear them chanting or singing. To have the reputation of a holy man is a mark of great distinction. The villagers are deeply religious, and it is no uncommon sight to see a muleteer or a man working in the fields stop at the appointed hour, take out his prayer-mat, turn towards Mecca, and say his prayers. This will happen even in the middle of a meal, and no one seems to feel any embarrassment about it at all. We sometimes attempted to explain that we were Christians, but the word seemed to have little meaning for them. The villagers thought that the fact that we washed so frequently must have something to do with our religion.

Many had not heard of England: those who had, thought it must be part of India. At times we must have been a source of wonder and amusement to them. Whenever we washed at night in the stream, they would cluster round giggling and pointing curiously at us. When we brushed our teeth and they saw the white foam on our mouths, they thought we were in some kind of ecstatic trance. And when we allowed them to taste the toothpaste for themselves, they were overjoyed and plastered it all over their faces.

In 1961 one of the members of our expedition brought a motor-bicycle into the Alamut valley and up into the village of Gazur Khan. I shall never forget his entrance into the village square, for this was the first time that many of the villagers had ever seen a motor-bike. The driver put on a crash-helmet, and he must have looked just like a man from Mars to the villagers. All the children ran away, terrified by the noise. Gradually they came back and then started to finger every part of the machine. However, their awe did not last long, for within three days they discovered what fun it was to let the tyres down.

We always found the people friendly, helpful, and courteous. They showed neither subservience nor excessive flattery. They treated us with respect, but as their social equals. We found this very refreshing, and we always knew where we stood with them. They were always deeply grateful for anything we, and particularly our doctors, could do for them. At the same time there was a distressing fatalism about their lives. They accepted misfortune or tragedy with resignation, even if it was avoidable. They did not wish to know about progress, and were not concerned with any attempts to improve their lot. The pattern of their existence has remained unaltered for centuries, and they do not appear to wish for change, even though they might benefit. This is reflected in every external manifestation of their lives: their methods of farming (which are surely even more primitive than those practised in England in the Middle Ages); their local industries, such as rug-making and wool-weaving; and their dress and customs. Time seems to have passed them by. They live for the moment, and their lives are as unchanging as the mountains around them.

The castle of Alamut stands on top of a bluff about 600 feet high, and was built in the year 860–861. Hasan, as we have seen, largely rebuilt it after 1090. Juvayni likened its appearance to a kneeling camel with its neck stretched out, and many other picturesque phrases have been used to describe it. Probably Freya Stark's —a ship, broadside on—is the neatest and best. From a distance the rock of Alamut looks unimpressive when seen against the great peaks of the Hawdeqan range, which tower behind it to a height of some 15,000 feet, and it is only as you get nearer that you appreciate its immensely strong position. The name Alamut means "Eagle's Nest," and eagles do, in fact, circle the rock.

Base-camp had been established at the northern tip of the village and from here it was possible, with the help of binoculars, to see most of the remains of the castle. The colour of the rock is grey—a contrast to the red sandstone of Maymun-Diz. Near the top there are two bright patches of green. These are grape-vines, and are popularly supposed to have been planted by Hasan-i-Sabbah. Even from the foot of the rock it is possible to appreciate its ideal strategic position, which enabled the castle to withstand so many sieges. The rock runs approximately north-west to south-east, and consists of the main fortifications and living quarters, about 450 feet long and varying in width from 30 feet to 125 feet, and a smaller south-eastern protrusion consisting of a rounded bluff of sandstone rock joined to the main part by a saddle of granite. The castle itself must have been of considerable size, and there are substantial ruins left of walls and subterranean rooms and caverns. The difficulty for the investigator is to decide to which period some of the remains belong, as it will be remembered that the fortress was used in the seventeenth

ALAMUT

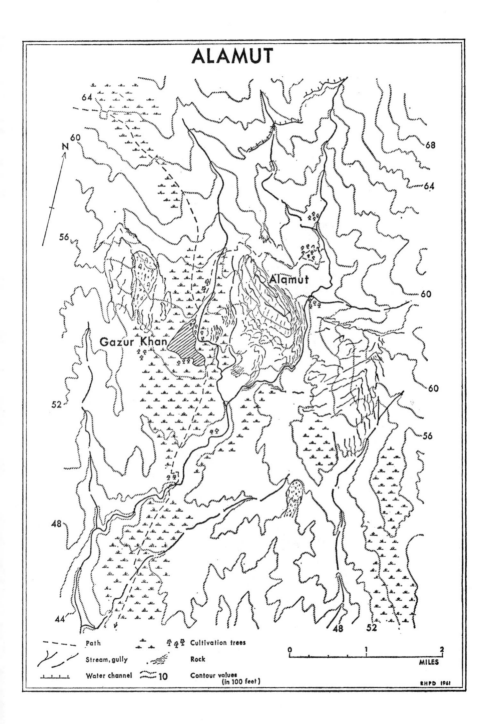

N

64

60

68

64

56

Alamut

60

Gazur Khan

60

52

56

48

48 52

44

Path   Cultivation trees

Stream, gully   Rock

Water channel   10   Contour values
(in 100 feet)

0   1   2

MILES

RHPD 1961

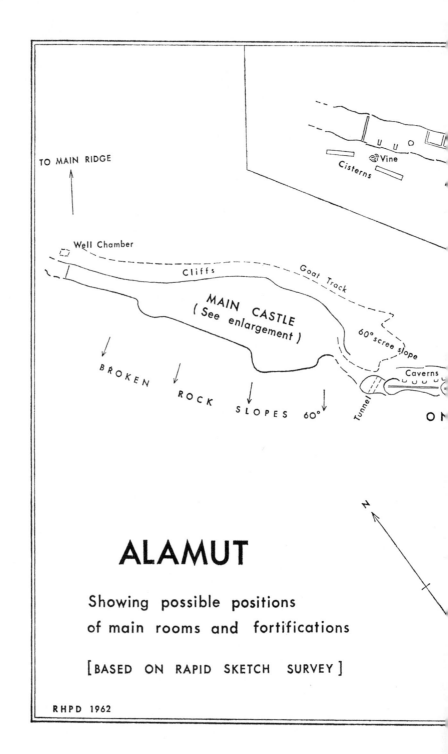

TO MAIN RIDGE

Cisterns · Vine

Well Chamber

Cliffs · Goat Track

MAIN CASTLE
(See enlargement)

60° scree slope

Caverns

BROKEN ROCK SLOPES 60°

Tunnel

O N

N

ALAMUT

Showing possible positions
of main rooms and fortifications

[BASED ON RAPID SKETCH SURVEY]

RHPD 1962

Main Castle

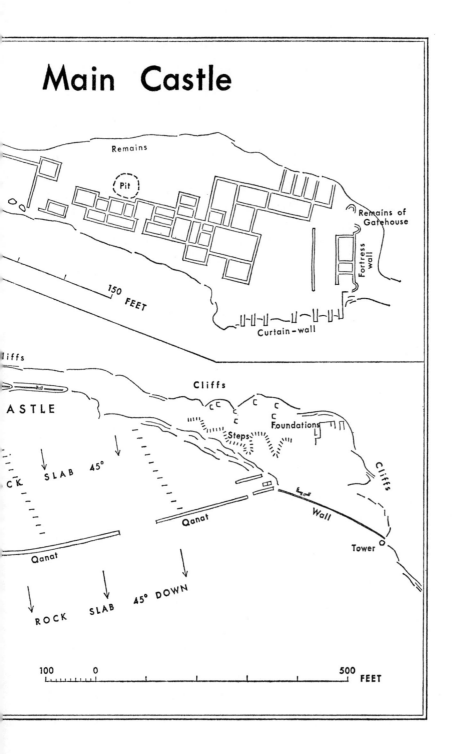

Remains

Pit

Remains of
Gatehouse

Fortress
wall

150 FEET

Curtain-wall

Cliffs

Cliffs

ASTLE

C C C C
C

Steps

Foundations

Cliffs

CK SLAB 45°

Qanat

Wall

Qanat

Tower

ROCK SLAB 45° DOWN

100 0 500 FEET

and eighteenth centuries as a prison for dissident members
of the ruling dynasty. There are still remains of the earlier
Daylamite fortifications, but, as a result of the complete
Mongol destruction, the different strata are mixed and
confused.

Let me first describe the topography. Immediately to
the north stands the massive Hawdeqan range, centring
around the peak of Siyalan Kuh, which is 15,000 feet high.
Beyond this, the Elburz mountains slope gradually away
towards Ashkavar and the Caspian. This range forms a
half-circle round the rock. Between the Hawdeqan range
and the rock is a smaller lava hill some 500 feet high
joined to the rock by a narrow neck. It is from this hill that
the stone used for building the castle may have been
quarried. On the western side there is a ravine, up which a
goat-track now runs, giving access to the castle. The
distance across the ravine is some 450 feet, after which the
ground rises gently again.

On the southern side the rock runs steadily down to the
foot of the valley, a drop of approximately 800 feet. From
this side the castle provides a magnificent view over Gazur
Khan to the main Alamut valley, and beyond the Taliqan
range the horizon is closed by the Chala Pass. On the
eastern side (where it is thought that the stables and
domestic quarters of the castle were situated) the rock
runs fairly steeply down to a ravine, which drops another
50 feet or so. There is no cover from which to launch any
direct assault on the castle, and one gets an impression of
overwhelming and tremendous strength.

Having climbed up the steep goat-track, which first runs
along the western end of the rock, and then turns north
until it joins the col of the lava hill before winding up to the
castle itself, one is struck by the extent of the castle area.
This is no mere fort, for there is evidence of a large number
of rooms both above the ground and inside the rock itself.
To attempt a proper examination of the castle would
require a great deal of modern equipment, including

power-drills and bull dozers, a large labour gang, and the expenditure of much time and money. Unfortunately, no one so far has been able to carry out more than superficial exploration. As the site of Alamut has been well known for the last hundred years, there have been many visitors who have caused great damage to the remaining structure. Their careless excavations have made it much more difficult to draw up an accurate ground-plan of the castle. Many of these marauders are Iranians who have heard legendary tales of hidden treasures buried in subterranean passages hollowed deep into the heart of the rock, and contemporary records do tell of such underground passages. It is even related that Hasan had a store-chamber hollowed out of the rock which he filled with honey and when one of the Mongol invaders entered the chamber he slipped and plunged headlong into it and was drowned. This is a nice Oriental version of the butt of malmsey wine.

We were continually being shown pieces of unglazed pottery, weapons, rings, and coins, which the villagers assured us had all been made at the time of Hasan-i-Sabbah. Our attempts not to appear incredulous were severely tested when among such so-called medieval relics there appeared a Queen Victoria halfpenny. At Gazur Khan there is a local notable who delights in the title of Sheikh, and who seemed to be regarded by some members of the village as slightly weak in the head. He brought along to show us a small phial containing a few grains of gold, which, he solemnly assured us, he had found at the castle. Some genuine remains are sometimes washed down from the top of the castle by the winter rains, and may be found at the bottom of the bluff, but one would be very lucky to come across anything of value. In the time of Hasan a mint was established in Alamut, and we hoped very much to find some of the Alamut silver coins, but we were disappointed. Most examples of Assassin pottery disappeared a long time ago, and the ground is now covered with the litter of obscure eighteenth-century lords who inhabited the castle after it ceased to be a prison and the remains of broken pots left by modern goatherds who take their flocks to graze on the mountainside.

Starting from the north-western end, there is first of all a narrow tongue of rock which does not seem to have been used for any building or living accommodation. There are certainly the remains of fortifications on each side, and on the northerly side a brick sentry box is perched precariously on the rock like a swallow's nest. This tongue is about 150 feet long and 30 feet wide. It could conceivably have been the site of Hasan-i-Sabbah's notorious garden of paradise, but probably it had a far more prosaic use. Near the western end of the tongue and on the south-westerly face are two water-cisterns. They lie some 50 feet down the steep rock wall and are cut into the side of the rock. Richard and Jah clambered down the extremely perilous descent to examine one of them, but there was no way of telling whether the water that was still in it came from a well, or a spring, or was accumulated rainwater. It is on the barren rock-face near these cisterns that grows the cluster of vines which can be seen from the bottom of the rock, a sight that is typical of the appearance of the whole valley—a few patches of luxuriant green among reddish-brown rock. A little farther to the east of the cisterns and some 60 feet down is a brick archway in a very good state of repair. It is built over a smooth-faced, narrow culvert, which runs straight down the mountainside. This could have been a sally-port for the garrison, although the descent was extremely steep.

Clinging to the hands of two guides, Ragnar and Roddie risked their necks by visiting a well-chamber on the north-easterly face. This must originally have had an internal entrance, but they had to scramble down the slippery rock and over a narrow, brick bridge. One false step would almost certainly have sent them hurtling down into the ravine below. The well-room is a low, vaulted chamber with three alcoves cut out of natural rock. The well is in the first alcove, and, although there is a lot of earth and brick inside, there was still 2 feet of deliciously cool water on top. The ceiling of this chamber seemed to be coated with soot, and Ragnar and Roddie took some samples, but their guides poured cold water on their hopes of having discovered some Assassin soot by telling them that occasionally the more athletic and rash village lads climbed into the well-chamber, where they lit fires and spent the night. Incidentally, the well-room affords another magnificent view of the southern slopes of the Hawdeqan range and probably served as a look-out post too.

There is a fairly steep rise from this tongue of land to the main part of the rock, which is on another terrace about 350 feet long and, at its widest point, some 125 feet across. This part of the rock contains most of what seem to be the principal rooms, and our party explored twenty of them. The biggest is in the central part of the castle, measuring 39 feet 6 inches by 20 feet. The south-east wall of this room is 9 feet high and 2 feet thick.

The southern side of the main block of the castle falls away to a terrace which slopes gently down for 50 yards before the sheer drop to the ravine below. It is covered with a coarse grass on which goats and sheep sometimes graze. The curtain-wall of the castle was built at the edge of the terrace and substantial remains still exist. One could easily imagine Hasan ordering his bodyguard to jump over this wall to their deaths in order to prove their loyalty.

The most complete part of the castle is the big fortress wall at the eastern end. It stands about 45 feet high and is approximately 10 feet thick. At each end are two quite well-preserved turrets faced with hard stone. Inside are the remains of staircases that wind down inside the rock, but are now blocked with fallen masonry and rubble. The turrets—to the imagination inflamed by the hot Persian sun—seem to stand guard like sphinxes over the treasure of Hasan-i-Sabbah. The main entrance to the castle was in this wall, and the remains of a gatehouse can still be traced.

The Alamut party next turned their attention to the south-easterly protrusion. This extension to the main part of the rock is sometimes called Piyaz Qal'a, or Small Fort, as opposed to Pila Qal'a, or Great Fort, which is the name given to the western half. A more picturesque name used by the villagers is 'Onion Castle,' because of the bulbous top that surmounts the narrow ridge. It has always been thought that Onion Castle was not fortified, but was used for stables and living quarters. Some previous explorers—and the villagers—have called the more easily accessible of the buildings on Onion Castle the stables, though there is no evidence that they were ever used as such. The present ascent to the castle is very steep, and it is unlikely that in Hasan's time it was any easier. After all, a garrison does not conveniently provide suitable paths along which its enemies can approach. Just at the entrance to the eastern side there are caverns hollowed out of the rock, but in Richard's opinion these were much more likely to have been storerooms than stables. A few mules could have been brought up to the castle and would be quartered here, but, from our reconstruction of the ground-plan of the castle, Alamut was far more difficult to approach by mule than Maymun-Diz, where a special track had been made to enable mule-trains to get into the castle. There is one other difference that must be borne in mind between Alamut and Maymun-Diz. Alamut had been built as a fortified castle and Hasan had never altered its character, whereas Maymun-Diz was first intended as a royal residence, which was fortified as well.

Near the storerooms a short tunnel had been cut through the rock so it would be possible for a sentry to watch both the northern and southern approaches to the castle.

Onion Castle is very difficult to explore. In some places the slopes are relatively gentle, but the parts that interested us often had slopes of 70° or more, and the limestone was covered with a fine layer of pebbles, which made it extremely dangerous. Shukrallah, who had accompanied

Richard's party as chief guide, had now become familiar with ropes and pitons, and he proved invaluable in helping the party to explore the sloping faces of Alamut. This is something that had never been attempted before on account of its danger and difficulty.

Richard first turned his attention to the top of the 'onion,' where, just under the thin surface of earth, he found the remains of a tower and a wall that must have run along the entire length of the ridge. Part of the wall ran at right-angles down the north-easterly slope to another tower, 150 feet down. Here, too, were the remains of steps cut into the mountainside. These were very interesting. An attempt had been made, presumably by the Mongols, to destroy them, but their general direction could easily be followed. To the east of this tower there is a flattish piece of ground before the hill drops sharply away to the stream below, and here our expedition found pieces of pottery that were quite clearly Assassin. Also around this area were the remains of water-pipes, but they were so broken that it was difficult to identify the direction in which the channel had run. At the far end of Onion Castle there are the remains of the foundations of houses, and a great amount of pottery, which suggests that quite a lot of people lived there.

Moving round to the southern slopes, a difficult and tortuous procedure that demanded much mountaineering skill, the Alamut party now proceeded to investigate every inch of the southern face. Professor Ivanow, in *Alamut and Lamasar*, pointed to the possibility of the existence of stairs or paths leading to lower defences, and suggested that it would be interesting to "make a careful, detailed and reliable search for them with the help of proper mountaineering equipment and mechanical aids." Richard decided to test this theory and to investigate any lower fortifications that might exist. Half-way up the southern slope, and running along its entire length, there is a great water-channel or qanat. This can be reached either from the top of the Onion or by climbing round the side. Richard employed both ways. The construction of this qanat is in my opinion the most impressive feature of the castle. Originally there was probably faulting in the rock, but the Assassins succeeded in cutting out a great channel some 600 feet long, with an almost constant width of some 12 feet, and a depth that varies betwen 11 feet and 13 feet. Parts of it had been destroyed by the Mongols. It was intended both as a water-channel and a natural water-obstacle for any attacking forces. Slightly above the qanat are four cisterns, hewn out of the rock, which were also intended for water-storage. The qanat peters out at the western end and it is impossible to tell where it led to. There are no fortifications below the level of the qanat. The Alamut party explored every inch of the steep, sloping ground and there was nothing to suggest any man-made defences. Two flights of steps led from the qanat to the top of the castle and are roughly hewn out of the rock. These stairs provided rapid means of communication, but in our opinion the principal means of approach to the qanat was round the eastern side.

The exploration of Onion Castle by Richard's party established four things. Firstly, it had been much better fortified than previous visitors had thought. Secondly, there is positive evidence that a considerable community had lived here. Thirdly, new information was obtained about the extent and nature of the qanat. And, finally, it can now be positively stated that there are no fortifications on either the eastern or southern slopes beneath the line of the qanat.

While these investigations were going on, Jah continued with his medical work at base-camp. By now everybody in the valley knew of the expedition, and each day the queue of sick and injured of all ages became longer and longer. Richard felt, however, that something was lacking in the reception he received from the villagers of Gazur Khan. This may have been due to the fact that he had brought Shukrallah with him, and so the villagers felt that they were deprived of direct contact with the expedition. At one stage Richard thought of sending him back, but his skill as a mountaineer was so great that it outweighed the minor artificial barrier that had sprung up between the expedition and the village.

Towards the end of their stay, the night before Richard was due to meet me at Shahrak, a wedding took place in the village, and this provided the opportunity for establishing good relations. As acting-leader of the expedition Richard presented the bride with a mirror and a set of cutlery. These, to her, were valuable gifts, and the whole party was invited to the wedding. The bride was to marry a man from another village, and so the ceremony did not take place in Gazur Khan itself. However, pre-wedding festivities began three days before the marriage ceremony and the bride was at home to all her relations and friends in the village. The village band was hired, and it played with only a few breaks for the whole three days. The night before the bride was due to leave a great feast was given in her house, and it was to this that the Alamut party was invited. Three sheep had been killed for the feast and all the delicacies that Gazur Khan could produce were prepared. At 7 P.M. about fifty people gathered inside the bride's house, and there was scarcely room to move. After the meal the band came in and dancing began. Everybody danced, jostling and bustling each other merrily. When the party broke up, at 5 A.M., most people remained where they were, sleeping on the floor of the room.

On the next morning Mike took the tape-recorder and Ragnar his camera so that they could record the bride's departure. For a long time all the village stood outside her house while her clothes and few possessions were packed into the gaily coloured wooden crates, which were then loaded on mules. The villagers had put on their best dresses, the men wearing bright pyjamas of all sorts of colours and the women wearing black trousers and printed aprons. When, after a long wait, the bride appeared, the band

C.A.–P

struck up and all the village chanted, clapped, and cheered.

The bride was accompanied by fifteen attendants, including her sisters, and they were followed by the rest of the village as they walked along behind the mules over the hills. Then, from the other direction, the dust of a similar cavalcade could be seen approaching from the east. When the two processions met, the bridegroom, a rather short young man with an aquiline nose and flashing white teeth, produced an apple and handed it to the bride. She accepted it and ate half. She then handed the rest of the apple back to her future husband, who consumed the remainder. After this symbolic sharing of food, both processions joined up together and headed for the bridegroom's village, which they entered an hour or so later. Here another band greeted the couple, and once more the whole village turned out. Rings were exchanged at the threshold of the bridegroom's house, and he then gave the bride a hearty kiss to the accompaniment of thunderous cheers from the villagers. The wedding-breakfast was then served, and it was even more substantial and longer than the meal of the night before. Dancing and feasting went on again into the small hours of the morning, and when the expedition members slipped away they were told that there were still two more days of festivities to come. During the ceremonies the expedition members were treated as honoured guests, and before they made their farewells Mike gave an appropriate speech, translated by Jah, during which he gave the married couple a further present of some water-containers.

It was now past the time when Richard was due at Shahrak, and as usual there was still work to be done—photographing and surveying—so it was decided that Richard should hurry down to meet Minou and me, leaving the others behind to finish the job. They would finish in two or three days' time and make for Shir Kuh, where Richard would leave messages telling them what Minou and I had done and what they were to do next.

11

Nevisar Shah
and Ilan

AFTER MINOU and I had bidden farewell to the Alamut party, we decided that we would journey to Garmrud along the floor of the valley, as this would be the quickest and easiest route. We had one mule and a muleteer, and we struck southward over the plain leading towards the village of Zavarak. The path was quite an easy one, and as we walked along we talked with our guide about Maymun-Diz and Hasan-i-Sabbah. He seemed to know quite a lot about the medieval history of the valley and told us two legends about the manner of the death of the Old Man of the Mountains. Probably neither of them is true, but it is worth while relating them, as we heard them again in Teheran.

The first account says that in 1116 Hasan felt that he was near his end and told his followers that he had not long to live. Before he died, he said, he wished to spend two or three days in meditation in his own room, and no one was to disturb him. At the end of the three days his servants must enter the room, but they would find no trace of his body. Instead, they would see a black raven, which would take his soul to heaven. Our guide told us that Hasan had prepared for himself a bath of oil of vitriol —sulphuric acid—and that after locking himself in his room he had plunged into this bath, with the gruesome result that when his faithful followers entered the room after three days there was no trace left of his body. He had arranged for a raven to be in his room, and it flew out as they came in.

The second story about his death illustrates the ferocious character of this warrior-priest. He used to order the sentries of Alamut to jump off the side of the castle to their deaths in order to prove their unquestioning obedience. This seems to be an historical fact, but the legend relates that one day he ordered a whole section of his guard to jump over the edge of the castle. Half of them did so, but the others refused, whereupon Hasan drew his dagger and killed three of them. The loyalty of the remaining two guards did not stand up to this test, and they are reported to have seized their Grand Master and hurled him over the edge. In any event it seems that Hasan's death was not a gentle one.

As we walked along listening to these somewhat bloodthirsty tales, we passed the ruins of what must have been quite a large town. This had nothing to do with Hasan-i-Sabbah, but it had been destroyed by a very localized earthquake fifty years before. Near the ruins of the town was a small oasis, and there we sat and rested and ate our lunch. Our loquacious guide, seeing that he had whetted our appetite, went on to describe how once the great poet Omar Khayyám came to Alamut. He had been summoned by Hasan and was met at the entrance to the valley by Hasan's servants, clothed in white garments with golden girdles. They conducted Omar to the castle of Alamut, where he was taken to the famous pleasure-garden that Hasan is supposed to have kept, although from our study of the rock there did not seem to be very much room for it. This garden is reputed to have contained sweet-smelling plants and flowers of rare beauty, and even nightingales were specially imported for it. The sybaritic poet, enchanted by these scents and sounds, fell asleep, and woke up in the middle of the night to find a girl of surpassing beauty beside him. She told Omar that she had been sent by Hasan because, although the Grand Master of the Assassins possessed power and wealth, he felt lonely and longed to have a sensitive spirit beside him, and it was for this purpose that he had summoned Omar. The poet would be rewarded with anything that he cared to ask for if he would stay in Alamut for six months. Beguiled, Omar said he would, only to find himself a prisoner in Hasan's hands. Every day he was shut up in a small room with barred windows, which was heavily guarded, and in the evenings he would be taken to Hasan's pleasure-garden to talk with the Grand Master and to sing to him. Wearying of his captivity, Omar decided to escape. He managed to bribe one of the attendants into lending him a uniform, the white uniform of Hasan's guards, and thus disguised he hastened down from the castle. The vigilant Hasan, however, spotted him before he had got to the foot of the rock and hurried after him with an armed escort. However, on this occasion Hasan showed great magnanimity, and promised to let Omar Khayyám go in peace provided he promised to return to Alamut for two days every year to read and sing to Hasan. This was a gentler story, and as we sat under the cool poplars it almost seemed true. Our guide told us many other kindred tales and these we carefully preserved.

After our rest we moved on, reached the river, and followed its sinuous course as it wound in an easterly direction towards Garmrud. The stars came out, and still we walked on, our guide singing in a low voice to himself. It must have been just about midnight when we reached the village of Zavarak, rather tired and footsore, but enchanted by the soft night around us. Nights in the valley were delightful. When we got into bed it was still quite warm. There was always, however, a pleasing breeze. The stars seemed to be a deeper gold than anywhere else. August is a month for shooting stars, and in whatever direction we looked we could see the quick flash of some meteor falling silently across the heavens, and often the words of Juvayni would come to our minds. We would look for and identify the star Capella, which Maymun-Diz rivalled in height. The crickets droned their monotonous song and in the distance we could hear the music of a waterfall or the gentle tinkling of a stream. Thus we had the feeling of ineffable peace, that we were thousands of miles away from modern civilization, and here was a repository of the ancient wisdom of the East, the quietness and balm of an unhurried way of life. Walking at night was a delicious experience too. Gone were the heat and clamour of the day and the choking clouds of red dust. Whenever we could we walked long distances by night and hardly ever felt tired.

Our arrival at Zavarak in this instance was heralded by the barking of many dogs. Most of the villagers had gone to bed, but they came out to meet us and we were escorted to the best house in the village. Here, to our surprise, we were courteously greeted by a man of noble countenance who introduced himself as Mr Alamuti, the owner of the whole region. As it happened he had come on a visit from Teheran and was staying in the house of one of his cousins. He had heard about us and seemed genuinely glad to be able to give us hospitality. A meal was quickly prepared and set before us. He spoke a little French, but most of the conversation was carried on in Farsi with Minou acting as interpreter. Mr Alamuti was a very rich and highly educated man. He had met Professor Ivanow and had heard of Samuel Stern. At the same time he showed remarkable *naïveté*. For example, he asked us if we had found the tunnel that connected Maymun-Diz and Alamut, and when we told him that such a tunnel just did not exist, he merely shook his head and said that we had not looked hard enough.

Soon afterwards a rather short, stocky man came on to the veranda of the house and was introduced to us as Aziz. I thought I recognized him and that I had seen a picture of him somewhere, and then it suddenly dawned on me that this was the famous Aziz who had been Freya Stark's guide. I politely asked if this was so and he assured me that it was. Eagerly I asked him all sorts of questions about Freya Stark, and his replies proved the boundless admiration and affection in which this gallant English-woman is held by all the inhabitants of the valley. I asked if I could take a photograph of him the next day to send to Freya Stark, and he agreed at once and wrote a letter which I promised to send too.

We sat up until nearly 3 o'clock in the morning talking to Mr Alamuti about the site of Maymun-Diz. He admitted that he had not heard of the castle of Shams Kilaya before the 1959 expedition. He had not gone to look at it, but from what he had heard it seemed to be the most likely site. He believed that Nevisar Shah was the next most likely site, and, if it was not, then the castle of Shir Kuh. Finally, we all went to sleep on the veranda. Fine woollen blankets were brought out for us, and our shoes were taken away and washed. We had not met such gracious hospi-tality in the course of our long wanderings.

On the next day, after an affectionate farewell from Mr Alamuti, who begged us to visit him when we returned to Teheran, we set off towards Garmrud. The path became steeper, the valley narrower, and in front of us loomed the impressive range of mountains that closes the valley at the eastern end. At midday we reached Garmrud, one of the most attractive villages in the valley. The houses are built on the side of a hill. There are no streets through the village, and the only way up or down is over the flat roofs of houses. We were taken to the house of the headman, a most forceful character with black hair and fierce, burning eyes. On the wall of his main room were pictures of the rulers of the world in the year 1939, and it was strange to see portraits of Hitler, Mussolini, and George VI adorning this peasant house. He had five wives, which is more than the number permitted either by the Government or by the laws of Islam, and how he squared this with his conscience I do not know. He was a rich man, as we could see by the quality of the bedclothes and the rugs on the floor. Most Persian peasants put their savings into expensive rugs, and it is easy to judge a man's wealth and status at a glance when you enter his house. The headman had a visitors' book and we were curious to see how many names this contained. Most of them were local tax-collectors and recruiting officials, but we soon spotted the name of Professor Ivanow. The Professor had stayed with him when he was examining Nevisar Shah but, so the headman told us, he had found the final 100 yards too steep, and so, to his great disappointment, had to content himself with examining the castle through powerful binoculars. When we said we wished to go to Nevisar Shah, he at once undertook to arrange everything for us. He was sitting in the middle of his room, rather like Bluebeard, and now he clapped his hands and two of his wives appeared. He gave orders with a ferocious expression on his face, and in five minutes mules and guides appeared at the door. He said that Nevisar Shah was a day's journey, and that we must be prepared to spend two or three nights away. He then told us exactly what we must pay the muleteers, and asked us for his commission. This seemed rather exorbitant, but by now we were just as terrified of him as his wives and every one else in the village, and paid up with alacrity, feeling rather glad to see the back of him. The whole village turned out to watch us leave. We said we would be back in three days' time and were promised that we would then receive a royal reception befitting the first two Europeans to climb Nevisar Shah.

It was about 2 o'clock in the afternoon when we left Garmrud. First we climbed north-west up a steep hill called Karafan Khak, "the Hill of Heretics." When we inquired about the origin of this name we were told that two years before the villagers had discovered some Zoroastrian graves on the top of the hill. They had excavated one and found the usual collection of pottery and bronze swords. Although we had learnt in Ashkavar to distrust the numerous tales that we were told about Zoroastrians, there did seem to be more evidence that some Zoroastrians had lived in Alamut. The graves, of course, if they had ever existed, could not have been Zoroastrian, for Zoroastrian dead were not buried, but left on hill-tops to be consumed by wild beasts.

From Karafan Khak we then turned northward and skirted the lower slopes of a vast white-domed hill called Boar Kuh, or White Mountain. The path led steeply upward, and after a climb of four hours we were rewarded with our first glimpse of the castle of Nevisar Shah on the peak of the mountain. We could just see the top of the central tower standing starkly against the eastern sky. It seemed to be perched on the top of a mass of boulders and rocks rising precipitously from the centre of the hill.

Darkness was falling, so we decided to camp for the night on a small green plateau, which was like an oasis in the middle of the red and brown mountains. We unloaded the mules by a small, wooden hut in the middle of the plateau. This hut was used by shepherds from Garmrud when they brought cattle up to graze, and the ground floor had been used as a sort of stable. This room was small and dark, but there was a hearth in one corner, and our muleteers gathered wood for a fire.

The upper storey consisted of a single low room with one or two rather dirty cushions and bedclothes lying around. As soon as I entered the door I had an itchy feeling, which forewarned me of the presence of numerous fleas, so Minou and I decided that it would be better to set up our camp-beds on the roof. One of our guides had brought a gun with him and said he would go off and try to get something for supper. We waited for an hour, until it became quite dark, and then he came back ruefully shaking his head and saying that he had been unable to find anything. So there was nothing for it but to open the inevitable tins of luncheon meat and bully beef and to wash this down with tea. Close by there was a mountain pool, formed by water cascading down from a miniature waterfall. We had a shower, although the water was intensely cold and we could stay under it only a minute or so. We retired to bed early, instructing our guides to wake us up in good time the next morning so that we could climb the remaining 4000 feet before the sun got too high. In the middle of the night I was awakened by a scuffling sound. I grabbed a torch and shone it in the direction of the sound. There was a large jackal rootling for food amongst the empty food tins. I hurled a boot at it, and it let out a cry and darted off. Minou must have been having a nightmare, because at the sound he shot out of bed and shouted, "The guns, fetch the guns, we are being attacked." We laughed a good deal and settled down to sleep peacefully for the rest of the night.

At about half-past four we woke up shivering. There was a heavy dew, and most of our clothes were soaked through. Our guides soon made some tea, and we then sent two muleteers back to the village as their services would not be needed during the next few days. We intended to make the remainder of our climb rather slowly not only because the way was very steep and difficult, but in order that we could study closely the topography of the area surrounding the castle.

It soon became clear that an invading army could not have approached the castle from this side. The defenders would have been in an unassailable position. The path got steeper and steeper, and I admired Professor Ivanow's pluck in getting so far.

By midday we had covered only 2000 feet and were feeling tired and hot. I had blisters, and Minou was obviously unwell. He complained of feeling hot and cold and said he had a bad headache. There was no shade on this side of the mountain and so the only thing to do was to keep climbing. The water in our water-bottles was getting very low and we could see no signs of a spring. We were left with two guides now, and it was impossible for our mule to go any farther. One guide said that there was a spring at the top, or at least there was one in winter and he hoped that it did not dry up in the summer. It took us another three hours to get to the top, and by this time we were exhausted. There could be no question of descending that night, and so we looked round for the spring. Fortunately there was one, although only a trickle of water was coming out. However, our somewhat flagging spirits were revived by the magnificent panorama of the valley, visible after we had climbed the last hundred yards of almost sheer, gravel-covered rock. The sun was setting, and the whole scene was suffused with a deep orange glow that softened the outlines of the mountains. At the same time the atmosphere was sufficiently limpid and clear for us to be able to distinguish all the familiar landmarks that were now spread out beneath us. The river wound like a silver thread among the jagged rocks. Through our binoculars we could clearly make out the gaunt rock of Alamut and beyond it the flaming red sandstone of Maymun-Diz. In between we could just discern the outlines of the watch-towers that the Assassins had set up as part of their communications system between the castles, and then far in the distance, right at the other end of the valley, we saw the jagged spine of the Taliqan range sloping down to the gorge. Over to the south loomed the massive peak of the Elburz mountain, from which the whole range takes its name, with three big patches of snow on its northern slopes. We asked our guide about this and he said that the snow was always there, and that during the summer it became so rotten that it was infested with maggots. We did not argue over the accuracy of this statement, but let our eyes gaze wonderingly at this miraculous scene. I could not help feeling that here, indeed, was a castle that reached up to the star Capella. As we sat there, gazing at this timeless scene, shadows came racing up the valley and obscured all our landmarks. There was no sound. We allowed ourselves to be enveloped by the gathering darkness, which falls so quickly in this part of the world. The stars came out, and the whole sky seemed to twinkle with the light of myriads of candles. The Milky Way stretched over our heads, and now a cricket began to chirp. This mood of enchantment was broken by a loud sneeze from Minou. Our guide brought up our rucksacks and we put on thick pullovers and looked around for a place to sleep. Where better to spend the night than in the ruined tower? So we clambered back up the last few feet and settled down among the roofless ruins of what must have been the keep of Nevisar Shah. Our guide fetched wood, and soon we had a roaring fire going—probably the first fire that had burned in these ruins at night for over 700 years. The flames cast a flickering shadow on the wall, and now our guide began to talk about the deeds of the legendary hero Rustum and his fight with the Turks, and then he began to sing. He sang an old love-song, a ballad that lasted for about five minutes. He had a pleasant voice, and, although I do not usually like Oriental music, I was fascinated by the melody of this song. Minou translated the words in a whisper, and it seemed to be quite natural for him to be whispering. When our guide finished we asked him for other songs, and for half an hour he sang songs of the hills and valleys, songs of life and death, timeless folk-songs that have been handed down from one generation to another. I suppose that this night was the most unforgettable of those I spent in the valley. I wished it could go on for ever, and the thoughts of castles and the sweat of exploration seemed almost to vanish as though by magic, and in our minds we were taken back in time to Hasan's garden of paradise. We both drifted off to sleep sitting where we were and without bothering to go to bed, lulled by the songs of our guide.

The next morning brought harsh reality. The sun soon beat down mercilessly on us. We did not have enough food to stay up there for another night, and so we got down to work quickly. The castle of Nevisar Shah is built in the form of an incomplete semicircle. From where we were standing at the tower we could see the two arms of the rest of the castle stretching out to east and west and descending the steep slope of the mountain at an angle of 45°. To the north lay the white top of Boar Kuh and about 3 miles away to the north-east we could just see the Pass of Salambar—the route of so many invading armies. The peak on which we were standing was called Anarak-Dangar and a small col linked it to a twin peak to the north. To the west lay the goat-track up which we had come. On the east the ground fell away precipitously for about 2000 feet, and on the north, beyond the twin peak, there was an equally sheer drop. We first went to explore the twin peak, crossing the narrow col, and found there many traces of outer fortifications. We also came across some clay water-pipes, and it was evident that apart from the spring on the top of the mountain most of the water had been brought by a channel from the neighbouring peak. We followed its course and eventually found a natural spring. We then proceeded to explore the castle ruins. The tower where we had spent the night was only some 10 feet high, and connected to this were the remains of five or six rooms. Some of the walls were 6 feet thick and the original arrow-slits were still evident. As we surveyed the scene our impression was one of the complete inaccessibility of the castle and its tremendous height. Even now the question that was continually occupying my mind was whether this could be Maymun-Diz?

But it did not take long to appreciate from the lie of the ground that, despite its height and remoteness, which corresponded more closely to Juvayni's description of Maymun-Diz than the situation of the castle of Shams Kilaya, the rest of the topography did not fit his description.

First of all, there was no place where the Mongol armies could have camped. Secondly, there is no real circumference to the mountain, and it was quite impossible to measure it in terms of distance, let alone to try to estimate the 4 miles that Juvayni mentions. Thirdly, where could the Mongols have set up their mangonels of war? There was simply no place for them to do this. The twin peak joined to the mountain by the col would have been in the hands of the Assassins. If mangonels had been set up on the plateau, 5000 feet below, the castle would clearly have been out of range; and even if the mangonels could have been brought to bear, where would the Mongols have found the trees in order to construct them? The slopes of the mountain are completely bare, apart from a few stunted thorn-bushes. Juvayni says clearly that the Mongols constructed their mangonels from trees at the foot of Maymun-Diz. The trees nearest to Nevisar Shah are in the village of Garmrud, and it would have been a superhuman task for these trees to have been brought to the top of the mountain. Fourthly, Juvayni mentions that Maymun-Diz had a crater-like mouth on the top, but Nevisar Shah is a sugarloaf hill. Fifthly, there was no trace of any spring inside the castle itself. Sixthly, Juvayni says that the ramparts of Maymun-Diz were built of plaster and gravel, and here there was not the slightest trace of either. The castle was built of dressed stone quarried at Boar Kuh and cemented together with limestone cement of quite high quality. Lastly, we know that the siege of Maymun-Diz took place at the end of November. As the reader will remember, Rukn-ad-Din had hoped that he would be saved from destruction by the winter, but that in the year 1256 the weather was unusually mild. There is no possibility of mild November weather on top of this peak! We were told that snow falls at the end of October or the beginning of November, and this was confirmed later in Garmrud, where the headman said that he had never known Anarak-Dangar to be without its mantle of snow during November.

All this seemed to be clear proof that Nevisar Shah could not be Maymun-Diz. In a way I was glad, because this vindicated our original choice of Shams Kilaya, and to have been forced to repudiate it at this stage would have been embarrassing to say the least. On the other hand I was sorry, because in a sentimental way I had become far more attached to Nevisar Shah than Shams Kilaya. However, sentiment cannot be permitted to play a part in these matters, and we were looking for scientific, geographical proof.

The rest of the day was spent scrambling round the ruins on the castle-site, and on closer inspection it proved to be far more extensive that we had first imagined. The most impressive part was the western side. Here, as on Alamut, every possible piece of ground had been built on, and some of the remains stretched right down the mountainside. There must have been a large community here, and although it is very difficult to estimate the population of a castle with its accompanying dwelling-places, there seemed to be room for 1500 to 2000 people. This is a very large number, more than could have lived on Alamut or Maymun-Diz. It is a pity that so little is known about the history of Nevisar Shah. Juvayni hardly mentions it at all, and of course one cannot possibly rely on the accounts of the villagers. We found a lot of pottery there, both glazed and plain. We looked carefully for water-cisterns, but failed to see any, although such a large garrison must have had other sources of water apart from the spring by the keep and the water-pipes. The western side of the castle-site stretches for about 800 yards, and at the end there are the remains of a large building with three arches perched right on the edge of a big drop. It was so extensive that it could have been a banqueting-room. The walls were solidly built and covered with smooth plaster. From here we climbed up the eastern side of the castle-site and saw the foundations of rooms that had been built on to the thick external wall and formed a series of five or six terraces.

Looking over the top we could see an eagle's nest some distance below, and the eagles were circling around, as though keeping guard over some hidden mystery.

By now it was about 5 o'clock in the evening and so we decided to descend to the plateau where we had slept two nights before. The return journey was even worse than our climb up. Our guide told us that he would take us down by an easy route, but his easy route turned out to be a matter of scrambling down slippery, jagged rocks. There was no path at all, and our guide insisted on going quickly. Quite often he would be out of sight, and Minou and I had to find our way down as best we could. The worst thing about the Elburz mountains is not so much the steepness of the rocks, but the fact that everything is covered with a fine film of gravel and shingle, so that you are in constant danger of slipping. If you do slip you will either slide down quite a long way or else you will land in a thorn-bush. By the time we arrived at the plateau we were covered with scratches and cuts, and in a very bad temper. Our guide was repentant and realized that he had let us down, so he did his best to make us comfortable for the night and cooked a wonderful omelette for us. Where the eggs came from I still do not know. The herbs he picked on the mountainside gave a delicious seasoning to our meal.

Early the next morning we set out for Garmrud. Reports of what we had been doing had already filtered down to the village, and when we arrived at the outskirts of the village we were met by the headman. He welcomed us back in solemn and relieved tones, and admitted that he had been rather anxious about us because he had not really briefed us on the difficulties of the climb. By this time our bad tempers had worn off, and we were feeling rather pleased with ourselves. We were invited in for a meal, and while Minou chatted with the headman about the local elections I sat back comfortably on a great pile of cushions and wrote feverishly in my notebook before I forgot everything. I then dozed off to sleep, and woke to find the whole room filled with curious villagers who were staring at me.

It was too late to push on that day: the wisest course was to stay the night in hospitable Garmrud. Minou was having the time of his life. It seemed that nowhere had he been listened to with such respect as here, and again I went to sleep with the sound of his voice echoing through the darkness.

Our next objective was the castle of Ilan. Freya Stark had visited the village but had not, it seems, explored the castle. It lies some way off the main valley and to reach it we had to descend once more through Zavarak, where we stopped for lunch, and then walk on to Koch-i-Dasht. We got there at 4 o'clock and had tea with the landlord. He was another member of the educated Persian class who spend most of the year in Teheran and then come up to the villages for summer. He knew Mr Alamuti well and we had met him on our first visit to Zavarak. His wife was present, dressed in Western-style clothes, but she was not completely at her ease, and, after talking for a while in the garden, she got up and said that she had some things to attend to. I caught a glimpse of her from time to time, peering at us from the house, and wondered how long it took Persian women who adopt the Western style of dress and manners to throw off all the remnants of their old way of life. I imagine that in cosmopolitan Teheran she would probably have sat with us the whole time, although on reflection I cannot remember ever having met Mr Alamuti's wife or any of the female members of his household. The Empress Farah sets a good example, encouraged by her husband. An educated Persian gentleman, with whom I discussed this question at some length, said that he had noticed that the wives of highly placed Persian officials, even, for example, the wives of ambassadors, always felt their position a trifle embarrassing in Teheran. It was as though people had to force themselves to live according to Western ideas, so that when a Persian couple go back to a

C.A.–Q

place like the Alamut valley in the depths of the country, even on a holiday, they easily and naturally return to a way of living dictated by thousand-year-old customs.

When I was in Iran in 1961 with the Stobart-Izzard expedition, the survival of the customary attitude towards women was amply demonstrated. An English girl, Jean, had asked if she might join us in the valley for two or three days before she set off on the long journey over the hills to the Caspian. At that time she was an undergraduate at Oxford, and when one day I went off to examine a mosque that might have contained the tomb of Hasan-i-Sabbah, she asked if she could accompany me and our Swiss interpreter. Of course we said that we should be delighted, and when we reached our destination we met Mr Alamuti and were entertained to lunch in the house in which he was staying. I was curious to see who would get served first. Normally it would be myself as the chief guest, then Mr Alamuti, then any other guests, and finally the family of our host; but would Jean now be given pride of place? She was not, rather to her dismay. I was served first, and politely passed my plate to Jean. This produced quite a sensation, and I regretted that I had done so because Mr Alamuti must have felt that I was gently reminding him of his manners. When the next course came along Jean was naturally offered the first plate. After that it was really a question of whether Mr Alamuti remembered or not, and we were all rather thankful when the meal came to an end. Western manners can sometimes be a little bit of an embarrassment and a handicap in these circumstances. When we all rose to leave the house there was another problem—who would go through the door first? Normally the host leads the way, and on this occasion Mr Alamuti started towards the door. He then remembered that Jean was following him, and so we had the ridiculous comic-opera situation of both waiting in the doorway and eventually colliding together. Although Mr Alamuti invariably kisses me when we meet—a custom, I must confess, which I find embarrassing and, when both parties have five or six days' stubble on their chins, slightly painful—he did not offer to shake hands with Jean. When we finally took our leave she offered her hand to Mr Alamuti in the usual English fashion, but Mr Alamuti pretended not to see it and turned round to see whether his horse was ready. Clearly he is prepared to conform to Western customs only to a certain extent.

It was pleasant in the garden at Koch-i-Dasht, but our host eventually remarked that if we intended to get to Ilan that night it was time to start moving. He warned us that it was a stiff climb, but by this time we were thoroughly in training and thought any ascent of less than 2000 feet a mere walk. We were given a guide and off we set.

It took us about four hours to reach Ilan, and our route lay through some of the wildest and most rugged scenery in the whole of the valley. It reminded us of the gorge at Shir Kuh, except that it was far steeper and much longer. After we had climbed up to the usual plateau covered with fruit-trees, we entered a narrow gully, which became narrower and steeper. On each side piles of jagged rocks lay, just as if an earthquake had thrown them up in one gigantic upheaval. It was like entering a fairy-tale country inhabited by wicked robbers, and to our surprise we saw in the rocks great gaping holes that were obviously the mouths of caves. We asked what animals lived there and were told that tigers had been seen, and bears and wolves often came down in the winter to prey upon the villagers' flocks of sheep and goats. In fact, during the winter Ilan is completely cut off, and the children do not dare to go down to any of the lower villages for fear of being devoured by wild beasts. We were also told that this was outlaw country, and that men from villages lower down in the valley and the Shah Rud who had committed crimes often took to these hills rather than face imprisonment, and they did, in fact, live as bandits and outlaws. We rather hoped that not too many had taken refuge in Ilan.

Eventually we rounded a bluff and saw before us the first houses of Ilan. By this time I was expecting a rather primitive village, but was amazed to find a most pleasant and well-laid-out community nestling under one of the big peaks of the Hawdeqan range. At the head of the village there was a great waterfall, and here children were bathing and splashing and calling cheerfully to one another. Our guide, who was called Cand Ali, meaning Sweet Ali, took us to the headman's house. This headman was the complete opposite of his counterpart, Bluebeard, at Garmrud. He was a dignified old man and lived quietly with his wife and family. They had just built a new house and it looked very clean and spruce. Tea was served, and we sat on the balcony watching the sun set.

Shortly afterwards a man came along asking to see Minou. His hand was fearfully swollen and was covered with mud and congealed blood. We asked what had happened and were told that he had cut his finger on a broken bottle and that in order to stem the bleeding he had coated his hand with a thick layer of mud. Naturally we were scandalized by this and I wondered why the man had not already died of tetanus. Minou at once asked for some water to be boiled and proceeded to examine the man's hand. It was a nasty cut, very deep, and already showed signs of infection. He could not flex his fingers, and it looked as though some of the nerves and muscles might have been damaged. Minou set up surgery and asked me to help perform a minor operation on the hand. This was the first time I had had the opportunity of watching him at work at close quarters, and I admired the dexterity and skill with which he worked. The operating-theatre was the living-room of the headman's house. Minou decided to give the patient a general anaesthetic, and I was instructed in the technique of administering this. All the time I was terrified that I would give the poor man too much and that he would never wake up again. A pad was placed over the patient's mouth and nose, and on this I had to pour drops of ether. However, Minou seemed to approve of what I was doing, and he set to work. Having got my patient safely to sleep, I began to worry in case he should wake up in the middle of the operation, and this would have been even worse. The rest of the village formed a dark circle outside the room. The headman held a pressure lamp high so that Minou could see what he was doing, and there were two steaming pots of water near by in which Minou had sterilized his instruments. After about twenty-five minutes he said that he had done as much as he could, that there was no further danger of infection, and that the man would probably be able to regain some use of his fingers. I then helped Minou bandage the hand and put on plaster. By this time the patient, to my intense relief, was showing signs of regaining consciousness, and a few minutes afterwards he woke up. My own impression of people recovering from anaesthetics had always been that they were either liable to be violently sick—so I kept a respectful distance away from him—or else they wanted to go to sleep again immediately, but our patient was a far tougher character. He woke up fighting and proceeded to strike out to right and left. Eventually the headman managed to calm him down and he was taken off by his family.

After we had cleared up the operating-theatre we were offered tea. Minou was, of course, the centre of attraction, but as his anaesthetist I felt that I was entitled to share a little of his glory.

"Not at all bad for a first attempt," he told me, and I expressed the hope that this would be the last time that I should ever be called on to act in a medical capacity.

A meal was produced, supplemented by a chicken sent by the patient's family. It was boiled in a delicious sauce. By now I had given up any good resolutions I had ever formed about being careful over the food that I ate. So far this policy had not proved too disastrous, and I hoped that this would continue. After three or four weeks in the valleys we seemed to acquire some kind of immunity. The first week was the most dangerous time, and when we had survived this we were able to eat more or less what we liked, exercising reasonable caution and always remembering that the greatest source of infection was likely to be water. We never relaxed our precautions over water and I am sure this saved us from contracting any serious illness.

We retired to bed at about midnight, feeling very replete and rather self-satisfied. The headman had promised to wake us up early in the morning and to provide another guide to take us to the castle. But at about 3 o'clock in the morning I was woken by the sound of Minou groaning next to me. I asked him what was wrong and he said that he felt dreadful. He was sweating profusely, his headache of two or three days ago had returned with renewed force, and he ached all over. I asked if there was anything that I could get him, but he replied that he preferred to stick things out and see how he was in the morning. By the time morning came he was no better and I took his temperature. It was 103·5° and I asked him to prescribe for himself. He said that he must have some form of local infection and his stomach was very hard and distended. When I heard this I had visions of myself performing an operation for appendicitis under the patient's directions, but he went on to say that an injection of streptomycin would probably help. I had never given an injection before, but I was now to learn. The needle was a little blunt and Minou squealed as it went in. I sat with him for two or three hours and his temperature began to drop. By evening it was almost normal again, and I repeated the injection on his instructions. He decided that he must have had one of those fevers that are common in this part of the world, and which hit like a sledgehammer, last for about twenty-four hours, and then go away very rapidly, leaving the patient weak and depressed. The next night was a better one for Minou and he slept peacefully. On the following day he seemed better still, so I felt justified in leaving him at the headman's house and going to explore the castle. I had almost forgotten the date, and when I asked Minou what it was, he said he had forgotten too, but we thought that it was approximately September 7 or 8. It is amazing how quickly one loses all count of time in these conditions. One day is exactly the same as another. Some expeditions make a point of celebrating on a Sunday night with a can of beer or fruit salad or something else special to eat. This can be done at a base-camp but is clearly quite impossible when moving about the country.

I approached the castle from the north, walking down through the village, crossing to the other side of the gully, and climbing about 500 feet until I reached a spur. At first I could see absolutely nothing at all, and the way was barred by two big rocks with a very narrow crack in between. I thought we were going to go through this crack, but my guides told me that I would have to crawl round the edge of the rocks and the castle lay on the other side. This was a very tricky manoeuvre as the rocks were jutting out almost over the valley, and there was hardly any room to crawl along. Having successfully reached the other side, I then saw a promontory sloping away from me at an angle of 65°. It was 600 yards long, and on the eastern side the ground fell away steeply, rising again half a mile away to another rather narrow plateau. My guide pointed to the plateau and said, "Bazaar." To begin with I could not make out what he was talking about, but when we returned to the village he told Minou that the villagers believed that in earlier times a small town had existed on this plateau, hence the word 'bazaar,' and that often shards of pottery and other objects were dug up under the plough. There could possibly have been a town there, but it seemed rather a long way from the castle, and it would also have been difficult to cross the gully quickly in order to get to the castle in times of difficulty.

Ilan has been mostly destroyed and I was told that the little remaining brickwork had been removed four or five years before when the village decided to build a new

Turkish bath. I don't think that it ever had been a particularly large castle, but it must have been an important intermediate fort forming one of the links in the chain of castles which stretched all the way down the valley. The most interesting part of the ruins was what was left of the water-system. At the top of the promontory on which I was standing there were two water-cisterns, 12 feet long and 4 feet wide, cut deep into the rock. The first was very deep, how deep I could not tell. The second had a depth of some 12 feet, and there was still some water in it. Looking around I estimated that we were at about the same level as the top of the rock of Alamut. I could clearly see the watch-tower at Koch-i-Dasht and, farther over to the south, the castle of Shir Kuh. Although Alamut and Nevisar Shah were invisible, this castle commanded a very good view of the central part of the valley, but its effectiveness in defence was limited. I imagine that it probably held reserve forces as well as guarding the back route from Nevisar Shah to Lammassar. There were a large number of fragments of pottery on the ground, but none of them big. Most were glazed—the usual yellow, green, and brown. I walked down the promontory, which was built in the form of terraces. The rock here was solid conglomerate with harder intrusions.

On the west side there were foundations of rooms, and I measured what remained of the outer wall, which was 30 feet long and 5 feet thick. It was built of gravel and plaster, but I could see no evidence of stone-facing as at Maymun-Diz. I asked if there was a quarry near by and was told there was none. At the southern end of the promontory there was further evidence of rooms and possibly a well. Right at the edge there was another very deep water-cistern, which was some 20 feet by 4 feet, and I estimated its depth to be 20 feet. Some of the remaining plaster-work looked rather older than Assassin work and I concluded that this castle has a long history dating back well before the Middle Ages. It could easily have been the stronghold of some robber baron or petty lord. When he shut himself up in this fortress, it must have been almost impregnable.

I returned by the eastern side. Much of what had remained of the walls had been quarried by the villagers, and there were many signs of recent digging. I asked if any treasure had been found or any weapons, and was told that only one or two rings had been recovered from the earth. I saw one, the design of which was much later than the Assassin period—somewhere between 1650 and 1750. Looking over the edge I could see some brickwork, which the villagers said were the remains of sentry-boxes. I rather doubted this, and managed to scramble down to have a look at one. It was a piece of wall built across a narrow chimney in the rock leading up to the castle. Between the bottom of the wall and the rock there was a gap of some 2 feet. This could possibly have been used as a means of exit from the castle under cover of darkness, but I think it much more likely to have been a defensive wall to prevent attackers using this method of getting into the castle unseen. It could be observed from the top and anyone rash enough to try and clamber under the wall could have been dispatched with the greatest ease by rolling a few large boulders down the chimney, which formed an ideal chute.

If I had had more time I should have liked to explore Ilan to a greater extent. Its water-system is not as fine as that of Alamut or the castle of Shir Kuh, but it would have been interesting to have attempted to determine the earliest date at which it could have been built, and to have excavated along the foundations on the western wall. Apart, perhaps, from Freya Stark, I think I was the first European to visit it. Alamut has been a hunting-ground of treasure-seekers for many centuries, but few people have bothered to search amongst the ruins of Ilan. I was pleased to have discovered that the back route of the valley was guarded in this way. The normal supply-route for the

Assassins was along the banks of the Alamut Rud, but
during times of siege this would have been impossible.
No one has attempted to say what other means of communication there were in the valley, and I had always
thought that the most obvious route lay along the
mountainside, and here it was, guarded by a series of
forts as I had expected. I spent most of the day taking
photographs and measurements, and I brought back some
samples of the matrices of the rock for later analysis. I did
not find any bones, nor did I really expect to, as there were
no buildings in which they could have lain undiscovered
and anything above ground had clearly been removed a
long time ago.

On my return from the castle I found that Minou was
much better, but he said that he still felt a bit weak and
wanted to spend one more day in the village before going
down to the mouth of the valley. I was due to meet Richard
at Shahrak on the following day, and as I was anxious to
find out how things had been going at Alamut I asked
Minou if he would mind if I went on alone. He said he
would not, and would follow me in twenty-four hours' time
by mule.

I got up early on the following day and, taking one mule
to carry my kit, set off down the gully in the direction of
the main valley. It was about seven hours' walk to Shahrak
and this would be quite a comfortable day's journey. I was
feeling very cheerful as I left, and enjoyed my walk down
very much. This was the first time I had been alone since
I had arrived in Iran and, although I had enjoyed Minou's
company, I was quite glad to have a chance of reviewing
the expedition, which, for me, was now nearing its end.
Soon, however, I stopped thinking of archaeological investigations and just let my eyes wander over the sheer
beauty of the valley. It was a lovely September morning,
still quite nippy, and there were wisps of cloud hanging
over Solomon's Throne. It looked as though it might even
rain a little later in the day. I did not know when I should

be returning to Alamut—in fact I was to pass this way again only twelve months later, but at that time I had no idea of this—and so wanted to impress on my mind the colours, the forms, and the shapes of the scenery so that I should not forget them.

A little shepherd boy joined me as I descended the steep slope towards Koch-i-Dasht, and he tried to make conversation. We did not get very far, but he insisted on skipping along beside me, every now and then giving me a friendly smile, his white teeth glistening and his dark eyes sparkling. When we got to Koch-i-Dasht he took me by the hand and insisted on leading me to his home. This was rather a poor house and the main room was shared by his family and their goats. I did not like the look of it very much but felt that politeness demanded that I should eat some grapes and have some *mast*. Lots of people say that *mast* is extremely good for upset stomachs. But in our view this is untrue, and on this particular occasion its effects on me were quite disastrous. Two hours later, as I was walking down the broad main river valley once more, I suddenly felt very ill. My mule and muleteer were out of sight round the corner and I had to stop. I sat there for about an hour, feeling just as Minou had two days before. I knew I had quite a high temperature and I crawled into the shade. My head felt heavy and I dozed off to sleep. When I woke up it was night, but I suddenly felt much better. I walked down to the river, splashed some water over my face and hands, and then started to walk slowly on in the direction of Shahrak. I wondered what had become of my muleteer and, even more, of my kit, and whether Richard was worrying about what had happened to me. I reached Shahrak at 3 o'clock in the morning. The barking of the watchdogs wakened some of the inhabitants, and I was directed to the house of the headman. There I found my muleteer fast asleep and completely unconcerned about what had happened to me. As far as he cared I could have been attacked by highway robbers and left for dead.

Richard had not yet arrived, and so I got out my camp-bed
and slept on the balcony until fairly late the following
morning. When I woke I found most of the village
collected in a half-circle round my bed. By now I was
feeling quite recovered, and my only embarrassment was
getting out of bed, as owing to the hot night I was wearing
very little. The villagers showed no sign of going, and so
the only thing to do was to get out of bed and start
dressing. I had breakfast and asked if there was any news
or sign of Richard. He still had not arrived I was told, and
so I decided to go and examine the castle at Shahrak while
waiting for him. This castle belongs to a far earlier period
than the Assassins and has very little association at all with
them.

Shahrak was probably the capital of the Daylamite
kingdom before the arrival of Hasan-i-Sabbah, and at one
time was supposed to have been a very rich and prosperous
township. It is built on an S-bend of the river and is a very
fertile spot. The castle stands on a mound no more than
50 feet high above the banks of the river, and it is really
rather refreshing to know that there is at least one castle in
the valley that can be entered with hardly any physical
exertion at all. I wandered down to the river, had a bathe,
and then walked up the mound to the castle. It is hardly
fortified, and it would probably be more exact to call it a
palace than a castle.

The length of the mound is 450 feet, and at its widest
part it is 60 feet. The western end still has the quite
well-preserved remains of a big rectangular room, 20 feet
wide by 35 feet long. Its four walls still stand, and there
are big holes in them at irregular intervals. The lower part,
6½ feet high, is made of rough stone, quite undressed, stuck
together by some form of crude cement, which has survived
the wear of the centuries extremely well. The upper part
of the wall consists of 4 feet of loose stones stuck together
with mud, and this part looks as though it has been
restored, perhaps a hundred or so years ago, when the

building might have been used to house some of the local inhabitants or their cattle. The western end of this hall is raised, and there are some foundations there suggesting that originally there were four small rooms with their dividing walls. At the eastern end of the castle-site, the buildings have been almost completely destroyed, but the foundations of some thirty rooms are still clearly visible. What fortifications there are stand on the southern or river side, and it looks as though an outer wall once ran almost to the edge of the river. I could not see any signs of water-cisterns, but perhaps these had been scarcely necessary. Even in summer there is quite a good volume of water flowing down the Alamut Rud, and so the inhabitants could never have been short. On the northern side there is a large rectangular hole, which could have been the remains of a well. I scratched around inside the hole and pulled out some well-baked bricks. I left these by the side of the well while I continued my investigations, but when I came back I found they had gone. I looked to see if there were any fortifications similar to those on the opposite side of the valley, but there were none. It is strange that most of the Assassin castles and forts are to the north of the river—the notable exception being the fortress of Shir Kuh. It would be interesting to explore the slopes of the Taliqan range. I very much doubt if there are any castles comparable to Maymun-Diz or Alamut, but it is likely that there are watch-towers and perhaps small fortresses similar to the one at Ilan.

12

Shir Kuh and back to Teheran

WHEN I had finished examining the castle at Shahrak there was still no sign of Richard, and so I walked along the floor of the valley towards the village of Gazur Khan to meet him. It was a pleasant walk along the river-bed. By now I was quite a familiar figure in the valley, and people would wave cheerily at me as I passed, shouting the traditional greeting, *"Salaam-e-lekum."* One man even offered to give me a lift on his mule, but I much preferred walking. Eventually, rounding a bend in the river, I saw Richard coming from the opposite direction. It seemed ages since we had parted. His beard had grown longer, and he seemed much thinner. We sat down by the river and I eagerly asked about what had been happening at Alamut. Then we walked back to Shahrak and I showed Richard round the castle. We decided to press on to Shir Kuh, leaving a message for Minou with the headman of Shahrak asking him to join us there.

After eating some grapes and melon, we pushed on through the village of Badasht and stopped at a small tea-house which we visited in 1959. The owner was a thin, gaunt man of about fifty, and we were surprised to see that he had recently made extensive alterations to his premises. The tea-house consisted of a low, rather squalid room built of wattle and branches. In one corner there was a smoky hearth where he made tea, and this was served in unwashed glasses. In 1959 it had cost us a rial (about a penny) a glass, but now he was clearly trying to cover the cost of his repairs, as the price had gone up to three rials, and we also had to pay for the sugar we used. But he was a friendly enough man, and he invited us to stay at his tea-house for the night. The house was a bit too dirty, so we set up our camp-beds on a flat piece of ground near the river-bed, and cooked our supper on solid-fuel cookers inside the tea-house. Our host had never seen these before, and was very pleased when we gave him a small quantity of tablets. We went to bed early, and then were awakened by the sound of mules. There seemed quite a lot of them and, as we watched from our beds, we suddenly realized that it was Minou riding at the head of a convoy. He looked quite impressive, and was obviously treated with great respect by the muleteers. The mule-team had come from Ilan and was going to Kazwin, so he had joined it and spent a leisurely day riding down. He had completely recovered and joined us for the rest of the night.

In the morning there was a great deal of discussion about our best approach to the castle of Shir Kuh. We had been the first people to investigate it when we had visited it in 1959, and on that occasion we had approached it from the Taliqan side. This had been a very steep climb, and we hoped to find an easier route from the Alamut side. Now that Minou had rejoined us, we were able to make some inquiries, and were told that the best way of approach was from the gorge. The owner of the tea-house, after he had given us breakfast, suggested that we should go to Gureh-Dar, a village at the extreme end of the valley, where we could get a guide, and this seemed a sensible idea. Minou's team of muleteers, who had also stopped the night at the tea-house, volunteered to carry all our equipment free to the end of the valley.

Gureh Dar is an interesting village. Besides holding the distinction of being the dirtiest village in the whole of the valley it is the home of the Meragis, who have curious religious beliefs, akin to those of their Zoroastrian ancestors. They are a small community, very much a state within a state, and keep to themselves. We found them rather reserved, and at the beginning less helpful than the other villagers. I think they were probably suspicious of our intentions, and we gathered that they believed they were subject to a certain amount of persecution by the Government and by the other inhabitants of the valley. We tried to find out as much as we could about their religious beliefs, but they were clam-like and refused to give away any of their secrets.

We set up camp on the roof of one of their houses, and, after a lot of discussion, we hired a guide. He was a taciturn fellow and would never speak unless it was absolutely necessary. He told us that he knew an easy way up to the castle, but, as we feared, this proved to be merely wishful thinking. Although the climb was relatively short, it was very stiff. By now we were in extremely good training and the muscles in our legs were like steel springs, but we found this climb almost as exhausting as any we had done.

The castle of Shir Kuh has three or four different names, and it is sometimes confusing when one reads the accounts of the few other travellers who have passed through this area, and have mentioned the castle without actually visiting it. Besides being known as Shir Kuh, it is also referred to as the castle of Badasht (as it stands on the opposite bank of the river to the village of this name), Bidelan, and Gureh Dar. There is another reason for confusion. Near the castle there are two forts at the extreme entrance to the valley, and these are sometimes mistaken for the main castle. Our chief purpose was to prove that the site of Shir Kuh could not be Maymun-Diz. As the reader will remember, the two alternative sites that are continually being advanced are Nevisar Shah, and Shir Kuh. Shir Kuh had always seemed to us less likely than Nevisar Shah, but Mr Alamuti had told us that it was a possibility.

This castle lies on the spine of the Taliqan range, and overlooks the valleys of Alamut and Taliqan, to the north and south. As we ascended the northern slope, we came across its water-system. Some 200 yards from the top of the hill where the castle is situated there is a catchment-area which is second only to Alamut in size and complexity. There are, altogether, eight water-cisterns, at intervals of 15 feet from each other and running diagonally down the slope of the hill. Like those of Alamut, they are cut into the rock, and their length varies between 20 and 50 feet. They are all about 5 feet wide, and with a depth of up to 20 feet. They are connected together by jubes, and these jubes act as an overflow-channel when the top cisterns are full. The cisterns are unlined, and in some of them we found stagnant water. The slope of the ground is about 50° to 60° at this point, and so it is quite difficult to climb up. The water-cisterns seem to lie outside the main defensive wall, which we thought rather odd. On the other hand, the natural slope of the rock would have made it difficult for anybody to approach the castle from this side, and the water-cisterns would have been in full view of the main castle garrison. At the highest level, across the top cistern, run the foundations of the outer wall. This is about 300 feet long. On the western side there is a well-preserved corner tower, and the wall runs north along the side of a deep gully. There are still the remains of battlements here, and there is an exceptionally fine archway in the centre of the wall. Just by the archway we were shown an 'oven,' which our guide told us was used for baking bread. It is built into the rock and is lined with stones and mud bricks. It is semicircular in shape, and is 4 feet high and 2 feet in

C.A.–R

diameter. It was around there that we found the greatest
number of shards of pottery, some of them much bigger
than we had found anywhere else.

At the top of the castle there is a keep, and near it
are two large boulders, which the Assassins used as
watch-towers. The core had been hollowed out and the
rest built up with brick and stone. From here there is a
superb view down both valleys and over the Chala Pass.
The rock itself is about 5500 feet high, and we estimated
the base to be 1850 feet above the floor of the valley. The
castle extends down the northern slope for 75 feet, and the
remnants of the curtain-wall still cling to some of the
rocks. It was obvious from the very start that this is no
possible contender for the site of Maymun-Diz. The height,
when compared with any of the other castles of the valley,
is not very great; there is no central tower; the remains
indicate that it was not large enough to have housed a
substantial garrison; and the topography does not match
Juvayni's description. It was an important castle of the
second rank, and must have been intended as a first defence
against an enemy entering the valley. I imagine, too, that
it probably saw more action than the other castles. Anyone
rash enough to descend the hills from the Chala Pass, or to
attempt to come along the floor of the Taliqan valley,
would have come under fire from the bows and mangonels
of Shir Kuh. They could certainly not have passed un-
noticed, and Shir Kuh was especially well situated to signal
information of this kind to Alamut and Maymun-Diz,
whence it could have been relayed to Ilan and Nevisar
Shah.

Shir Kuh would have been in even closer contact with
the two forts that guarded the very entrance to the gorge.
These go by the names of Borj and Borjak, which reminded
us of two giants in a fairy tale. The fort of Borjak is the
smaller, and is situated on the northern side of the gorge,
400 feet up the rock, that is, about two-thirds of the way up
from the base. The entrance must have been from the top,

as we could see no way up from the foot. We studied the
ruins through binoculars, and found these were very few,
so it did not seem worth risking a broken leg by climbing
down from the top to examine them more closely. We
could see foundations of a tower made of the usual brick
and stone. It was about 15 feet high, and on a corner of the
wall there were the remains of a dome. We could see
curious slits at the foot of the tower. These, we assumed,
were used either for pouring down burning oil, or,
possibly, for dropping a cascade of rocks and boulders on
anybody coming through the gorge.

The fort of Borj, which we visited, was on the south side
of the gorge, some two miles west of the castle of Shir Kuh.
Obviously it had been manned by an outpost from the main
castle, although the garrison must have had a tricky time
getting to it along the top of the Taliqan range. It was
situated on a saddle of overhanging rock some 20 yards
square immediately opposite the village of Gureh Dar, and
overlooked the Taliqan valley as well as the gorge. We
could see no definite signs of walls or fortifications, but
there was a small amount of plaster lying on the ground
and some brown and yellow pottery. There were also some
brown bricks that the villagers found too large to take
away. This must have been the "castle" Freya Stark
mentioned seeing when her guide first took her through
the entrance to the gorge. She assumed that it was the
main one, but we discovered that, in fact, two forts and
one fairly large castle had guarded the entrance. In winter
it would have been impossible to enter the valley this
way, and the Mongol armies did not attempt to do so.

To add to the difficulties, most of the gorge is filled by
the foaming torrents of the Alamut Rud. Richard once had
to wade through it late in September and found that he
could only just make his way across. In winter it would be
even deeper. Those who did not know the dangerous
currents would run the risk of being drowned, even if they
escaped the formidable cross-fire in the form of arrows,

rocks, and boulders that the Assassins would have sent down on them.

After we had investigated these two forts, we decided, as this was my last day, to return early and bathe in the river before the sun went down. We had our bathe at about 5 o'clock and then lay on the sun-baked rocks. Then we returned to the village and ordered a chicken apiece to celebrate. The chickens that were brought were scraggy, so we promptly ordered three more. We cooked them over an open fire, and although they were not very tasty, we enjoyed our first roast chicken for over a month. We were in bed before the sun set and watched the shadows covering one well-known peak after another. It was a sad thought that this was my last night in the valley, and we stayed awake for a long time chatting over all we had done, as well as our future plans.

The party from Alamut was not due to arrive at Shir Kuh for another two days, and so Richard, Minou, and I decided to return to Teheran. I could then take a proper farewell of all our acquaintances there and Richard could get fresh supplies of food and essential stores. Minou would have to come with us as our interpreter, and he seemed to be looking forward to seeing the bright lights of the capital once more.

I left a note with the headman for the remainder of the party, thanking them for their work, and anticipating our reunion in England. The note was addressed to Roddie and I had a special word of farewell and thanks for Jah. I outlined the remainder of the programme as I saw it, although the leadership of the expedition in the field now devolved upon Richard and he would have the final say. While we were in Teheran they were to make an extensive study of Shir Kuh with particular reference to the water-system. This, I estimated, would take them about three days. I asked Ragnar to photograph the two forts at the entrance to the gorge and to see if he could film the village of Gureh-Dar. The party would then move to Lammassar.

I was sorry that I should miss this part of the expedition, but as I had spent about a week there in 1959 I knew that it was unlikely that anything more of real importance would be discovered. However, there was no accurate ground-plan of the castle or map of its topography, and if we were to complete our survey of all the castles in the valley Lammassar could not be omitted. I estimated that the work at Lammassar would take five to seven days.

They would then return to Teheran for a refit before setting out on the last stage of the expedition, which was to return to Samiran to complete the map-making and then to strike eastward into the mountains of Daylaman. Daylaman adjoins the valley of Ashkavar, and we felt it would be worth excavating there to see if the riches of Ashkavar had been shared by Daylaman. We were optimistic about this as people we had met at all stages of our travels had told us that Ashkavar was merely a fringe area, and that the most rewarding place for excavation was Daylaman. We also hoped to find further traces of the Assassins, and, by following the course of the Chaka Rud, to complete our investigations of the route that Hasan-i-Sabbah had taken to Alamut. We were not sure at this stage if Minou would be able to spare the three or four weeks necessary to complete the last part of the programme. We were not sure if Jah would either, and so one of our jobs when we reached Teheran would be to find an alternative interpreter. Roddie would just have time before the period expired for which he was seconded by Military Survey. Richard, Mike, and Ragnar were not due back in England till December, and so for them time was not so pressing. They were due to bring back all the equipment in the Land Rover and were also charged with stopping in Greece on the return journey to start editing part of the film. Ragnar had a friend in Athens who could offer him the necessary facilities in his studio.

As usual, we awoke early the next morning, and I knew

that there was a gruelling climb in front of us over the
Chala Pass. We had heard that Mr Alamuti had started
constructing a new motor road, which was to open up the
valley, and that it had been completed as far as the Pass
itself. Although we should not be spared the steep climb
up, at least we should escape the long tedious descent the
other side if we were fortunate enough to catch the so-
called bus, which left the village of Hasanabad every day at
6 o'clock for Kazwin. This would save us twenty-four
hours. Richard was not at all well that morning. He might
have eaten too much chicken the night before, but in all
probability it was a recurrence of the dysentery which had
been plaguing him throughout the expedition. He said that
he could not possibly face the climb, and so we agreed that
he should go by mule while Minou and I walked. We
elected to climb out of the valley and over the Pass by the
Fort of Borj rather than walk through the gorge. This
would be a strenuous climb, but I wanted to have a last
look at the other castles and to take compass-bearings on
them from Shir Kuh to demonstrate the inter-visibility of
the fortresses of the valley. I rather regretted this decision
later, as it turned out to be a boiling-hot day and the climb
was exhausting. However, I took bearings with Minou's
help. We climbed down into the Taliqan valley, and then
started the climb up the other side. This was sheer agony,
but with each step we knew that we were getting nearer
the top. By 4 o'clock we still had another 10 miles to go,
uphill all the way. If we missed the bus there would not be
another for twenty-four hours, and so, summoning up our
last reserves of energy, we struggled on. We were about
half a mile from the village when people came running
towards us, shouting that the bus was about to leave.
"Tell them to wait," we yelled. "We are important people
and must get back to Teheran to-night." The bus did wait,
and we got to its starting-point just in time. We bought
our tickets to Kazwin, and then, to our horror, we found
that the bus (which was a converted truck) was absolutely

full. There just was no room to squeeze anybody else in. This was really very embarrassing, and we explained our predicament through Minou to the man who was acting as ticket-agent, rather hoping that he would persuade three of the occupants already seated in the bus to postpone their journey to Kazwin. We felt a bit selfish about this, but a day's delay would probably have meant very little to most of the other travellers, whereas to us it meant a great deal. Fortunately, three people were quite willing to give up their seats to us, and with charming smiles they climbed down from the bus. We thanked them as profusely as we could, but the bus-driver was obviously in a hurry to leave and cut short our thanks by setting off with a tremendous jerk.

When I returned in 1961 I was very interested to find that the road had been extended right down to Shir Kuh, and there was a usable track for Land Rovers and jeep-type vehicles as far as Shahrak. This meant that we were able to get to Maymun-Diz in the Stobart-Izzard Land Rover. I must confess it seemed a very odd experience to drive into the valley instead of going on foot. The making of the road as far as Shir Kuh is undoubtedly quite an engineering feat, and one of which Mr Alamuti can justifiably be proud. He told me that he had borne all the expense himself and that the Government had not been able to contribute anything. When I asked him what was the principal object of the road, he replied that he hoped it would open up the valley and so increase its economic prosperity. He hoped that there would be a market in Kazwin for the glut of grapes and melons that formerly went to seed or rotted on the ground. Personally, while admiring his initiative and his faith in this enterprise, which must have cost him a great deal, I have serious doubts as to whether the road will bring the desired benefits. Kazwin and Teheran are already well supplied with fruit of all kinds. In fact there are so many melons in Teheran that, at the height of the season, they can be bought for almost nothing. The quality

of the Alamut grapes is poor, and far better ones are
produced around both Teheran and Kazwin. Also, upkeep
of the road will be an expensive matter. In 1961 we met
the chief engineer of the project, a charming man who
spoke English and who was full of praises for the new road.
We asked how it had been constructed, and if a surveyor
had been employed. He replied that he was both engineer
and surveyor and that he had planned the course of the
road by eye. One bulldozer had been used and this had cut
out the road in great, sweeping curves from the sides of
the hills. Some of the bends are extremely sharp and most
vehicles have to take them in two bites. These corners are
built up on the outside with stones, and the surface is
generally poor. Frost and floods in winter could cause
severe damage, and part of the road is liable to subsidence
and may be blocked by landslides. In the valley itself, the
road can be used only in summer. For most of its length it
runs alongside the river, and is just a track over the dried-
up river-bed. We asked many villagers what they thought
about the road, and if they intended to export some of their
produce to Kazwin. Most of them agreed that production
would not increase. A great deal of capital would be
required to improve the very primitive system of irrigation. The natural lethargy of the inhabitants must also
be taken into account. For centuries they have been
used to scratching a living from the soil, and there is
little incentive for a higher standard of living. The
younger and more enterprising of the villagers will
stand by the side of the road hoping that a vehicle will
come along and give them a lift into Teheran, but there
is no sign of the Alamuti highway being used for its
real purpose. All this may sound pessimistic, but in my
own opinion the valley's first need is the improvement of
its irrigation-system. From some of the castles we could
see terraces that had obviously once been cultivated. Now
they are just fallow lands. In Hasan-i-Sabbah's time the
valley must have been able to support a much greater

population than it has now, and in our own archaeological researches we continually came across evidence of
the wise and enterprising use of water—the diversion of
streams and the creation of water-channels and jubes. It
seems a pity that the present-day population has not the
same vitality and energy as their illustrious forbears. But
if they can be given a real incentive and shown the way by
competent engineers, then perhaps they will want to grow
more valuable crops than fruit. For instance, I am quite
sure that the production of rice could easily be trebled, and
then perhaps Mr Alamuti's road will come into its own.

At all events, in September 1960 we were heartily
thankful to Mr Alamuti for his road. Soon we left the
Taliqan valley behind and plunged down the steep
mountainside to Kazwin. We reached the city at about
7 o'clock in the evening, and it took us a little time to
readjust ourselves to the sights of a civilized community.
We went to the best hotel in the town and greedily drank
three bottles of fizzy orangeade, which we normally
disdained, but which now tasted quite delicious. It was
beginning to get dark, and the pressure lamps in the shop
windows were being lit. There was even electric light, and
this really seemed quite strange. However, the last thing
we wanted was to linger in Kazwin, and so the three of us
piled into a taxi and told the driver to take us to Teheran
as quickly as he could. Although the distance is about a
hundred miles the journey in a taxi is very cheap. It cost
us £1 each and we felt that this was well worth it. The
taxi-driver was anxious to return to Kazwin that evening,
and he sped quickly along.

We reached the city limits of Teheran some two hours
later, and Minou invited us to spend that night and the
next two or three days at his house. He lives in a northern
suburb of the town with his mother and two brothers, and
they were obviously overjoyed when they saw us. Persian
hospitality is well known, but the Sabetians surpassed even
this high standard. In a moment they put up beds for us on

the veranda and lit a boiler so that we could have baths and—best of all—wash our hair. We were filthy, and the dusty ride from Chala to Kazwin had not improved our appearance. We were provided with a splendid meal and clean clothes, although we looked a little odd in pyjamas that were either far too big or far too small. We slept soundly that night, and it was not till late the next morning that we woke up. It was delicious to lie back again, realizing there really was no great hurry. I thought, reluctantly, that now I was back in civilization I should have to shave off my beard. I was rather proud of it, although one side had caught fire when I was attempting to blow out a pressure stove that had burst into flames, and so it looked rather moth-eaten. With a heavy heart I set to with shaving-soap and a new razor-blade, but found that despite all my efforts I was making no impression whatever. Minou had decided to follow my example, and after an hour's hard labour he had managed to shave off only one-quarter of his thick, luxuriant growth. It was obviously hopeless, and we should have to go to a professional barber. Minou was a bit shy about this, as he thought everybody would remark on his extraordinary appearance now that he had lost a quarter of his beard. We laughed at him, and his brother whisked us round the corner to a modern and very elegant barber's shop. I sat in a chair and watched my normal face gradually reappear in the mirror, and very strange it seemed. We took the opportunity of having our hair cut too, and when we emerged we hardly knew one another.

Richard and I then began our round of visits. The first was to the British Embassy, where we called on Arthur Kellas and got a change of clothes from our store in his garage. Our next call was at the Museum. We had brought back two bronze swords and three or four specimens of the pottery we had found in Ashkavar. The rest of the pottery would be brought back by Roddie and the others. The Museum officials were naturally extremely interested in all that we had to tell and show them, and asked us to write a provisional report for their journal. This we promised to do, and then set off in search of Mr Hannibal, our contact with the Museum. Scarcely had we left the building than we ran into him hurrying to meet us. We told him at length all that we had achieved and his excitement knew no bounds. I asked if it would be possible for me to take the pottery to London to show the Department of Oriental Antiquities, and he was sure there would be no difficulty about this.

On the next day we went to Iran TV to tell them that we were willing to appear on television, if this could be arranged soon, and give an account of the expedition. Our offer was accepted with alacrity, and we were asked if we could appear the following evening at 7 o'clock. This suited me well. My plane was due to leave at 11 P.M. and so there would be time for a farewell party after the programme and before I left for the airport. It was agreed that the programme should take the form of question and answer, and that we should show the pottery and swords we had brought back. They asked us to come on the following day at 6 o'clock, when the final details would be arranged. The rest of the day and most of the next was taken up with formal leave-taking. I called once more on the Director of the Museum and on Dr Alavi, who had kindly arranged for Jah to join us, and sent a letter of thanks to the Minister of Education. I made a special point of visiting the Minister of Court, who had been so helpful in overcoming all our initial difficulties. Unfortunately he was engaged, and so I had to leave him a note. I cannot speak too highly of the part played by His Excellency Husain Ala. He followed the affairs of the expedition with the closest interest and sympathy, and even after our return to London authorized the release of aerial photographs and other documents, which have been of the greatest help to us. My final visits were to Mr Alamuti, of whom I took an affectionate farewell, the Faculty of

Oriental Studies at the University, and the National
Iranian Oil Company. Just before we left for the television
centre I gave a final report to Arthur Kellas and told him
of our plans for the next stages of the expedition. Then we
took a taxi to Television House. Originally, we had been
scheduled to speak for half an hour, but the controller of
the programme was so interested in our findings that we
appeared for almost an hour. By the end of it we were quite
exhausted. Time, as usual, was getting short, and we
hurried down to the town where we were to join the
Sabetian family for a final meal. At half-past ten I said
farewell to the Sabetians and got into the Land Rover,
which had been fully serviced by N.I.O.C., and drove to the
airport. Formalities were few, and very soon I found
myself in the departure lounge. The customs officials had
been warned that I was due to leave, and allowed Richard
to accompany me on to the apron. There was even a Press
photographer there, who asked me to pose for a final
photograph and to say a few words. I tried to say how very
grateful we were for all the kindness we had received in
Iran. A last handshake with Richard, and a hurried review
of what he was to do at Lammassar and Daylaman and my
own activities in London, and I climbed into the plane. A
few moments later it roared into the air, leaving behind the
lights of Teheran. For me, the expedition in the field
was over.

13

Lammassar

RICHARD AND Minou spent the day after I had left
Teheran in collecting fresh supplies, then they collected
the Land Rover which had been picked up from Rahimabad
and serviced, and set off for Alamut. By now they were
familiar with the drive through Kazwin and over the
mountains to Hasanabad. Here they left the Land Rover
and walked down the long hill. They found the rest of the
expedition encamped in the village of Gureh Dar. They
were in good heart, had received our letters, and had
completed the survey and photography of the castle of
Shir Kuh. So it was decided that they should all move on
the next day to Lammassar. Camp was struck, the equipment loaded on mules, and with a new guide called Aqa-ye
Maleki they set off down the valley of the Shah Rud and
into the district of Rudbar.

The valley of the Shah Rud is quite different from the
Alamut valley. The gorge opens out after only 300 yards
into a broad river-bed some 1000 yards wide. The hills on
either side are far less steep, and on the left or southern
bank the ground is relatively fertile and there are numerous

small villages. In some ways it is reminiscent of Ashkavar, except that the river is much broader and the valley is flatter. The atmosphere of the Rudbar, too, is much softer and less rugged and awe-inspiring than that of Alamut. The people are more prosperous and better clothed, housed, and fed. This is probably due to the fact that it is a relatively easy journey to Kazwin, from the western end of the valley at least, and so there is much more contact with the life of the city.

When Freya Stark visited Rudbar in 1931 it was unhealthy and malarial; since that time the houses have been extensively sprayed by travelling medical-teams and, although the expedition was badly bitten at times by mosquitoes and other insects, they were never really worried about the possibility of getting malaria. Richard wanted to go along the river-bed, thinking that this would be an easier route and so would help to preserve the diminishing strength of his team; but their guide had other ideas and took them up through the hills on the southern bank until they reached the village of Koramchal. Here they stopped the night in a rather dirty house, which belonged to a friend of Maleki's, and this social visit was evidently the reason for the long detour. In fact the house was so dirty that the party preferred to sleep out on the roof in company with cats, chickens, and goats rather than risk being eaten alive inside, but even on the roof there seemed to be more insects than ever. It was a relief when morning came and they were able to continue on their way. The next stage of the journey was a nightmare. Their indefatigable guide, followed by the mule-team, set off at 7 o'clock, and did not stop, even for a rest, until 2.30. They descended again to the river, crossed it below Koramchal and then walked either beside the river-bed, which at times was quite white with deposits of salt, or along a track a little way up the northern hills. The northern side is far less fertile, and occasionally they passed a small deserted settlement whose mud-brick dwellings were rapidly

LAMMASSAR

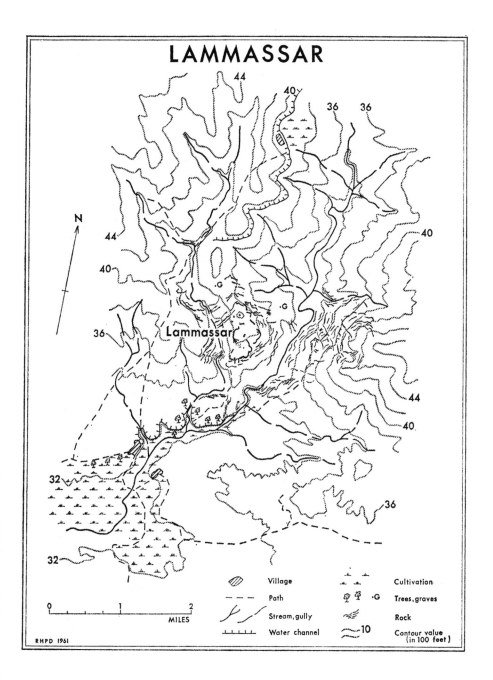

N

44

40

36   36

44

40

40

36

Lammassar

44

40

32

36

32

	Village		Cultivation
- - -	Path	·G	Trees, graves
	Stream, gully		Rock
	Water channel	~10	Contour value (in 100 feet)

0   1   2
MILES

RHPD 1961

crumbling away. The springs tasted very salty too, and for
a long time there was little sign of vegetation. At about
half-past two they reached a small, isolated village, where
they stopped for lunch and rested their aching limbs. From
here they climbed the last hill and then descended a long,
gentle slope into the attractive village of Sharistan Bala.
This is the centre of another fertile area, and the ricefields
all around must have covered 1500 acres. Here they turned
north, following the course of a small tributary of the
Shah Rud, the Naina Rud.

Very soon the impressive outline of Lammassar came
into sight, and they could see at once that it looked quite
different from any of the other castles we had visited
earlier. Instead of being hollowed out of the rock as at
Maymun-Diz, or perched on the top of a great bluff as at
Alamut or Nevisar Shah, Lammassar stands no more than
450 feet above the Shah Rud. It occupies a large area, and is
some 600 feet long by 200 feet wide. It is set on a rounded
rock, which is tilted at an angle of 30°, so the traveller may
take in most of its details at once. In addition, it suffered
less than the other castles at the hands of the Mongols.
From Sharistan Bala one can see the keep at the northern
end of the hill and, on each side of the tilted table of rock,
the ruins of towers, walls, and other fortifications. At a
distance it could well be mistaken for a Norman castle, and
it is an imposing sight.

Richard decided to stop in the small village of Mansurbagh below the castle and the party set up camp in the
garden of a large house belonging to Mr Yaq'ubi, a local
landlord who remembered Freya Stark well and had also
given hospitality to Professor Ivanow. He had an attractive
house and, as he was a rich man, it had two storeys. He
was married and had five sons. His wife was an unusual
woman, of striking personality, and it soon became clear
that it was she who ruled the household. The party was
frequently invited in for a meal and, instead of being
relegated to the kitchens, Mrs Yaq'ubi presided. She even

scolded her husband and her sons in front of her guests for coming in to eat with unwashed hands, and the family accepted these rebukes as a matter of course. Staying in the village was a party of soldiers engaged in signing on conscripts to take back to Teheran. Minou asked them how they had been faring, and gathered that they had had little luck and were obviously rather anxious about the reception they would receive on their return.

The expedition spent the next five days in photographing and surveying the castle.

Juvayni says that there had been a castle at Lammassar for some time before Hasan came into the valley and that the lord of Lammassar refused to be converted to Hasan's faith. Consequently a small body of troops was sent under Buzurg-Ummed—who later succeeded Hasan as the second Grand Master of the Assassins—to take the castle. Juvayni relates that these men climbed up by stealth in the night of September 10, 1102, and slew the inhabitants. Buzurg-Ummed resided for some years at Lammassar, until Hasan-i-Sabbah fell ill and sent for him to be appointed as his successor.

The castle was suitably situated to guard the valley of Alamut from attack by way of the valley of the Shah Rud, so it was important in the general system of defence of the Assassin strongholds. Buzurg-Ummed enlarged the castle and strengthened its fortifications. Juvayni mentions a library, but there seem to have been no other great treasures there. It is relatively isolated, so it did not play a large part in the history of the Assassins, despite its impregnability.

After the fall of Maymun-Diz and Alamut, Lammassar continued to hold out for another year. Hulagu Khan stayed for some time in the village of Mansurbagh, and in the end the castle surrendered to his besieging armies.

There are two ways of approaching the castle from the village of Mansurbagh. Richard chose the shorter and steeper, walking over the fields, scrambling across a series

C.A.–S

of irregular ditches, fording the Naina Rud, and climbing
to the castle over steep scree.

The principal gateway is at the southern end of the
castle, and it is relatively small—no more than 6 feet high
and 3 feet wide—and must have caused loaded pack-mules
difficulty. Just beside the gateway are the remains of two
towers, which were probably used for signalling purposes.
Since the ground rises from south to north by a series of
terraces interspersed with depressions—so that not even
from the northern gateway is the whole castle-area visible
—a system of internal communications was necessary.
Two or three other towers, similar to those by the gateway, were probably part of this system.

The outer wall—of which there are some remains—
runs around the site, rises steeply at the western end, and
skirts a massive stone building with an apsidal-projection
built on the edge of sheer cliffs which former travellers
have supposed to be either a residence or a serai. Professor
Ivanow suggested that it is much more likely to have been
part of the fortifications of the ridge, and with this we
agree. We called it the small keep. Near by is the catchment-area for rainwater, and the ground is covered with
numerous cisterns dug into the rock and connected together
by channels designed to prevent each cistern from over-
flowing. Little round holes dug into the lips of the cisterns
once held posts, which supported rough shelters to prevent
the water from being evaporated by the sun or polluted by
dirt and dust. Around the great tanks the marks left by
countless picks could still be seen. The tanks were often 18
feet deep, and sometimes three or four times as long, and
the connecting channels were 6 or 8 inches wide.

The garrison also drew water from the river, and by the
river there is a small tower guarding a tunnel hewn into
the rock for about 1800 feet. This tower overhangs the
river and contains a trap-door above the water through
which buckets could be let down. There is a story that once,
when the garrison was besieged and the tower was in the

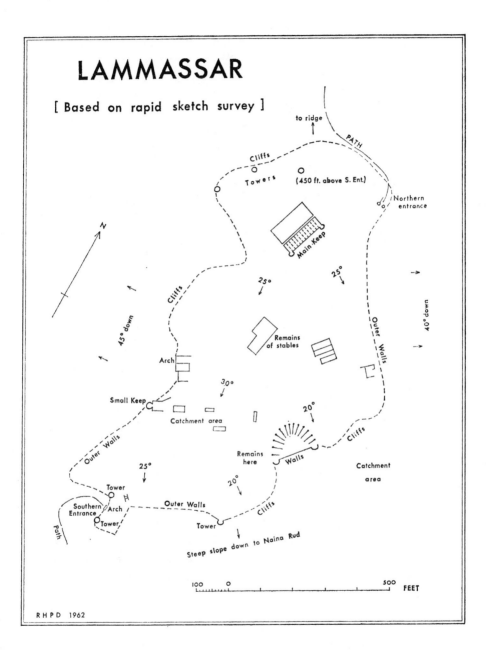

LAMMASSAR

[Based on rapid sketch survey]

to ridge

PATH

Cliffs

Towers (450 ft. above S. Ent.)

Northern
entrance

N

Cliffs

Main Keep

25°

25°

40° down

45° down

Arch

Remains
of stables

Small Keep

30°

20°

Catchment area

Outer Walls

Remains
here

Walls

Cliffs

Catchment
area

25°

20°

Tower

Southern
Entrance Arch

Outer Walls

Cliffs

Path

Tower

Tower

Steep slope down to Naina Rud

100   0   500
                                      FEET

RHPD 1962

hands of their enemies, sheep were sent down through the tunnel to the river. The sheep had water-bags strapped beneath their bellies and filled them in the river. A shepherd in the pay of the garrison stood near by, unsuspected by the invading forces, and, as soon as the water-bags were filled, he set a wolf to chase the sheep back up the channel. The channel is, in fact, far too steep for this to have happened, but it is a picturesque story.

To the north of the catchment-area and the small keep ridge are the stables, which can be seen from practically every point in the castle. The present structure is built on the ruins of the old stables and is a recent one made of mud bricks built on a stone foundation. Even taking into account the greater size of the original building it could not have accommodated many horses or, more probably, mules.

Near the northern end is the main keep, still in quite a good state of preservation. This was where Buzurg-Ummed lived in a simple and unpretentious style. Its single storey is built of stone, and the walls are covered with rubble. The entrance has a rounded arch, and inside there are two rooms. The left-hand room has a fine vault and it is 10 feet high, 6 feet wide, and 12 feet long. The walls are 4 feet thick, and the floor is covered with rubble and shards of pottery. Behind the keep are rooms of other houses, or possibly storerooms. The ground rises again to the ruined tower of the northern gateway.

Ragnar decided that he would like to photograph the castle from one of the surrounding hills. He therefore enlisted Mike's assistance in carrying the photographic equipment up to the hill he had in mind. They set out, but soon the route became very difficult. There were no goat-tracks or paths, and after two hours they found themselves confronted by a sheer cliff. The equipment was heavy, as we had not expected to carry it long distances. They separated, each trying to find the best route up to the top. Luck was with Mike, and after some scrambling he found a steep track that led to the top of the hill. After a brief rest on the summit he tried to locate Ragnar by shouting. Eventually he saw him working his way along a narrow rock ridge ending in a terrifying abyss. Mike managed to guide Ragnar back, and after a painful climb he was able to join Mike at the top. The view from here was superb, and showed clearly the fantastic natural strength of the castle. Looking down they could see the great curtain-walls on the southern and eastern sides, the signalling towers and the southern gateway, the small keep, and the main keep, and finally the ruined towers of the northern defences. The very plateau out of which the castle grew was a natural fortress in itself. Set aside from the surrounding land, it rose, a solid rock mass, a tilted slab with sheer sides that scarcely needed fortifying. The eastern side is perhaps the most vulnerable, although this is a relative description, and it is easy to trace the line of the continuous wall on this side. The river is to the east of the castle, and there is a legend that when Buzurg-Ummed rebuilt it, he had a water-channel cut to the upper reaches of the Naina Rud, a distance of about 10 miles. It is possible that this channel did exist, as we had already learnt much of the great engineering skill of the Assassins. Richard did, in fact, find the remains of a tunnel that certainly led in the right direction. He was able to follow its course for about 800 yards, but whether this was Buzurg-Ummed's water-channel or not it was impossible to say.

From their vantage point Mike and Ragnar could see that the surface was gashed with regular black cuts; these were the water-catchment tanks that the garrison had hewn. Every detail of this great fort stood out clearly. It was more than just a fortress, it was a triumph of man's ingenuity, and it had an aesthetic quality, fitting superbly into the magnificent background of the mountains and hills.

Ragnar was dancing like a small boy. Never had he seen such a view as this before or anything so photogenic. He spent the next hour or so using every device he knew to record this magnificent sight. When at last he was satisfied,

Mike helped him to pack up the equipment and, happy in
the knowledge that they had recorded and seen everything,
they climbed down and trudged back to the camp. Here
Richard, Roddie, Minou, and Jah were waiting for them,
and were eager to hear all they had to tell.

A little while after Mike and Ragnar's return Richard
said that he was feeling unwell and wandered off. After an
hour he had not come back and the others began to get
anxious. A search round the camp was made, Roddie and
Jah walking down to the river along the irrigation-dikes
and terraces shouting, looking, and listening. Still there
was no sign of Richard. By now the party was beginning to
get seriously worried, especially when the villagers who
had accompanied them to the castle said that it was
dangerous to go farther afield because of snakes. The
whole party returned to base-camp thinking that Richard
might have made his own way back there, but still there
was no sign of him. By now it was beginning to get dark,
and Mike set off with a guide and a torch back in the
direction of the castle. Having reached the castle gate, the
guide became frightened and left Mike, who continued on
alone.

Mike shouted, but heard only his own echoes in reply.
The castle seemed utterly deserted and forbidding,
garrisoned by countless ghosts, but he went on and, having
made a complete tour of the castle, went down to the river.
The moon was now rising, casting hard shadows from the
distorted crags. As he picked his way over the fallen
rubble he saw an entrance to a tunnel about 3 feet 6 inches
high with a pointed arch. Mike entered it and climbed
steeply for a few yards, then he heard a loud hiss. Startled,
he jumped back in time to see a snake disappearing
beneath the rocks. This experience made him hasten back
to camp. He followed the course of the river, splashing in
and out of the water. Tired out and desperately worried
about Richard, he struggled back into camp. A happy
laugh greeted his entry into the pool of light cast by the

"Tilley" lamp. Half an hour after Mike had set out, Richard had been discovered asleep on his bed. Nobody had thought of looking there!

With the examination of the castle completed, the whole party returned to Samiran to complete our unfinished survey, which I have already described in detail. From Samiran they motored back in the Land Rover to Teheran. It was now time for Roddie to fly home, for his leave was almost up. Minou wanted to spend some time with his family, and Ragnar was anxious to go to Athens and start developing the film. Jah, too, had to return to work soon although he wanted to accompany Richard and Mike on at least the first stage of their journey to Daylaman. This was sad news, for every one had liked Jah. Quiet and infinitely patient, he was a complete contrast to the dashing, gay Minou. He had inherited many of the qualities of the fearless, wiry warriors who were his ancestors. But his greatest characteristic was his sense of dedication to the people he served as a doctor. He won our affection and respect, and is a man who is not easily forgotten.

Richard decided to postpone finding another interpreter for the time being. The Land Rover was serviced, and soon the small party was again ready to leave Teheran. Daylaman was the last site due to be explored by the expedition, and as the task now devolved entirely upon Richard and Mike I shall let Richard tell this part of our story.

14

Daylaman

by RICHARD MORDAUNT

MR ALBUYEH had fired our interest in Daylaman during the afternoon we had spent in his garden before leaving Teheran for Ashkavar. His dramatic stories of the treasure-bearing earth in his mountain villages—the proof of which lay in the sacks of Luristan bronzes, Caspian pottery, and metal statuettes that he proudly displayed—prompted us to seek the centre of this unknown civilization.

After the other four had flown home, Mike, Jah, and I recharged the Land Rover with food and films. Then, with our letters of introduction, we set off on the 250-mile journey to Siachal on the Caspian Sea. Our maps showed us that this was the only possible entrance up into this part of the mountains. How true were the villagers' tales in Ashkavar when they had talked of the silver and gold of Shavak? And was Marabbu still the seat of a powerful feudal lord?

We reached Siachal late in the evening. Intent on wasting no time, we avoided the hospitality of Albuyeh's brother, a devout Sufi, and moved through the muddy village to the house of Mr Delarchand. He, we had been

informed, was the headman of the town and kept contact
with the hinterland and with the absentee landlords in
Teheran. This was an excellent start.

He welcomed us into his gabled, clean house, built on
chubby stilts, like so many of the Caspian houses. This
elevation is to safeguard the inhabitants from the wild
animals and from the waters of the winter. On one side a
parapet led from room to room while the other half was a
shuttered balcony designed for summer sleeping. Mr
Delarchand, like all Iranians, was overwhelmingly charming. Jah questioned him carefully as to our chances of
penetrating the mountains. He knew what we wanted from
the letters of introduction, but for us to interpret his
thoughts was impossible. He told us the rains had
devastated the crops in this region, and the swollen waters
of the rivers were impassable. Abate they might, but in two
weeks' time it would be too late in the year to make the
130 crossings of the river, which, he said, were necessary
to reach Daylaman.

Was he for some reason trying to prevent us from
travelling into this area with our permits? Almost
immediately, while the subdued preparations for the
evening meal came from the adjoining room, the noise of
voices below broke the discouraging silence. We walked
out on to the balcony in time to see wooden crates being
carefully loaded on to two trucks which were drawn up
under the low eaves. We had not noticed these on our
arrival, but now the lights of "Tilley" lamps lit them up.
Heavily coated figures removed padlocks from the doors,
and then a swinging lamp lit up the words "Japanese
Willie" on the mudguard. Five minutes later three men
and a woman climbed the steps, and their weathered faces
were Japanese. We were introduced, and realized that
Albuyeh's story of foreign archaeologists working in this
area was indeed true. Conversation was awkward and uninformative—their success was obvious, but our intrusion
was clearly unwelcome. The dampness prevented them

from leaving immediately as their jeeps would not start. However, after ten minutes they were joined by a fourth man. Jah told us that he was the Government representative from the Internal Security Department. As soon as dinner was finished, they said they wanted to reach Teheran by the next morning and left. We slept uncomfortably, awaiting the morrow.

Still it was raining, and such was our obvious unwantedness that we decided to return to Teheran also, but not before two things had happened. Delarchand showed us an exquisite gold necklace, which had, he said, been removed from one of the tombs in Daylaman. Secondly, on our way back through the village we used one other introduction which produced invaluable information. In such a community secrets become small talk and then legend as they pass from hand to hand, but our informant had a reliable, trustworthy face; not a man of to-day, but a believer in the glorious past of the Daylaman empire. Between deep, ponderous suckings on his hashish pipe he told us that the Japanese had been digging. However, the inhabitants, secure in their inaccessibility, had demanded a high price from the archaeologists for the disturbance of their land.

On our return to Teheran, Jah went back to his medical practice. Luckily, through friends, we made contact with another Iranian who agreed to be our interpreter for three weeks. His past record was unimportant to us, as the likelihood of finding anybody who was prepared to spend three weeks away from modern civilization was so small that we were prepared to accept the first comer. We shall call him K. He was middle-aged, pock-marked, and indirect in his speech, which came slowly in a much-practised broken English. In Iran, a country of romantic tribal life, there still exist uncontrolled migrations, huge bodies of humans and cattle moving their pasturing grounds with the sun. Entirely isolated from the evolution of mankind, they resent the intrusion of alien customs. Governments

have failed to enforce any permanent rule or organization
on their lives where the sky is their roof and the earth
their floor. K told us he had been financial adviser to the
Kashgai tribe until the banishment of the Khans from Iran.
He had then been asked to leave the country at the time of
the Mossadeq *coup d'état* and had taken shelter in Geneva.
His linguistic ability had enabled him to return to his
fatherland and act as interpreter to an American geological
team working in northern Iran during the later fifties.

While in Teheran we returned to Albuyeh's villa and
told him of our difficulties in getting permission to dig in
Siachal. He replied that we could enter Daylaman from
the Ashkavar end of the valley, 20 miles due west of the
Pul-i-Rud down which we had travelled to enter Ashkavar.
With more letters of goodwill we set off again.

The long, jolting ride to the mountain village of Amlesh
added years to the life of K, just as it did to ours, but
he told us stories of tribal warfare in the plains and
mountains around Isfahan and Shiraz, and of the problems
of the undernourished peoples, which reminded us of Old
Testament stories. We hired our mules and, leaving the
Rover in the hands of the grocer, we set off into the wooded
foothills. The climb was steep, but the scenery beautiful.
Lizards and snakes darted across the zigzagging route, and
butterflies of blue, crimson, and gold added brilliance to
the mountain scene. From time to time we met mule-
trains passing out of the lawless countryside on their
descent to the towns, each man fit and cheerful now that the
rains had ceased. We stopped for tea at a *chai-kh'anae*
(tea-house) a mere stone's throw from the summit of the
mountain. The Iranian devotes many hours every day to
copious tea-drinking; it has become a ritual of rich and
poor alike. On the wooden benches carved with the marks
of generations of muleteers, there was little room for
strangers, but, avoiding the warm sheets of bread moving
from hand to hand, we sat on the floor, crossing our aching
legs beneath us. Looking up, we saw that the faces were

warm and happy, and that tough, dirty hands gripped the chipped lumps of sugar and the small, grubby, thumb-stained glasses. The empty tea-glasses clinked and trembled beside the bubbling samovar. A teapot blackened with charcoal was removed from the embers of the fire; with a basis of this potent brew the water was added from the sitting samovar. Nobody ever kept count of how many glasses he had drunk, but the crouching figure of the *chai* seller quietly operated a bead counter; at 1 rial a glass, nobody questioned his good faith.

Before leaving, Mike recorded on tape the delicate melody of a young boy playing a flute. On hearing the result, one after the other the tea-drinkers vied for the title of champion flute-player. We were rescued by a dervish whose skill was beyond dispute. The rest of our journey to Buyeh was made in the company of this dervish who sang beautiful folk-songs, tales of love and hatred, the simple birth of a king and the jealousy of two brothers. We slept the night in an old feudal building, now a resthouse for muleteers, while close by the remains of a Shah Abbas bridge spanning the river showed the route to a disused caravanserai.

We arrived in Buyeh at midday and straightway were given a house to stay in and an old woman to minister to our needs. The excitement of hearing the reason for our arrival was considerable, and many of the more learned men of the village offered themselves as our guides. We learnt that there had been digging in Buyeh, but nothing of great value had been found. By this the villagers meant that nothing more exciting than pots and swords had been unearthed; but, though they were keen that we should work in the village, they talked of Marabbu, Shavak, Diarzan, Espeyli, and the stories which had floated down-wind from the villages of Daylaman. Later, when trying to locate the centre of this civilization, it was significant that the finds of real value were being dug up in the villages close to the Chaka Rud, which links the districts of Daylaman and Ashkavar. In the centre of this string of what were probably the most important towns, we heard of a village called Pir Kuh, which means "Head of the Grave."

From time to time information trickled into our cold little room. The natural secrecy of important finds provided a curtain between neighbouring towns, while the sight of dealers and long-absent landlords travelling up into this area brought tales of gold and silver to the lips of all we talked to. K translated all this with a peculiar quietness, only now and then mentioning how much he wanted a sword studded with jewels for his children.

Mike and I woke the following morning to find that the mists had clamped down tightly on top of the village; the swirling clouds occasionally broke so we could pick out a patch of ground. We set out to see what work had already been done around Buyeh. The spectacle that met our eyes came as a shock to us both. Suddenly the ground became a desolation of pits and holes, a chaos of slabs of stone and humped-up earth. No semblance of order or system was present. This devastation of the ground extended over an area 150 yards square. Quite stunned by this sight, we were then informed that, little success having been met with, the villagers had moved to another area. This was in fact nearly twice the size and also resembled rabbit-warrens and fox-holes scratched and dug out of the sandy earth. The villagers could see no reason why they should not benefit from what was lying a few feet under the very ground from which they took their livelihood.

Through K we were told that since the second dig had taken place, namely six months ago, the Government had forbidden all digging. Police prowled the mountains, and had frightened the majority of villagers sufficiently to keep them from further plundering, but the more we saw, the more we were appalled by the lack of respect and the ignorance that accompanied the pillaging of these graves. Excavation-fever seemed to have spread through the villages. Now, only the bravest of the villagers indulged, but in some places landlords defied the long arm of the law and organized digging parties.

At lunch we talked of the advantages of using our permit in Buyeh. The village did not suffer from the influence of dealers and landlords; they were in need of our help, while a larger community might resent it. It seemed that money was still a star of the future and that the dealers had not visited this outpost of the community.

We organized teams, the blacksmiths made levers and picks, and soon we had chosen an area at one end of the pot-hole district. While surface-digging was taking place I went to examine the work already done by the villagers. The graves were mostly 5 feet beneath the ground, some big, while those towards the perimeter of the area were smaller. Like a house of cards they varied in levels, some consisting of three levels, each separated by a 2-foot-thick stone and approached from the side. They extended 15 to 25 feet beneath the ground, and it seemed unlikely that nothing should have been found inside them. But the villagers insisted that nothing important had been brought to light. However, to determine exactly what period they belonged to, systematic excavation and the recovery of pottery was necessary. Our men worked manfully for several hours. On one occasion work stopped as a peasant strode into our midst and angrily protested that it was his land we were digging. The sweating diggers took no notice, but retorted it was all the land of Albuyeh and that the man was only working a patch. But, as they dug, more and more potatoes were shovelled from the earth, and the man, calling for the help of Allah, darted to and fro with a sack retrieving his potatoes. We moved to another place.

Wherever we looked there were graves all built in lines or squares. A slight rise in the ground, a platform, a cluster of bushes growing singlemindedly in the middle of nothing, or a king-sized weed were all signs of places to be dug. During the course of the afternoon, before the mists became a suffocating blanket and the air too cold to bear, we uncovered what seemed to be a warrior's grave. The thick earth clung to the pots crudely worked in black clay. These crumbled in my fingers and, working like a sculptor removing useless material, I struggled to save the other buried objects. A bronze buckle, rings, amulets, and a long, corroded bronze sword crested and chipped—all survived. I quietly cursed the blameless inhabitants for their irrigation-channel, which had flooded the graves in this place. As evening wore on, it became obvious that objects of archaeological importance almost certainly rested in the lower graves, but time was against our being able to excavate these.

Already the weather had turned and the galloping clouds momentarily stood between the weak rays of the sun and the dried-up earth. Looking towards the village of Daylaman, I could see the sinuous silver thread of the Chaka Rud, which had run so peacefully throughout the long summer months. Focusing my binoculars on the nearer reaches of the river, I noticed that the small rivulets, which had so recently been zigzagging down the dry bed, had swollen into swirling waters. No longer silver or brown, but a muddy, roaring torrent bounding along, a respecter of nothing, carrying boulders, logs, and mud down to the great meeting of the rivers at Sipul. The omens were poor. Once the monsoon weather started there would be no leaving the mountains. Snow and rain would turn the district into a slushy morass from which one could not escape.

Early the following morning I discussed the situation with Mike, and we decided that since time was short we must learn as much about the area as possible, so that evidence of this civilization could be recorded. But this was not the only reason that Mike and K left for Marabbu at 7 o'clock that morning. Our confidence in K was waning every day; with only a small Persian vocabulary we had to trust implicitly his translation of everything that we asked and were told. If his integrity was to be doubted, it was better that I should be left alone to continue work by myself. We had already heard in Teheran that every moment of our trip through Ashkavar and Alamut had been carefully checked. In these areas, which are normally restricted zones, one is usually accompanied by an escort from the Internal Security and the Archaeological Institute.

My diggers continued work. Every hour brought further signs that we were near the centre of this undiscovered civilization which, in all probability, stretched as far as Ashkavar, and thus linked with our early discoveries at Lotosan and Kashan. By carefully scraping with trowels and knives I succeeded in unearthing several pots after the excavators had dug down into the graves. Sometimes the pots and lamps fell limply apart like overripe pears, but others, beautifully shaped yet musty with the cobwebs of time, remained in their original form and let the warm sun touch their damp surfaces for perhaps the first time for 3000 years. One grave surely belonged to a large family, for a set of earthenware bowls was unearthed from the four walls. One was an impressive vessel, 15 inches high, its bowl measuring 10 inches across the top and 8 inches deep. Small, rounded pieces protruded like ears, forming two handles by which the delicate object might be held. With no joins visible, the stem supported the bowl above a rounded base. It was not difficult to imagine a hand squeezing the stem into shape and then moulding the lower and upper halves. Another small object, also made of Caspian clay, was a jug; strangely proportioned, it resembled a teapot without its lid. From the bowl projected a long, beak-like spout, which had split, on the upper surface. Did this represent some extinct bird? When it was cleaned, geometric patterns were revealed on the side, some of which suggested birds with long necks and long beaks. A hard day's work produced several interesting pieces, but nothing of great significance.

I ate dinner with Ali Shukavar, the only shopkeeper in the village. The air of the room was sickly, but this was natural since no windows pierced the mud-brick walls, and the cold night air entered only through the door. The floor, like the walls, was made from straw and mud, but felt rugs and mountain *gleems* (carpets) were part of the normal peaceful existence. I wondered if I should produce my insecticide spray to give the fleas a moment's warning before they bit. Tea, *mast*, and bread formed the meal with a few sweets brought up from Resht as a dessert before *chai* was served again. With shoes removed (a much-respected Middle Eastern custom) friends pushed open the small wooden door every few minutes. The family—which numbered seventeen—took their places in the main room, which was a corridor to the whole house. The family consisted mostly of sniffling children with long, unkempt hair, dressed in red, green, and orange baggy pyjama-trousers and rough scarves delightfully worn from shoulder to waist; little buttons down their waistcoats glittered under the light of the candles. Some of these buttons had been removed from the graves and were many hundreds of years old.

First there was a lesson in Persian, but the crowded tea-drinkers soon became bored with this, and it turned into an amusing kindergarten English lesson. Of course we must all count to ten and say "Good morning": this delightful elementary education went on far into the night.

There continued two days of careful work, followed by tours of the village. On the second day I was amazed to see a mounted, uniformed gentleman, carrying a rifle, ride by the graves we were digging. Sensing trouble, I turned to beckon to the organizer of the diggers, but they had all vanished. Deeming it unwise to appear the only target for investigation I walked away also. No sooner had the policeman disappeared than, one by one, terrified unshaven faces appeared from the holes they had been digging. The landlord at Marabbu had sent for the police.

Half an hour later Mike arrived. His tale was one of continual frustration and, of course, amusing and colourful incidents. He insisted I should leave Buyeh for Marabbu, which, he said was a revelation and an eye-sore, since before the no-digging order had been issued the excavation accomplished there was unbelievable—and it still continued. At Marabbu there were no longer graves, but tombs; vaults several feet underground were connected by small crawling tunnels. He had not been allowed more than a glimpse of their contents, and K assured him the dealers had taken everything away. The villages beyond Marabbu were in a similar state, but the village of Pir Kuh, on the other side of the Chaka Rud, was now out of reach as the river had become impassable.

They had stayed in the house of a man named Mona Jimi. Mike's description of "a rambling feudal mansion, with courtyards and living quarters for the servants, set in the centre of a timbered oasis" sounded most unlikely for this area, but, on reaching it later, I found that his description could not have been more accurate. Mona Jimi was an old and educated man whose life had alternated between the mountains and the civilization of the plains. He had been the financial adviser to the predecessor of the Shah's father. A man of many parts, he had sheltered Reza Shah in his home at Marabbu when the Shah had fled from the Government. Mona Jimi had welcomed Mike and, hearing of our interest in Assassin pottery, he had sent off to friends in the valley who, he believed, had entire glazed pots. Although he supplied all the necessary tools and men for Mike to dig, something invariably cropped up at the last moment to prevent it; or was this K's translation? Mike was also not certain that Mona Jimi did not understand English at least as well as K.

Mike stayed the night and the following day. We shared one camp-bed, as the dampness in the floorboards would have given us rheumatism for life. The night was uncomfortable, but we talked quietly for many hours, taking sides in this tactical game of chess. On the second day an unexpected realization of our earlier hopes was heralded by "Good morning" and no longer "*Salaam-e-lekum.*" As the day progressed the villagers' apparent suspicions that we had been sent by the Government seemed to have been allayed. Although it was certainly not a valuable collection which began to assemble, our room became full of pieces of pottery and bronze. At first, to test our reaction, the villagers brought specimens that were crude and poorly shaped, but as time progressed, slightly more impressive jugs appeared through the window and door. By 3 o'clock the stream had become a mere trickle. By no means rich ourselves, we were able to buy only a few of these objects, which would remain as souvenirs of our trip. The few pieces of value were priced by the exorbitant hand of rumour, while the stubbornness of our hosts was proof against any argument.

Boxes were made and straw provided. Our finds, priceless to us, were wrapped up inside, each labelled with the location and type of grave it had come from. Our mules, loaded with anonymous boxes lashed tightly to the hand-woven saddle-bags, set off in front of us. Wishing one and all "*Befarma-ri*" (God be with you) we were pleased to hear them reply with one accord in English.

The journey to Marabbu was rough; dogs twice the size of the Western conception of the canine family rushed out from behind walls as we entered villages, but the muleteers were used to them and kept them off with staves and stones. My heart went out to Mike when I thought that he had already completed this foot-wearing slog five times by himself. Inquisitive faces, some old, some young, watched us as we moved through the homesteads, each one stricken with the digging plague. On one of Mike's earlier trips the headman of Umam had promised to show him some animal-jugs on his return. Each time Mike had passed through the village the man had apologized and said that they had been lost, but on this occasion, as we waited to buy some newly baked bread, he sent a messenger to meet us. The rare pieces that lay in front of the smiling headman were of exquisite work. There were four in all; two were made of clay and two of bronze. All stood 5 inches high, while those in clay were elongated—perhaps to enable the potter to work more easily; or was it that these four animals, each of which resembled a cross between a cow and a wild pig, were representations of animals that flourished 3000 years ago but are unknown to-day? An oval hole in the centre of the back was connected with a spout running through the nostrils of the beast. The two in bronze were especially fine, both perfectly worked and, unlike so many children's toys of to-day, they stood firmly on all four legs.

We arrived in Marabbu just as the light was failing and the policeman was leaving.

Mona Jimi had promised Mike that he would gather together some of the rings, beads, plates, bowls, and unusual swords that had not left his area, so we had naturally looked forward to our arrival with great excitement. We unloaded the crates behind the large, studded gates in the great courtyard of this lord of the mountains. We climbed the stairs, and were shown through three disused rooms, dark and rank with dust and seed of bygone harvests. Each room was entered by a slim, decorated archway, and these panelled rooms were linked by dark stained-glass windows. Along a communicating passage-way, off which stemmed many more rooms, we followed the flickering lamp of our guide as its flame licked the crumbling plaster of the low, vaulted ceiling.

Finally we were shown into a sparsely decorated room in which sat Mona Jimi and K, bolstered and already in night dress. They received us with offerings of *chai*. The talk was strained and uninformative. Sadly, nothing had been collected for our viewing, except a few bronze knives and spearheads. K pressed for an immediate return to Teheran, as he claimed that his time was at an end, and, in any case, he felt in his aged bones that the rains and snow were upon us. We finally agreed with him, as even Mona

Jimi with his stilted French—although apparently open-minded towards our digging—was, I feel, secretly anxious to see the back of anybody with a permit. Over dinner Mona Jimi talked of the land and its problems. He was devoted to the simple life of the mountains; but if he had real aesthetic appreciation, why had he allowed the objects of rare value from the tombs of his forefathers to fall into the greasy fingers of dealers and not filled his residence with cabinets of these priceless relics? Time was too short to tell; we agreed to leave early in the morning.

To satisfy my curiosity, Mike and I went down to the tombs late that night. They were exactly as Mike had described, scattered in long lines wherever we shone the lamps. Some were square, some were oblong, a catacomb of disgracefully excavated holes of the dead. We walked and groped between the huge tombstones, up-ended and motionless in the light of the moon. The tombs, approachable from all angles, measured as little as 2 feet by 4 feet in places, but Mike already knew where to find the more extensive ones. One grave, 6 feet by 3 feet, would lie on top of a slightly larger one, not always directly underneath, while the chamber beneath measured in one case 10 feet by 8 feet. Small pigeonholes cut into the rock wall of the tombs were used as shelves.

But this was no place to spend the night! We hurried back, wrapped in thoughts and painful frustration, knowing that we could do nothing to stop this unlawful and no-longer-ignorant destruction.

At 4.30 A.M. next day we were awakened by a servant and had a quick breakfast of tea and bread while the animals stamped restlessly in the darkness outside as they were loaded and fed. With twelve hours' hard walking it was possible, we were told, to cover the seven *parasangs* to the town of Amlesh, our starting-point. K was to ride the whole way and we paid for our mules before leaving. This was only a matter of tomans, as Mona Jimi was delighted to help us on our way! He lent us two fine steeds to convey Mike and myself to the top of the pass; from whence they were to be returned. With the cocks crowing and the bark of distant dogs, we left the still sleeping outskirts of Marabbu, discussing the unrealistic possibilities of returning one day and building a house.

The morning was bitterly cold, but as we reached the summit at Shalkumark at nearly 9000 feet, dawn was beginning to spread over the rich, isolated area of which we had only caught a glimpse. We were once again witnesses of the beauty of daybreak over the Caspian, but this time the loaflike peaks penetrating the creamy whipped-up clouds were all covered by snow. We moved quickly down through steep, wooded hills. Mike began to feel faint and weak through violent dysentery, while I stupidly twisted my ankle. The hours vanished, but our chance of reaching Amlesh that night was still just possible. We hurried along the way, noticing nothing of the surroundings. When we arrived at the river-bed it was with amazement that we heard K suddenly order the mules to trot, and then, without a word, he followed them. We realized that K had no idea what was inside the crates on the mules, and that his intention was surely to arrive in Amlesh before us and order the police to open them. However, we tottered after him and arrived in Amlesh before he could contact the police.

When we reached the Land Rover, which was lacking several of its more necessary pieces, we bundled K into the front, while Mike took charge of our boxes in the back, and thus we returned to Teheran. Mike was desperately ill for four days, so I decided to contact K at the address he had given us. As we had expected, he was not there—and they had never heard of him!

Epilogue

Think, in this batter'd Caravanserai
Whose Portals are alternate Night and Day,
How Sultán after Sultán with his Pomp
Abode his destin'd Hour, and went his way.

Omar Khayyám

WE HAVE now come to the end of our story. Richard, Mike, and Ragnar arrived back in England at the beginning of December. Robert Moss and I drove down to Dover to welcome them. We were held up by traffic on the way, and when we got to the docks the Land Rover had already passed through the Customs. As we warmly greeted the three travellers we were both relieved to see that no harm had come to them, and that, although they looked tired, they were obviously in good spirits. But they could not rest yet, for borrowed stores had to be cleaned and returned, accounts settled, field notebooks checked, and the film edited. The aftermath of an expedition can go on for months—or even years—and ours has been no exception.

Throughout the winter we met at frequent intervals to discuss our results and to draw up a provisional report. When we had finished we could not help feeling a warm glow of satisfaction. We had established with certainty the site of Maymun-Diz, and we had entered and explored it despite all the obstacles and difficulties. We had made a thorough survey of a large number of other castles in the valley, including Alamut, Lammassar, Shir Kuh, and Nevisar Shah, and for the first time a complete description of the historical topography of the valley could now be given. In addition we had examined the great fortress of

Samiran, and had penetrated into the valleys of Ashkavar and Daylaman, never before visited by Western travellers. Here we had found the sites of lost cities, and pottery and bronzes prove the existence in these parts of an unsuspected civilization, dating back to 1000 B.C. or even earlier. At the same time we had been able to study the way of life of the people, and to record on film and tape their music, customs, and ceremonies.

These were our concrete results, and we can say that we may have added to the sum of human knowledge. But what had all this meant to the seven of us? Each one of us would probably give a different answer. For myself I had gone back into a very real past, and the past had taught me its eternal lesson: it is not power that rules the earth, for power (symbolized for me by the gaunt, soulless ruins of Samiran and Maymun-Diz) is, in the long run, neither strong nor holy. It is the rich warmth of human emotions, friendship, and respect for others that builds and sustains. And this perhaps is the greatest lesson a man can learn.

APPENDIX A

Hasan-i-Sabbah and the Nizari Ismailis

THE ISMAILIS take their name from Ismail, the son of the Imam Ja'far, who died in A.D. 763. The present head of the Nizari Ismailis, the descendants of the Assassins, with their two centres in Africa (Mombasa) and India (Bombay and Calcutta), is the Aga Khan. The Ismailis are a branch of the Shi'ite sect, which is one of the three main sects of the Moslem world and the official creed of modern Iran. The Shi'ites—excluding the Ismailis—number about 12,000,000. To put it very briefly and simply, the Shi'ites regard the family of Ali, the fourth Mohammedan caliph, who married Mohammed's daughter Fatima, as the only true descendants of the Prophet and hence the only lawful caliphs or successors to the temporal and spiritual powers of Mohammed.

Ali was murdered in 661 and succeeded by his son Hosain, who, when trying to assert his claim, was killed by troops of the rivals of his house, the Omaiads. Ali's other son, Hasan, rather than risk civil war, resigned the caliphate. He retired to Medina, where he died eight or nine years afterwards, but it was widely believed by his supporters that he was poisoned by the Omaiads. The great majority of the Islamic world, the Sunnites, accepted the subsequent changes in the caliphate with equanimity, believing that this office was primarily an elective one, although it must be occupied by a member of the tribe of

Quraysh. The Shi'ites, however, refused to accept this, and insisted that the caliphate was a divinely appointed office invested by God in Ali as a direct descendant of Mohammed. His descendants alone could correctly interpret the will of God. Behind this principle of an absolute personal and hereditary monarchy lay as well feelings of wounded national pride. The Persians had not accepted conversion to the Islamic faith with anything like the same readiness as, for example, the Christians in Syria. Moreover, they had clung tenaciously to many of their former beliefs which were incorporated in the new faith in much the same way as Christianity incorporated some of the practices of the religions it superseded.

The unity of the Shi'ite world was also to founder on this thorny question of succession. One group, the Ithna'ashariyya, believe that Ali had twelve descendants known as the Twelve Imams; the twelfth imam, Muhammud, is believed to have disappeared about the year 870, but to be still living. One day he will reappear and re-establish the Shi'ite faith over the whole world.

The Ismailis believe that Ismail, the son of the Imam Ja'far, was wrongfully deprived of his inheritance. For them Ismail is the seventh imam, and not his younger brother, Musa, who is accepted by Ithna'ashariyya. Later, the Ismailis also broke up into groups supporting different claimants to the caliphate.

Behind the recognition of different lines of succession lurked political motives. The fifth descendant of Ismail succeeded in forming an independent state, known as the Fatimid caliphate, in Tunisia in 909. At one stage Fatimids aimed at capturing Bagdad, the capital of the orthodox caliphate, but their plan came to nothing and they had to content themselves with power over Egypt alone. However, the very existence of the Fatimid caliphate gave tremendous impetus to Ismailism. Moreover, the Ismailis were able to systemize a lot of the rather vague Shi'ite beliefs and to present them as a living and rational credo.

They were a reforming movement, and as such earned the hostility of orthodox Mohammedanism, but by the middle of the eleventh century the ruthless energy and vitality of the early founders of the Fatimid State had been sapped. If Ismailism was to survive in the face of the attacks of its enemies a leader of exceptional calibre was needed. Hasan-i-Sabbah's hour had come.

What sort of man was he? There is no doubt that he was a man of exceptional gifts—intellectual, ruthless, imbued with a visionary and yet intensely practical sense. He was a reformer like Luther or Calvin, but lacked their integrity. He liked power for its own sake and firmly believed that the end justifies the means. He had none of the appreciation of the arts which humanizes the cynical harshness of the Renaissance princes whom he also resembled. He was the equal of Frederick the Great in military strategy and political opportunism, and, like the Prussian king, could make much out of little. There was not a trace of charity or affection anywhere in his make-up, even towards his family. Both his sons were executed by his orders and he exiled his wife and daughters. He was a complete ascetic, scorning anything that gives other men pleasure or joy, including music and wine. In this respect he was utterly different from Hulagu Khan and the Mongols who were to destroy all his work. He was an authoritarian, and he believed in and propagated the doctrine of personality cult, of the *Führerprinzip*, as assiduously as any twentieth-century tyrant. From his followers he demanded blind obedience as a necessary means to his goal of absolute power.

But it was not only power for himself that he wanted. It was power for the community. The concept of community permeates the whole of Nizari philosophy and is at the very base of its authoritarian hierarchy. His goal was that of a new Ismailism purged and purified from the decadence that tainted the Fatimid empire. This was puritanism in its most extreme form. Religion was to be severe, cold, all-embracing, centring round the doctrine of *ta'lim* or authoritative teaching. This fundamental principle of the Shi'ites and Ismailis (on which they based their belief in the absolute revealed authority of the imamate) became a deadly weapon in the hands of Hasan-i-Sabbah. In his theological writings on the nature of truth and reason he argued that in fact the Shi'ites were as illogical as the orthodox Sunnis in allowing truth to be distorted by reason, and that his doctrine of the absolute authority of the imamate was the only valid one.

The lack of an imam after the disappearance of Prince Nizar, the heir to the Egyptian caliphate, in 1095 came as a godsend to Hasan. He was now the leader and supreme teacher until a new imam appeared who would conveniently be recognized and proclaimed by Hasan himself. There is a story that a son of Nizar was secretly smuggled out of Egypt and taken to Alamut to live as the new imam under the protection of Hasan. This would certainly have increased Hasan's authority still more, but Juvayni does not mention this. Describing Hasan's death, he simply relates that Buzurg-Ummed and three other generals were told to act together in harmony until a new imam should come to take possession of his kingdom. In 1164 Hasan II declared himself to be the imam but Hasan-i-Sabbah could scarcely have anticipated this turn of events.

Based, then, on the doctrines of the absolute authority of Hasan until a new imam, a descendant of Prince Nizar, should appear, strengthened by a reformed code of religious beliefs, intensely militant, and proud of their individuality, the Nizari Ismailis formed a close, compact community united against the Seljuk Turks and the Sunnis. Geographically, however, they were divided, with their centres in Daylaman and Rudbar, Quhishan, Fars, and Syria. Their methods of assassination soon produced equally bloody counter-measures. Possible converts were frightened off, and the recapture of the fortress of Shahdiz by the Seljuks was a considerable setback. It was now clear that Hasan could not unite all Islam, or even the Ismailis, under his leadership or by his teaching. The initial impetus had been spent and could not be revived. The forces of tradition were too strong, and so after Buzurg-Ummed's succession the Nizaris ceased to be a revolutionary movement and a period of relative stability ensued. The Mohammedan world at large, however, continued to regard the Nizaris as dangerous heretics and a menace to the existing order. The measure of the hatred and fear which they inspired can rightly be seen in the ferocious joy with which Moslems received the news of the fall of the Assassin state.

Were this hatred and fear justified? It was not just the physical fear of the weapon of assassination (which had never before been employed on the same scale or deliberately used as a political weapon) or the seeming hopelessness of defeating the Nizaris in pitched battle, which they always wisely avoided, but the fear of a continual menace to their settled and ordered way of existence. The rest of the Islamic world realized full well that Hasan-i-Sabbah's aim was to impose his faith on them. Basically, then, this was a religious struggle, similar to our own in the Western world, and if any judgments have to be passed they should be considered in this light. The character of Hasan-i-Sabbah and the stresses and strains of the time imposed the direction that the movement took and the means that it employed, but it is undeniable that at a time when Islam was weakened and disrupted by internal conflicts many Ismailis believed that the strong leadership, order, and discipline offered by the Nizari Ismailis would bring badly needed peace and unity. The subsequent current of religious development in Persia owes much to their influence. Nizari Ismailism now fulfils a vital and creative part in the lives of the subjects of the Aga Khan. In order to keep our perspectives right we should not forget this.

Some Geographical Aspects of the Valley of the Alamut Rud in the Rudbar District of the Elburz Mountains

By COLIN VOLK

ALTHOUGH ONLY 75 miles from Teheran, the quiet and undisturbed Alamut valley has no reliable published survey or map, and the region is still accessible only by mule-track. There are two main reasons for this isolation. Firstly, the rocks that make up the Elburz mountains are predominantly of Tertiary age, and geologists (who have pioneered so much of Iran) have so far considered that these young strata are not likely to yield oil. Oil has proved so important to the economy of Iran that development has been closely geared to the opening up of new oilfields, and the Elburz mountains, apparently lacking in oil, have therefore been largely ignored.

The slow development of the Alamut area may secondly be attributed to the inaccessibility of the valleys between the high mountain ranges, for the most striking feature of the Elburz is the steepness of slopes. This is especially true in the zone alongside the Caspian's southern shore, where the mountain range is both at its narrowest and its highest. The mountain zone here, in the midst of which Alamut lies, and which separates the Caspian (35 feet below sea-level) from the Central Iranian Plateau (*c.* 4000 feet above sea-level), is only 50 miles wide. Yet, within that distance, the mountain ranges frequently reach 10,000 feet, the highest peak being the 18,000-foot extinct volcano of Demavend. The mountain-knot of Alamkuh/ Takht-e-Suleyman, to the east limit of the Alamut valley, is also over 15,000 feet, and a neighbouring peak marks the source of the Alamut Rud. This stream descends precipitately to Garmrud (*c.* 5500 feet) at the foot of the castle of Nevisar Shah, and then flows westward along a valley approximately 25 miles long and 12 miles wide, with mountain ranges up to 10,000 feet to the north and south, before joining the Taliqan in the gorge overlooked by the castle of Shir Kuh.

This stretch of valley between Garmrud in the east and the Shir Kuh gorge in the west is therefore bounded by mountain-walls to the north, east, and south. Furthermore, the 1000-foot-deep Shir Kuh gorge itself is impassable for half the year, for it becomes filled with floodwater during the rainy season of winter, and also with the meltwater of spring. The valley of the Alamut Rud could thus be defended as a viable economic entity, and the fort of Shir Kuh, guarding the western gorge entrance, and the castle of Nevisar Shah, commanding the eastern approaches via the mountain passes, no doubt played an essential role in maintaining that entity. Between these two fortresses lies an area which, if not immensely fertile, at least contains some comparatively flat land for both dry crops and irrigation. And herein lay the agricultural basis, protected by castles and mountain-walls, of the Assassin power.

Geology

Actually, the Alamut Rud has not so much carved its own valley as made use of one of the downfolds or synclines in the Elburz strata. Much of the younger strata was compressed and therefore hardened in the downfolds, while the upfolds (where the younger strata have been cracked open and eroded away) were weakened so as to expose older rocks. In the highest parts of the district, therefore, and especially east of Garmrud, Devonian rocks are exposed, while very ancient Cambrian rocks have been found on Alamkuh/Takht-e-Suleyman. However, the majority of the rocks of the mountain ranges that run parallel with the Alamut Rud are green Eocene volcanic rocks which, when exposed, give the mountain ranges bare, cragged, and jagged crests of poor agricultural value.

Between the two east-west 10,000-foot ranges of the Eocene volcanics lies the red Miocene sandstone-conglomerate; this covers most of the lower parts of the downfolded valley from Garmrud westward, and consists of alternating hard and soft bands of pebbles and sand, dominating the valley landscape. Furthermore, where this stratum becomes steeply tilted at the sides of the valley the hard bands may stand out as small ridges overlooking the lower parts of the valley. Some of those ridges may rise as much as 1000 feet above the surrounding plain, and, if divided into blocks by streams breaking through from the main Eocene volcanics crest behind, have great potential value as sites for fortresses, of which Alamut and Maymun-Diz are outstanding examples.

Before that point is developed, however, two other geological features are interesting. Firstly, the stratum between the Miocene conglomerate and Eocene volcanics is Oligo-Miocene limestone; thus lime-mortar for castle-building is easily accessible from the uptilted, conglomerate ridges. Secondly, there is a lava dyke, probably associated with the Eocene volcanics, which runs through the Oligo-Miocene sedimentary rocks from the vicinity of Andij to Alamut. This lava dyke constitutes the hill to the north of the 'neck' of Alamut, and the natural jointing in the rock is such that bricks of about 6 by 3 by 3 inches may be readily quarried. Evidence of their use may be seen in the small areas of brickwork visible on Alamut's southern face below the 'throne room,' and on the northern face they are used in a bridge over a gully.

Lieutenant-Colonel J. Sheil's description of Alamut in 1837 is, as far as it goes, accurate.[1] Alamut is indeed a "bare naked rock, exceedingly steep," standing "alone" about two miles north of the village of Gazur Khan; but the rock is approximately 800 to 900 feet high above the village, in contrast to the height of 200 feet given by Sheil, who was perhaps referring merely to the height of the ridge above the "neck." The site, from every aspect, is truly a commanding one, and Nevisar Shah in the east and Shir Kuh in the west are visible from it. As for the building stone, the bricks from the lava dyke have already been mentioned, while to the north and west of this dyke lies the narrow outcrop of Oligo-Miocene limestone that undoubtedly provided the mortar. However, most of the building remains are made up of sandstone rubble, which is obviously derived from quarries on the rock of Alamut itself. The quarries might have been used as places for storing goods or as tombs (which would explain the various regular-shaped cavities on the north-east face). The rubble itself, held together by the Oligo-Miocene mortar, was used in the construction, for example, of the south-east tower of the inner keep. In this instance the rubble has been squared off with some care, but the rubble-walls of the 'throne room' seem to have been built very hurriedly and carelessly, and probably denote a different period of building.

The castle of Maymun-Diz affords an interesting comparison with Alamut in the use of local geological features. As at Alamut, use has been made of an uptilted Miocene conglomerate ridge. In the case of Maymun-Diz, however, the 1000-foot sheer southern face is not a natural 'dip' slope, but is so abrupt as to be more characteristic of a fault line. Maymun-Diz thus has a horst-like character with

[1] *Geographical Journal* viii, 1838, pp. 430–434.

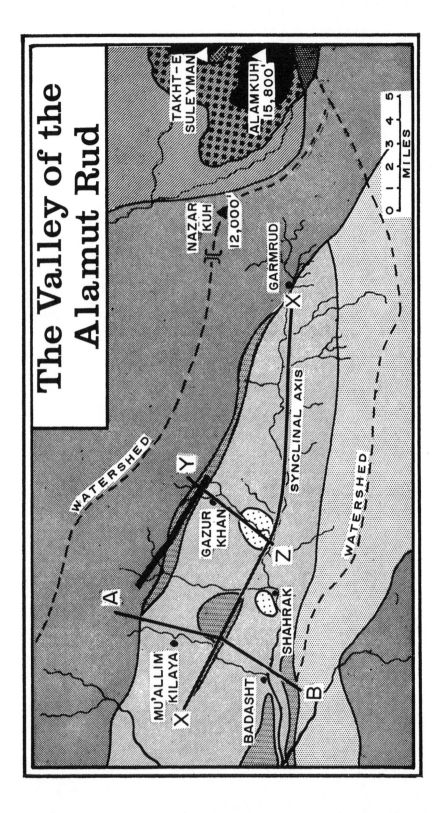

The Valley of the Alamut Rud

TAKHT-E SULEYMAN

ALAMKUH 15,800'

NAZAR KUH 12,000'

WATERSHED

GARMRUD

X

SYNCLINAL AXIS

Y

GAZUR KHAN

Z

A

SHAHRAK

WATERSHED

MU'ALLIM KILAYA

X

B

BADASHT

0 1 2 3 4 5
MILES

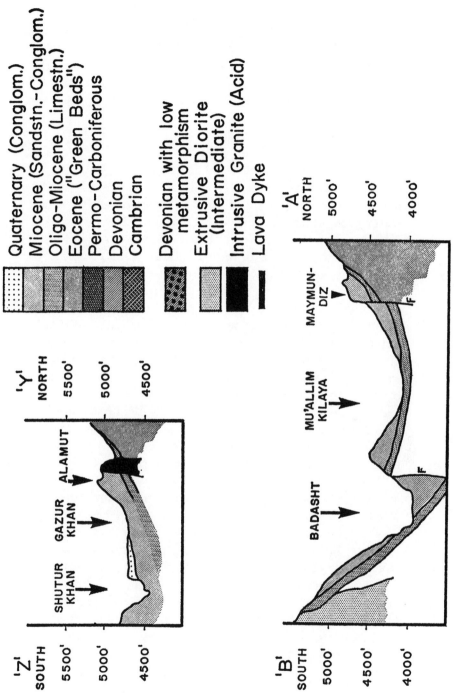

Quaternary (Conglom.)
Miocene (Sandstn.-Conglom.)
Oligo-Miocene (Limestn.)
Eocene ("Green Beds")
Permo-Carboniferous
Devonian
Cambrian

Devonian with low metamorphism
Extrusive Diorite (Intermediate)
Intrusive Granite (Acid)
Lava Dyke

'Y'
NORTH
5500'
5000'
4500'

'Z'
SOUTH
5500'
5000'
4500'

SHUTUR KHAN
GAZUR KHAN
ALAMUT

'A'
NORTH
5000'
4500'
4000'

'B'
SOUTH
5000'
4500'
4000'

BADASHT
MU'ALLIM KILAYA
MAYMUN-DIZ

F

F

1000-foot-high cliffs on either side of a plateau some 100 feet wide. Indeed, Maymun-Diz stands above the valley like some vast Gothic cathedral, with buttresses separated by channels, which, when it rains, become great waterfalls.

The Maymun-Diz conglomerate is significant also for the high content of lime in the matrix. This lime could, of course, be quarried and used as a cementing-mixture for building and plasterwork. The lime in the conglomerate has also encouraged the natural process of underground water erosion by solution, and the rock of Maymun-Diz is distinguished by a network of caves inhabited by bats.

These caves are all on the south side. Thus, if any cave water were to overflow, it would do so down the angle of dip and come out along the faulted southern face. But, even allowing for this type of erosion, the conglomerate, free of any jointing or faulting, has a cave-system unusually extensive for that type of rock. There are no lime beds large enough to encourage solution on the scale even of, say, the Cheddar caves, though Maymun-Diz possesses caves of the same order of size. Except for very limited areas of curtain-like accretions on the walls, no stalagmites or stalactites were seen, and any 'natural' cave-formation that may have existed has been severely tampered with, as is shown by the brickwork in and about the caves.

The question is to estimate how far the caves are natural, and to what extent man-made. That the caves have been inhabited is shown by such evidence as pottery and plaster-work, though the latter is sometimes difficult to differentiate (at least on the rock surface) from the natural lime accretions of the cave walls. It is probable that, after the superb site and defensive potential of the rock had first been realized, there was a later artificial development and enlarging of the cave-system. This would have been accomplished quite easily since the conglomerate at Maymun-Diz is very coarse. The matrix does not bind the pebbles very solidly, and the tunnels may have been made by any simple tool that would extricate the pebbles from the matrix. Deeper caves cut out in this way would have provided useful strongrooms, as well as providing a safe and secure supply of drinking water in time of siege.

After the utter destruction of the castle by the Mongols, the caves were left to underground water erosion. This has since destroyed much of any planned layout that may have existed, for streams have cut down through floors and caused the collapse of cavern ceilings. Thus the present cave-system is highly tortuous and dangerous. The continual process of natural destruction is upheld by the witness of local villagers, who said that they knew of other, larger caves that were, however, no longer accessible.

The evidence points to an important fortress on this site. The brickwork facing of the cliff alone necessitated much hard labour and implies that a strong political and economic organization governed Alamut at that time. No wonder then that this region, of all areas in northern Persia, proved the last obstacle to the Mongol invaders of the twelfth century. Hulagu Khan was rightly reluctant to try to storm a valley deep-set in mountain territory (and therefore inhospitable to steppe-trained Mongolian horsemen) and which he knew was not only well defended, but also united in its cause.

The relationship between, on the one hand, the various physical, geological and climatic features and, on the other, the agricultural and domestic economy of the valley over which the castle-rulers had sway may therefore be considered as significant. With regard to geological features, it is evident that although the Alamut Rud for most of its course flows along the alignment of the downfold in the Miocene conglomerate, from Shahrak westward the river moves south of that axis and cuts into the rock and eventually into the 1000-foot-deep gorge of Shir Kuh, guarded by its Assassins' castle. The reasons for the gorge, with pot-holes high up on each side, may be either superimposition and/or antecedent drainage. Such factors are undoubtedly important lower down the river, since the latter eventually turns a right angle northward and, cutting through the main range via fantastic gorges, empties into the Caspian. However, locally around the Shir Kuh gorge itself, faulting has been a vital factor.

The faults are made obvious by the dispersed distribution of the narrow Oligocene limestone stratum. To the east of the Shir Kuh gorge on the north bank of the Alamut Rud between Badasht and Shahrak, the limestone appears tilted northward. Thus even here, where gorge characteristics are less obvious, the river is south of the synclinal axis. That it follows a fault seems to be proved by the presence of the younger Miocene sandstone on the south bank at the same level as the Oligocene limestone on the north bank.

The Quaternary beds also have a special significance in the local economy, for they seem to be widely scattered throughout the Elburz, and are characteristic of areas immediately upstream of any gorge section, such as those where the rivers cut through the east-west ranges. The gorges, by restricting the volume as well as the carrying power of the rivers, cause deposition in front of their entrances. Indeed a lake might be hemmed in by the ranges before the river could make a gorge for an exit, because lakes would have occurred where, in spite of an earlier drainage pattern, the eroding power of the rivers was weak compared with the faster uplift of the mountains.

In Rudbar the Quaternary beds are obviously the result of very swift deposition of the coarse Miocene sandstone conglomerate. They are exactly alike, both in colour and consistency. However, the difference between them is proved by unconformities; the level bedding planes of the Quaternary rocks contrast with the dips associated with the synclinal structure of the Miocene series. The flat surfaces of the Quaternary rocks, as in the Kalar Dasht,[1] form valuable farmland in this mountainous region, and are very

[1] About 15 miles north-east of Alamkuh.

distinctive on aerial mosaics. But, because of the height above river level (about 250 feet), these areas in the valley of the Alamut Rud are not yet irrigated, and the coarse conglomerate soil is used only for very low-grade cereal culture.

However, the bedding is not always quite horizontal, and sometimes has a slight southerly dip of 2 to 3 degrees. Indeed, there seem to be two groups of Quaternaries to be borne in mind: the level beds associated mainly with the principal river, and the dipping beds. The first are remnants of an earlier stage in the river's erosive down-cutting, and the second are tributary fans associated with that stage. These fans were built up from unsorted material brought down by the short, swift streams from the wetter northern mountain ranges. Meltwater conditions in a glacial epoch would accelerate such a process. The fans, furthermore, had the effect of pushing the river southward so as to expose terraces high and dry on the north side as at Shahrak.

In sum, the fact that the Alamut Rud is not accordant with the synclinal axis seems due primarily to the presence of a fault south of the axis, west of Shahrak, an alignment endorsed by the effect of north-bank tributary fans. Such forces have undoubtedly offset any counter tendency of uniclinal shifting, whereby the Alamut Rud would seek a more northerly course along the axis. The drainage development is distinguished by other features also, such as the stream-capture and wind-gap south of Mu'allim Kilaya, while the fertile old-lake basin of Kuchinan seems due to the lava dyke at Andij, which holds up the river there.

Such features have been fundamental to the growth of the valley's economy, and none more so than the fact that the principal river has migrated southward. The area north of the river is consequently less rugged than the steep Miocene dip slopes to the south, and has therefore a far greater area of tillable land. Also, the watercourses from the wetter northern range of mountains are more reliable

than those to the south, and the alluvial fans that those
tributaries make with the Alamut Rud form valuable areas
for irrigation. No wonder, then, that the population with
its villages and castles has tended to favour the north bank.
Further, the *adret*, south-facing slopes to the north of the
river have more sunshine than those to the south. While
this is probably a disadvantage during the heat of summer
(the daily maximum being over 100°F.), it is undoubtedly
important to the north-bank villages in spring and autumn
when the extra hours of sunshine become vital for crops.

Climate: Geomorphology: Natural Vegetation: Crops

The Elburz do of course constitute a natural boundary
between the hot, yellow desert-elements of Central Iran
(rainfall less than 10 inches per annum) and the cold, green
forest-elements of the Caspian slopes (rainfall about
60 inches per annum). The fact that the mountains rise up
to 18,000 feet makes the difference emphatic, but this very
altitude ensures also that the vegetation of the boundary-
zone itself is common to neither. Thus, for example, the
forests that are claimed as typical of the northern Elburz
slopes are limited to the northern *lower* slopes and foothills.
As shown by H. Bobek's map illustrating his essay "Die
Tahkht-e-Sulaimangruppe . . . Nordiran" (1959),[1] the
tree limit is around 7500 feet, with stunted growth and
scrub characteristics up to about 9000 feet. Such limits are
gradual unless there is some relief form to make the limit
bold, and in these terms it is significant how the Tange
Gali gorge east of Alamkuh marked the limit of the scrub
and, at the time of our visit, of the Caspian cloud also. The
gorge is obviously an important barrier to any further upward seepage of damp Caspian air and associate vegetation.

Although valley configuration may have local effects, in
general the cloud limit is controlled by two factors: firstly,

[1] *Festschrift zur Hundertjahrfeier der Geographischen Gesellschaft in
Wien.*

the heaviness of the Caspian air mass due to its northern and colder origin, and, secondly, the relative strength of the air mass from the south. On September 10, 1959, on a 13,000-foot ridge, the southerly wind was estimated at force 5, and a strong *foehn* was in accompaniment. Thus the limit of the Caspian cloud was the result of a balance between a strong south wind boosted by the descending *foehn*, and the cold Caspian air mass; the cloud itself was the result of condensation of the warm *foehn*. It is probable also that the consequent air instability at this altitude of *c.* 10,000 feet increases the virility of the upper-air westerlies.

In winter, of course, the Caspian air mass is colder, more dense, and with very little inclination to rise. Wintertime, too, marks a period of higher pressure over the Persian Desert, so there is little chance of the Caspian air being drawn across the mountains. Nevertheless, the southern slopes, including Teheran, experience very cold winters[1] and the higher southern slopes regularly get a cover of snow. Ivanow complained of the snow in Alamut during his winter visit of 1928, while the extinct volcano of Demavend (18,000 feet) has snow all the year round. Moreover, it may be assumed that Hulagu Khan was handicapped by the common knowledge that an attack could only be timed before or after the winter snows. This type of climate, with maximum precipitation in winter and spring,[2] can only be attributed to the upper-air westerlies, and the extent to which the mountains protrude into this air is therefore vitally significant, not only as regards the present climate, but also as regards geomorphological relics resulting from different climates of earlier epochs.

Evidence for this last point may be observed in the high-mountain zone where ice has been an important erosive agency. Even in August ice-pockets occur at about

[1] Teheran: average January temperature, 34°F.

[2] Teheran: 46 per cent. of the annual precipitation occurs in the three months February to April.

C.A.–X

12,000 feet on north-facing slopes, and are surrounded by ample evidence of solifluction and other periglacial phenomena. Even the south-facing slope of the 15,000-feet peak of Alamkuh/Takht-e-Suleyman is scarred by a magnificent series of corries culminating in a corrie lake, while the northern slopes are still covered by a system of glaciers. Nevertheless, there are few of the glacial features (such as U-shaped valleys and steps) that characterize the extension of glaciation in a former Ice Age, for these have been eroded away by the powerful downward-action of the steeply cascading Caspian torrents. Indeed, the erosion could have been such as to explain shoulder-like masses observed as much as 1500 feet above the valley east of Nazar Kuh, each representing a former stage of erosion.

Stream and ice erosion are then the principal landscape forces on the well-watered (*c.* 60 inches p.a.) Caspian slopes and high-mountain zone respectively. However, sub-arid landforms are characteristic of the sheltered valleys such as Alamut, as well as the south-facing slopes, where the rainfall is irregular and amounts to only about 30 inches a year (compare Teheran: 9·3 inches p.a.). In Alamut, stony plateaux are divided by gorges of irregular flowing streams which have not the eroding power of those on the Caspian-facing slopes. Thus, within the fifty-mile width of the mountains, there is a great variety of landform and, consequently, of farming economy. Further, because of the past changes in climate, there has been migration of the landform zones.

In sum, much of the landscape has a composite geomorphology, although past effects of a cooler climate in the present dry areas of the southern ranges seem easier to recognize than in the wetter north. Thus, for example, near Teheran there are hills surmounting the gravel piedmont which may well be eskers, while in Alamut itself a well-developed corrie is situated in the north face of the lava mountain adjacent to Alamut rock, incidentally thereby making the latter still more impregnable.

The lack of any strongly marked geomorphological boundary on the southern ranges between the high cold and the low dry is emphasized by a similar lack of any boundary of vegetation. On the southern slopes the high cold desert leads straight down into the hot desert, the latter resulting from the lack of any regular supply of rain from the Caspian side. In this context the relatively high annual rainfall of Alamut, about 30 inches, is somewhat surprising, but precipitation is occasionally due to a breach of Caspian cloud through the Elburz, similar to the way in which the clouds filter up the Sefid Rud valley into the Central Plain above Kazwin. This type of movement probably occurs most frequently in spring and autumn when the two air-masses either side of the Elburz are least stable. In wintertime, precipitation increases when the upper airstream of westerlies comes lower and contacts the mountain ridges.

Thus, in early September in Alamut, an occasional cloudy morning was experienced, heralding the winter rain. These clouds soon dispersed, but they showed potential precipitation. An exceptional day was September 2, 1959, when 106°F. was reached at Mu'allim Kilaya between 3 and 5 P.M., with the relative humidity as low as 38 per cent. (8 A.M.) and 16 per cent. (an hour later). Otherwise, however, the relative humidity during September was quite high, measuring on average 68 per cent. (8 A.M.) and 54 per cent. (8 P.M.), with average morning and evening temperatures 67°F. and 71°F. respectively. This compares with the average September temperature in Teheran of 77°F., but the above humidity figures show that the air was moist in Rudbar compared with the desert plain. Furthermore, the minimum temperature during the night was about 58°F. (absolute minimum 54°F.) and dewpoint was often reached. The resultant condensation provides a supply of ground moisture to plant life. The barrenness of much of the landscape is therefore unexpected, and the presence of a few isolated trees on a high plain near Andij emphasized this. If these few trees could withstand drought, then why all the barrenness around? Furthermore, trees flourished in the 'gardens' of the villages, but were totally absent elsewhere along water-courses. The only explanation is an exploitation of timber for building and fuel purposes, and insufficient allowance for regeneration of trees.

Nevertheless, the trees in the villages, in contrast to the bare landscape around, are carefully tended. Two walnut-trees by the 'graveyard' at Gazur Khan had a very great girth, and might have been a century old, but, in general, the trees were young poplars whose economic value un-doubtedly lay in house-building. Immature trees are most needed since their straight, slender trunks make excellent crossbeams for the roofs, as well as the verandas that are characteristic of Alamut. Village youths also bring extra tree-trunks on their shoulders from the villages higher up the valley-side, and this shows the great need for wood.

Except for the use of timber for roof and veranda con-struction, the basic method of building is by means of mud bricks. These are carved out of mud beside a stream and then stacked with spaces between to allow the air to circulate and harden them. This method is common to much of the Middle East, and the brick walls are often smothered with mud daub. In Alamut the bricks, in any case distinctive with their reddish tinge because of their red Miocene sandstone conglomerate origin, may alter-natively be lime-plastered both inside and out, thus illustrating again the local importance of the Oligo-Miocene limestone. Furthermore, the plaster may be tinted red in decoration, a redness originating again from the surrounding sandstone.

Grazing is a major agricultural pursuit in the drier parts of Alamut. Indeed, quite large flocks of sheep and goats are kept on the steeper land of the higher mountain slopes that are too inaccessible to be tilled. The milk of the flocks is largely curdled into yoghourt or *mast*, and the dung for fuel is carefully made into cakes by the women-folk, who stack it on the roofs to dry. The wool is hand-spun, sometimes for carpets; but as for clothes, these were mainly cheap textiles brought in from outside.

Besides *mast*, the other staple food is bread, and all the land, including the various Miocene and Quaternary conglomerate terraces, that could not be irrigated without great effort is devoted to dry crops such as millet, wheat, and barley. Thus the threshing-floor with its bullocks or oxen is characteristic of every village in Rudbar. Hay also must be stocked to feed the animals in wintertime, and this is brought down from the hillsides on the backs of men, to be kept on the flat roofs of the houses.

Yet this cereal culture and the overgrazing of flocks and herds, have forbidden the regeneration of vegetation. Cereals are particularly characteristic of the unirrigated lands, and contrast with the irrigated riverside areas. These, green with young rice in August, are limited generally to the well-watered alluvial fans, where tributaries join the Alamut Rud, as at Shir Kuh, Shahrak, and Zavarak. The rice-growing areas of Mu'allim Kilaya, the valley's "capital," are a significant exception, while the "capital" is also well situated for grazing herds in the adjacent mountains. Mu'allim Kilaya no doubt owes part of its leadership to this dual role, for most villages seemed to specialize either in lowland irrigation or in hillside grazing, the highland village receiving rice in exchange for its produce from hillside flocks and herds. This inter-village trade is undoubtedly endorsed by the climatic contrast between the *ubac* and *adret* slopes. The villages of the latter have their harvests early, and can supply food to the *ubac* villages still waiting for their crops to ripen; these in their turn can supply food to the *adret* villages in midsummer when water is scarce.

Furthermore, these exchanges have developed beyond the basic foods. The riverside villages with irrigated fields 'export' other crops: Andij takes special care over bean-production and Shams Kilaya deals with onions. At Gazur

Khan, a highland village, a small stream is led through a series of mills for grinding corn. Here, too, *gives* are made. These shoes consist of strongly woven wool-waste for the uppers and sliced hide for the soles—that is, materials entirely taken from local flocks and herds. These shoes are sent to all parts of Alamut, and are bought in exchange or for cash. This small-scale exchange is notable since a feature of most primitive societies is the self-sufficiency of each village. Yet in the Alamut valley inter-dependence seems to be the rule, and seems also in no small way due to the close juxtaposition of contrasting environments and landforms. This variety within the valley could well have encouraged the area to become an important economic unit in the twelfth century, and any inter-dependence and specialization that developed then would have no doubt since become traditional.

Some of the special products may, moreover, be sent beyond Alamut to pay, for example, for extra rice. Rice has become part of the staple diet and the Alamut valley is not nearly self-sufficient because of its limited possibilities for irrigation and its degenerate cereal and grass lands. It is found easier to import much of the rice from the Caspian shores of Gilan by way of mule-trains. There is, however, a special relationship between Alamut and Gilan, for the former, with its comparatively dense population, is a vital labour reserve for reaping the rice-harvest in early summer in the latter. The complementary timing of the Gilan rice-harvest and the Alamut corn-harvest is all-important, for the rice-harvest occurs during the slack period in Alamut between the spring harvesting and the autumn sowing of the corn. Gilan thus provides a source of revenue during the crucial time of summer when the poorly yielding Alamut fields, particularly of the *adret* slopes, are producing their minimum.

In these terms can be seen the present dependence of Alamut on areas outside its own confines. This is in contrast to the greater degree of self-sufficiency that may have existed in former centuries, as during the Assassin movements. At that time, in the attempt to make Rudbar an economically viable unit, the agricultural potential, from the mountain slopes to the valley terraces and alluvial fans, would have been used to the uttermost, protected as the valley was by a series of castles and fortresses, themselves cannily utilizing the natural features of the land.

To-day, however, the clothing for Alamut, and much of the rice, one of its staple foods, come from beyond. The clothing is largely manufactured, and rice is imported from the Caspian. Further, each entails a migration of people. But while the Caspian migration is seasonal and is balanced according to the rice-harvest, the migration to the manufacturing industries of Teheran is generally outward. The latter is encouraged by such factors as military service, after which young men find village life dull, and the attraction of Teheran's economic boom. It is well realized by the villagers that their landlords (Gazur Khan was exceptional in that the villagers held their own land) are investing any interest that might accrue from village success not back into the village, but rather into the city boom. There is here, therefore, a double incentive to leave the village: the decreasing prosperity of the rural community and the increasing prosperity of the nation's capital.

The social and economic pull of Teheran is, of course, felt all over Iran. Nevertheless, it is interesting to observe its effects on an isolated community that is only 75 miles from the capital. There is in Alamut to-day very little sense of self-containment, and each house has many items brought from the manufacturing world beyond. Indeed, trade with the outside world has ensured that the distinction of Alamut is limited to its unique castles, and, while Alamut continues to look out to the world with envious eyes, above all on the wealth of Teheran, nobody looks in; and here lies the tragedy that is typical of isolated rural areas undergoing depopulation.

APPENDIX C

Persian Pottery at the time of the Assassins

By Ralph Pinder-Wilson

At the time when Hasan-i-Sabbah was establishing him-self and his followers in the mountains of Mazanderan, the administration of the Seljuq sultans was inaugurating an era of prosperity in Persia. The revival of commerce and industry was accompanied by developments in architecture and the arts. New religious institutions required new types of buildings. Such a one was the *madrasah* or school mosque providing for the teaching of theology and law according to Sunnite rules to which the Seljuqs adhered. Prosperity in the great cities created wealthy patrons for the products of artists and craftsmen. In the course of the twelfth century the decorative arts, in particular pottery, textiles, and metalwork, reached full maturity, and the style of decora-tion developed in this period directed the subsequent course of Persian art.

Seljuq decoration developed in part out of the style created by previous generations of Moslem artists and craftsmen; for it must be remembered that since the seventh century A.D. Persia was a part of the Islamic world with its own distinctive art. The extent to which the religion of Islam contributed to the creation of this art is not easy to determine. Nevertheless, certain features of Islamic art are the result of religious beliefs. Because he was forbidden by orthodox opinion to represent human beings in the round, the Moslem artist turned to the embellishment of surfaces—whether of buildings or objects. In religious buildings representation of living creatures, human or animal, was absolutely prohibited, and decoration was restricted to floral, geometric, and abstract patterns and inscriptions, mostly of religious content, in the Arabic script.

In the Seljuq period the artists of Persia realized splendid compositions in line and colour. In these the constituent elements might be many and various, but the overall effect harmonious. In pottery the decoration is always appropriate to the vessel's form. The artist prefers to break up his surface into a number of areas, such as bands, roundels, or cartouches, each contrasting with the other and emphasizing a single facet of the vessel. Apart from arabesque scrolls and geometric figures like the star and interlacings, he introduces, either singly or in procession, animals, birds, or human beings, which he sets, not in a recognizable landscape, but rather in a stylized scrolling ground. Sometimes he includes one or more bands of Arabic writing either in the angular Kufic or cursive Naskhi script. These inscriptions may be of a religious nature, verses of Persian poetry, or merely conventional good wishes to the man for whom the vessel was destined; more rarely, they include the date when the vessel was made and the potter's and the patron's name.

Two qualities distinguish the glazed pottery of this period—harmony of colour and vitality of design. Technical mastery of glazes made possible a wide range of colours; and the discovery of underglaze painting allowed for greater flexibility of drawing.

The potters of the Seljuq period inherited ancient traditions: painted pottery vessels were being made on the Persian plateau as early as the fifth millenium B.C. It was not, however, until the beginning of the Christian era that potters learnt the art of glazing pottery, and for several centuries the only glaze colours known to them were turquoise blue and turquoise green.

In the ninth century A.D. great advances were made in Mesopotamia, and some of these newly discovered techniques reached Persia. The luxury that surrounded the caliphs of Baghdad will be familiar to readers of *The Arabian Nights*; and what we know of the pottery of the period of Harun-ar-Rashid and his successors confirms this picture. One of the causes of this renewed ceramic activity was the import of stoneware and porcelain from T'ang China. The difficulty of bringing such delicate and fragile wares from distant China made them exceedingly rare and costly; and because they were in such demand, the Mesopotamian potters turned their hands to producing substitutes rivalling if not excelling the originals. Although unable to achieve true porcelain, they simulated its smooth white surface by the application of an opaque white tin glaze to the pottery body. In the same way they succeeded in producing a passable imitation of the famous celadon glaze. Where they were most successful was in imitating the T'ang mottled wares. In these, floral designs were incised in the vessel's surface, which was then splashed with brown, green, or yellow glaze. Nor were the Meso-potàmian potters content merely to imitate, for their designs are quite distinctive. Moreover, to them is due the credit for inventing the technique of painting in a metallic lustre on a white tin glaze.

Mottled wares were soon being made in Persian centres[1]; and native potters were developing their own distinctive wares. One of these is the so-called sgraffiato ware. A thin coating of white clay usually called a slip was applied to the vessel's surface; and through this slip the design was scratched, revealing the underlying body clay. Finally, the whole vessel was covered with a transparent glaze with or without colour and fired in the kiln. It has been suggested that this ware was inspired by the engraved metal objects

[1] See centre illustration opposite p. 209.

of the period, and certainly the designs employed both in pottery and in metal are similar. This relatively simple technique was practised in Persia in succeeding centuries and the only indication of date is the style of decoration. From the large number of finds it must have been a popular and inexpensive ware. In eastern Persia and Transoxiana, a fine and distinctive ware was made in which the designs were rendered in coloured slips under a transparent glaze. As simple as the sgraffiato technique, it spread to other parts of Persia, although the finest examples come from the kilns of Nishapur and Samarqand.

In the twelfth century the potters of Persia again had to face the challenge of imported Chinese porcelain; this time the exquisite wares of the Sung dynasty. We have seen how the Mesopotamian potters had simulated the surface appearance of porcelain by applying an opaque white glaze to the earthenware body. The Persians now succeeded in producing a hard white body clay much closer in appearance to porcelain. Bowls and beakers with carved or moulded decoration and covered with a transparent colourless glaze are clearly imitations of the Sung "ying-ching" porcelain. Some of these are enhanced by the addition of little holes which, filled with glaze, are revealed against the light as tiny windows. A fragmentary bowl of this type in the British Museum is decorated with a procession of horsemen against leafy scrolls with transparent interstices; above is an inscribed band in light relief with good wishes to the owner.[1] A small fragment of this ware was also found in the castle of Alamut.

The Persians do not appear to have made lustre-decorated pottery before the second half of the twelfth century. The Mesopotamians had been the first to paint in lustre in the ninth century, and the tradition was preserved by the potters of Egypt. Indeed, it is possible that after the fall of the Fatimid dynasty in 1171 some of the potters of Cairo found asylum in Persia. In support of this there is

[1] See upper illustration opposite p. 208.

certainly a relationship between the lustre wares of twelfth-century Egypt and Persia. In Persia there is evidence of two centres producing lustre pottery: at Rayy, a few miles outside Teheran and an important city in the Seljuq period, and at Kashan, south of Teheran.[1] The expedition was able to recover a few fragments of lustre painted ware from Alamut.

The most important contribution made by the Persian potters of this period was the technique of underglaze painting. Up to this time the only method of painting on pottery was with coloured clay slips as in the wares of eastern Persia and Transoxiana or on the surface of the glaze as in lustre ware when the metallic lustre was fixed in a second firing. Now a method was discovered of painting in glaze colours under a coloured or transparent glaze. The Kashan potters seem to have played an important part in this discovery, and a particularly beautiful ware is attributed to their kilns.[1] The decoration is in black and blue under a colourless glaze. Characteristic is a plant spray with sinuous leaves, such as appears on a fragment found at Alamut (Fig. 1). Another fragment is painted

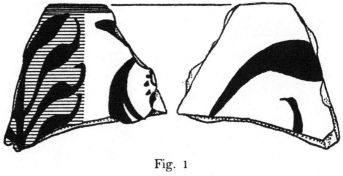

Fig. 1

Scale 1 : 1

[1] Examples of lustre ware and of underglaze painted pottery made in Kashan are shown opposite pp. 208 and 209.

with Persian letters (Fig. 2). Also from Alamut are a number of potsherds painted in black under a turquoise glaze; designs are too fragmentary to allow reconstruction,

Fig. 2   Fig. 3

Scale 1 : 1

but these include a characteristic trefoil leaf and the curling stem and tendrils of the arabesque (Figs. 3 and 4).

At about the same time the Persian potters were developing a more complicated technique combining underglaze and overglaze or enamel colours. By this means it was possible to employ no less than seven colours on a single vessel. The expedition found no sherds of this kind in Mazanderan, though one fragment painted in black under a turquoise glaze has the remains of white overglaze enamel.

Fig. 4

Scale 1 : 1

Of course the wares described above were probably accessible only to the rich. Simple monochrome glazed wares were made at many centres. Commonest are vessels with a plain cobalt or turquoise glaze, sometimes applied over relief decoration obtained by means of a wooden mould.[1] Plain turquoise vessels were current at Alamut to judge by the fragments found there.

A popular ware at this period was the sgraffiato ware. Several sherds were found by the expedition in the Assassin country as well as an almost complete bowl at Samiran. The typical shape of vessel is a large conical bowl standing on a footring. Descended from the Mesopotamian mottled wares, these combine incised decoration with splashes of coloured glaze. These splashes only roughly correspond to the incised design. Similar wares were being made in Azerbaijan and Armenia as well as the Caspian provinces. The decoration except in the particularly fine pieces is summarily drawn, some motifs being taken from the current decorative repertory, others being no more than hastily 'doodled' patterns (Fig. 5).

An interesting find at Ashkavar was a number of turquoise glazed tiles. These included fragmentary star-shaped tiles and complete cross tiles. These must have served as an exterior or interior wall revetment, consisting of alternating rows of cross and eight-pointed-star tiles forming a kind of mosaic. Such tile facings suggest a considerable degree of refinement. We can also infer that

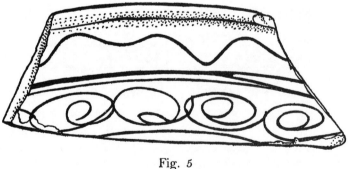

Fig. 5

Scale 1 : 1

[1] See example illustrated opposite p. 209.

there was a *hammam* or steam-bath system, since the expedition found a charming strigil or skin-scraper carved of greyish-white marble in the form of a dove. The

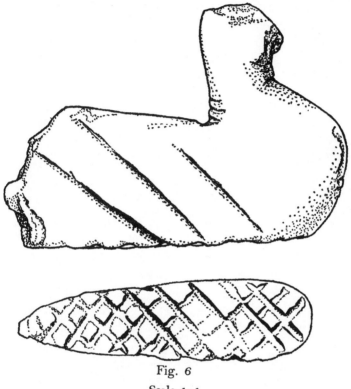

Fig. 6

Scale 1 : 1

rendering is rather stylized, but sufficient to indicate that it is a bird (Fig. 6).

It is doubtful whether any glazed wares were made in any of the Assassin centres; the expedition found no trace of kilns. But a great deal of ordinary unglazed domestic pottery was to be seen and no doubt some of this was locally made. This is confirmed by the chance find of a seggar, a small three-pointed clay object placed between bowls when firing in order to keep them apart and thus to prevent them fusing together in the heat of the kiln.

These finds from the Assassin castles are valuable inasmuch as they show that the finer wares were available to the Assassins. All appear to be of twelfth or early thirteenth century date. It is significant that no sherds of a later date and reflecting the Mongol style of decoration were found. It would seem that Hulagu's warriors executed their work of exterminating the heretics with remarkable thoroughness.